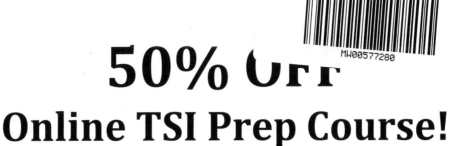

50% Off
Online TSI Prep Course!

By Mometrix University

Dear Customer,

We consider it an honor and a privilege that you chose our TSI Study Guide. As a way of showing our appreciation and to help us better serve you, we are offering **50% off our online TSI Prep Course**. Many TSI courses are needlessly expensive and don't deliver enough value. With our course, you get access to the best TSI prep material, and **you only pay half price**.

We have structured our online course to perfectly complement your printed study guide. The TSI Prep Course contains **78 lessons** that cover all the most important topics, **110+ video reviews** that explain difficult concepts, over **600 practice questions** to ensure you feel prepared, and over **300 digital flashcards**, so you can study while you're on the go.

Online TSI Prep Course

Topics Covered:

- Mathematics
    - *Elementary Algebra and Functions*
    - *Intermediate Algebra and Functions*
    - *Geometry and Measurement*
    - *Data Analysis, Statistics, and Probability*
- Reading
    - *Literary Analysis*
    - *Main Idea and Supporting Details*
    - *Inferences in a Text or Texts*
    - *Author's Use of Language*
- Writing
    - *Foundations of Grammar and Punctuation*
    - *Essay Revision and Sentence Logic*
    - *Agreement and Sentence Structure*

Course Features:

- TSI Study Guide
    - Get content that complements our best-selling study guide.
- 9 Full-Length Practice Tests
    - With over 600 practice questions, you can test yourself again and again.
- Mobile Friendly
    - If you need to study on the go, the course is easily accessible from your mobile device.
- TSI Flashcards
    - Our course includes a flashcard mode consisting of over 300 content cards to help you study.

To receive this discount, simply head to our website: www.mometrix.com/university/courses/tsi and add the course to your cart. At the checkout page, enter the discount code: **tsi50off**

If you have any questions or concerns, please don't hesitate to contact us at universityhelp@mometrix.com.

Sincerely,

FREE Study Skills DVD Offer

Dear Customer,

Thank you for your purchase from Mometrix! We consider it an honor and a privilege that you have purchased our product and we want to ensure your satisfaction.

As a way of showing our appreciation and to help us better serve you, we have developed a Study Skills DVD that we would like to give you for <u>FREE</u>. This DVD covers our *best practices* for getting ready for your exam, from how to use our study materials to how to best prepare for the day of the test.

All that we ask is that you email us with feedback that would describe your experience so far with our product. Good, bad, or indifferent, we want to know what you think!

To get your FREE Study Skills DVD, email <u>freedvd@mometrix.com</u> with *FREE STUDY SKILLS DVD* in the subject line and the following information in the body of the email:

- The name of the product you purchased.
- Your product rating on a scale of 1-5, with 5 being the highest rating.
- Your feedback. It can be long, short, or anything in between. We just want to know your impressions and experience so far with our product. (Good feedback might include how our study material met your needs and ways we might be able to make it even better. You could highlight features that you found helpful or features that you think we should add.)
- Your full name and shipping address where you would like us to send your free DVD.

If you have any questions or concerns, please don't hesitate to contact me directly.

Thanks again!

Sincerely,

Jay Willis
Vice President
<u>jay.willis@mometrix.com</u>
1-800-673-8175

TSI

Study Guide
2020-2021

TSI Secrets Test Prep

Full-Length Practice Test

Step-by-Step Review
Video Tutorials

Written and edited by Mometrix Test Prep

Printed in the United States of America

This paper meets the requirements of ANSI/NISO Z39.48-1992 (Permanence of Paper).

Mometrix offers volume discount pricing to institutions. For more information or a price quote, please contact our sales department at sales@mometrix.com or 888-248-1219.

Mometrix Media LLC is not affiliated with or endorsed by any official testing organization. All organizational and test names are trademarks of their respective owners.

Paperback
ISBN 13: 978-1-5167-4780-1
ISBN 10: 1-5167-4780-1

DEAR FUTURE EXAM SUCCESS STORY

First of all, **THANK YOU** for purchasing Mometrix study materials!

Second, congratulations! You are one of the few determined test-takers who are committed to doing whatever it takes to excel on your exam. **You have come to the right place.** We developed these study materials with one goal in mind: to deliver you the information you need in a format that's concise and easy to use.

In addition to optimizing your guide for the content of the test, we've outlined our recommended steps for breaking down the preparation process into small, attainable goals so you can make sure you stay on track.

We've also analyzed the entire test-taking process, identifying the most common pitfalls and showing how you can overcome them and be ready for any curveball the test throws you.

Standardized testing is one of the biggest obstacles on your road to success, which only increases the importance of doing well in the high-pressure, high-stakes environment of test day. Your results on this test could have a significant impact on your future, and this guide provides the information and practical advice to help you achieve your full potential on test day.

Your success is our success

We would love to hear from you! If you would like to share the story of your exam success or if you have any questions or comments in regard to our products, please contact us at **800-673-8175** or **support@mometrix.com**.

Thanks again for your business and we wish you continued success!

Sincerely,
The Mometrix Test Preparation Team

> **Need more help? Check out our flashcards at:**
> **http://MometrixFlashcards.com/TSI**

TABLE OF CONTENTS

Introduction

Thank you for purchasing this resource! You have made the choice to prepare yourself for a test that could have a huge impact on your future, and this guide is designed to help you be fully ready for test day. Obviously, it's important to have a solid understanding of the test material, but you also need to be prepared for the unique environment and stressors of the test, so that you can perform to the best of your abilities.

For this purpose, the first section that appears in this guide is the **Secret Keys**. We've devoted countless hours to meticulously researching what works and what doesn't, and we've boiled down our findings to the four most impactful steps you can take to improve your performance on the test. We start at the beginning with study planning and move through the preparation process, all the way to the testing strategies that will help you get the most out of what you know when you're finally sitting in front of the test.

We recommend that you start preparing for your test as far in advance as possible. However, if you've bought this guide as a last-minute study resource and only have a few days before your test, we recommend that you skip over the first two Secret Keys since they address a long-term study plan.

If you struggle with **test anxiety**, we strongly encourage you to check out our recommendations for how you can overcome it. Test anxiety is a formidable foe, but it can be beaten, and we want to make sure you have the tools you need to defeat it.

Secret Key #1 – Plan Big, Study Small

There's a lot riding on your performance. If you want to ace this test, you're going to need to keep your skills sharp and the material fresh in your mind. You need a plan that lets you review everything you need to know while still fitting in your schedule. We'll break this strategy down into three categories.

Information Organization

Start with the information you already have: the official test outline. From this, you can make a complete list of all the concepts you need to cover before the test. Organize these concepts into groups that can be studied together, and create a list of any related vocabulary you need to learn so you can brush up on any difficult terms. You'll want to keep this vocabulary list handy once you actually start studying since you may need to add to it along the way.

Time Management

Once you have your set of study concepts, decide how to spread them out over the time you have left before the test. Break your study plan into small, clear goals so you have a manageable task for each day and know exactly what you're doing. Then just focus on one small step at a time. When you manage your time this way, you don't need to spend hours at a time studying. Studying a small block of content for a short period each day helps you retain information better and avoid stressing over how much you have left to do. You can relax knowing that you have a plan to cover everything in time. In order for this strategy to be effective though, you have to start studying early and stick to your schedule. Avoid the exhaustion and futility that comes from last-minute cramming!

Study Environment

The environment you study in has a big impact on your learning. Studying in a coffee shop, while probably more enjoyable, is not likely to be as fruitful as studying in a quiet room. It's important to keep distractions to a minimum. You're only planning to study for a short block of time, so make the most of it. Don't pause to check your phone or get up to find a snack. It's also important to **avoid multitasking**. Research has consistently shown that multitasking will make your studying dramatically less effective. Your study area should also be comfortable and well-lit so you don't have the distraction of straining your eyes or sitting on an uncomfortable chair.

The time of day you study is also important. You want to be rested and alert. Don't wait until just before bedtime. Study when you'll be most likely to comprehend and remember. Even better, if you know what time of day your test will be, set that time aside for study. That way your brain will be used to working on that subject at that specific time and you'll have a better chance of recalling information.

Finally, it can be helpful to team up with others who are studying for the same test. Your actual studying should be done in as isolated an environment as possible, but the work of organizing the information and setting up the study plan can be divided up. In between study sessions, you can discuss with your teammates the concepts that you're all studying and quiz each other on the details. Just be sure that your teammates are as serious about the test as you are. If you find that your study time is being replaced with social time, you might need to find a new team.

Secret Key #2 – Make Your Studying Count

You're devoting a lot of time and effort to preparing for this test, so you want to be absolutely certain it will pay off. This means doing more than just reading the content and hoping you can remember it on test day. It's important to make every minute of study count. There are two main areas you can focus on to make your studying count:

Retention

It doesn't matter how much time you study if you can't remember the material. You need to make sure you are retaining the concepts. To check your retention of the information you're learning, try recalling it at later times with minimal prompting. Try carrying around flashcards and glance at one or two from time to time or ask a friend who's also studying for the test to quiz you.

To enhance your retention, look for ways to put the information into practice so that you can apply it rather than simply recalling it. If you're using the information in practical ways, it will be much easier to remember. Similarly, it helps to solidify a concept in your mind if you're not only reading it to yourself but also explaining it to someone else. Ask a friend to let you teach them about a concept you're a little shaky on (or speak aloud to an imaginary audience if necessary). As you try to summarize, define, give examples, and answer your friend's questions, you'll understand the concepts better and they will stay with you longer. Finally, step back for a big picture view and ask yourself how each piece of information fits with the whole subject. When you link the different concepts together and see them working together as a whole, it's easier to remember the individual components.

Finally, practice showing your work on any multi-step problems, even if you're just studying. Writing out each step you take to solve a problem will help solidify the process in your mind, and you'll be more likely to remember it during the test.

Modality

Modality simply refers to the means or method by which you study. Choosing a study modality that fits your own individual learning style is crucial. No two people learn best in exactly the same way, so it's important to know your strengths and use them to your advantage.

For example, if you learn best by visualization, focus on visualizing a concept in your mind and draw an image or a diagram. Try color-coding your notes, illustrating them, or creating symbols that will trigger your mind to recall a learned concept. If you learn best by hearing or discussing information, find a study partner who learns the same way or read aloud to yourself. Think about how to put the information in your own words. Imagine that you are giving a lecture on the topic and record yourself so you can listen to it later.

For any learning style, flashcards can be helpful. Organize the information so you can take advantage of spare moments to review. Underline key words or phrases. Use different colors for different categories. Mnemonic devices (such as creating a short list in which every item starts with the same letter) can also help with retention. Find what works best for you and use it to store the information in your mind most effectively and easily.

Secret Key #3 – Practice the Right Way

Your success on test day depends not only on how many hours you put into preparing, but also on whether you prepared the right way. It's good to check along the way to see if your studying is paying off. One of the most effective ways to do this is by taking practice tests to evaluate your progress. Practice tests are useful because they show exactly where you need to improve. Every time you take a practice test, pay special attention to these three groups of questions:

- The questions you got wrong
- The questions you had to guess on, even if you guessed right
- The questions you found difficult or slow to work through

This will show you exactly what your weak areas are, and where you need to devote more study time. Ask yourself why each of these questions gave you trouble. Was it because you didn't understand the material? Was it because you didn't remember the vocabulary? Do you need more repetitions on this type of question to build speed and confidence? Dig into those questions and figure out how you can strengthen your weak areas as you go back to review the material.

Additionally, many practice tests have a section explaining the answer choices. It can be tempting to read the explanation and think that you now have a good understanding of the concept. However, an explanation likely only covers part of the question's broader context. Even if the explanation makes sense, **go back and investigate** every concept related to the question until you're positive you have a thorough understanding.

As you go along, keep in mind that the practice test is just that: practice. Memorizing these questions and answers will not be very helpful on the actual test because it is unlikely to have any of the same exact questions. If you only know the right answers to the sample questions, you won't be prepared for the real thing. **Study the concepts** until you understand them fully, and then you'll be able to answer any question that shows up on the test.

It's important to wait on the practice tests until you're ready. If you take a test on your first day of study, you may be overwhelmed by the amount of material covered and how much you need to learn. Work up to it gradually.

On test day, you'll need to be prepared for answering questions, managing your time, and using the test-taking strategies you've learned. It's a lot to balance, like a mental marathon that will have a big impact on your future. Like training for a marathon, you'll need to start slowly and work your way up. When test day arrives, you'll be ready.

Start with the strategies you've read in the first two Secret Keys—plan your course and study in the way that works best for you. If you have time, consider using multiple study resources to get different approaches to the same concepts. It can be helpful to see difficult concepts from more than one angle. Then find a good source for practice tests. Many times, the test website will suggest potential study resources or provide sample tests.

Secret Key #4 – Have a Plan for Guessing

When you're taking the test, you may find yourself stuck on a question. Some of the answer choices seem better than others, but you don't see the one answer choice that is obviously correct. What do you do?

The scenario described above is very common, yet most test takers have not effectively prepared for it. Developing and practicing a plan for guessing may be one of the single most effective uses of your time as you get ready for the exam.

In developing your plan for guessing, there are three questions to address:

- When should you start the guessing process?
- How should you narrow down the choices?
- Which answer should you choose?

When to Start the Guessing Process

Unless your plan for guessing is to select C every time (which, despite its merits, is not what we recommend), you need to leave yourself enough time to apply your answer elimination strategies. Since you have a limited amount of time for each question, that means that if you're going to give yourself the best shot at guessing correctly, you have to decide quickly whether or not you will guess.

Of course, the best-case scenario is that you don't have to guess at all, so first, see if you can answer the question based on your knowledge of the subject and basic reasoning skills. Focus on the key words in the question and try to jog your memory of related topics. Give yourself a chance to bring the knowledge to mind, but once you realize that you don't have (or you can't access) the knowledge you need to answer the question, it's time to start the guessing process.

It's almost always better to start the guessing process too early than too late. It only takes a few seconds to remember something and answer the question from knowledge. Carefully eliminating wrong answer choices takes longer. Plus, going through the process of eliminating answer choices can actually help jog your memory.

Summary: Start the guessing process as soon as you decide that you can't answer the question based on your knowledge.

How to Narrow Down the Choices

The next chapter in this book (**Test-Taking Strategies**) includes a wide range of strategies for how to approach questions and how to look for answer choices to eliminate. You will definitely want to read those carefully, practice them, and figure out which ones work best for you. Here though, we're going to address a mindset rather than a particular strategy.

Your chances of guessing an answer correctly depend on how many options you are choosing from.

How many choices you have	How likely you are to guess correctly
5	20%
4	25%
3	33%
2	50%
1	100%

You can see from this chart just how valuable it is to be able to eliminate incorrect answers and make an educated guess, but there are two things that many test takers do that cause them to miss out on the benefits of guessing:

- Accidentally eliminating the correct answer
- Selecting an answer based on an impression

We'll look at the first one here, and the second one in the next section.

To avoid accidentally eliminating the correct answer, we recommend a thought exercise called **the $5 challenge**. In this challenge, you only eliminate an answer choice from contention if you are willing to bet $5 on it being wrong. Why $5? Five dollars is a small but not insignificant amount of money. It's an amount you could afford to lose but wouldn't want to throw away. And while losing $5 once might not hurt too much, doing it twenty times will set you back $100. In the same way, each small decision you make—eliminating a choice here, guessing on a question there—won't by itself impact your score very much, but when you put them all together, they can make a big difference. By holding each answer choice elimination decision to a higher standard, you can reduce the risk of accidentally eliminating the correct answer.

The $5 challenge can also be applied in a positive sense: If you are willing to bet $5 that an answer choice *is* correct, go ahead and mark it as correct.

Summary: Only eliminate an answer choice if you are willing to bet $5 that it is wrong.

Which Answer to Choose

You're taking the test. You've run into a hard question and decided you'll have to guess. You've eliminated all the answer choices you're willing to bet $5 on. Now you have to pick an answer. Why do we even need to talk about this? Why can't you just pick whichever one you feel like when the time comes?

The answer to these questions is that if you don't come into the test with a plan, you'll rely on your impression to select an answer choice, and if you do that, you risk falling into a trap. The test writers know that everyone who takes their test will be guessing on some of the questions, so they intentionally write wrong answer choices to seem plausible. You still have to pick an answer though, and if the wrong answer choices are designed to look right, how can you ever be sure that you're not falling for their trap? The best solution we've found to this dilemma is to take the decision out of your hands entirely. Here is the process we recommend:

Once you've eliminated any choices that you are confident (willing to bet $5) are wrong, select the first remaining choice as your answer.

Whether you choose to select the first remaining choice, the second, or the last, the important thing is that you use some preselected standard. Using this approach guarantees that you will not be enticed into selecting an answer choice that looks right, because you are not basing your decision on how the answer choices look.

This is not meant to make you question your knowledge. Instead, it is to help you recognize the difference between your knowledge and your impressions. There's a huge difference between thinking an answer is right because of what you know, and thinking an answer is right because it looks or sounds like it should be right.

Summary: To ensure that your selection is appropriately random, make a predetermined selection from among all answer choices you have not eliminated.

Test-Taking Strategies

This section contains a list of test-taking strategies that you may find helpful as you work through the test. By taking what you know and applying logical thought, you can maximize your chances of answering any question correctly!

It is very important to realize that every question is different and every person is different: no single strategy will work on every question, and no single strategy will work for every person. That's why we've included all of them here, so you can try them out and determine which ones work best for different types of questions and which ones work best for you.

Question Strategies

READ CAREFULLY

Read the question and answer choices carefully. Don't miss the question because you misread the terms. You have plenty of time to read each question thoroughly and make sure you understand what is being asked. Yet a happy medium must be attained, so don't waste too much time. You must read carefully, but efficiently.

CONTEXTUAL CLUES

Look for contextual clues. If the question includes a word you are not familiar with, look at the immediate context for some indication of what the word might mean. Contextual clues can often give you all the information you need to decipher the meaning of an unfamiliar word. Even if you can't determine the meaning, you may be able to narrow down the possibilities enough to make a solid guess at the answer to the question.

PREFIXES

If you're having trouble with a word in the question or answer choices, try dissecting it. Take advantage of every clue that the word might include. Prefixes and suffixes can be a huge help. Usually they allow you to determine a basic meaning. Pre- means before, post- means after, pro - is positive, de- is negative. From prefixes and suffixes, you can get an idea of the general meaning of the word and try to put it into context.

HEDGE WORDS

Watch out for critical hedge words, such as *likely*, *may*, *can*, *sometimes*, *often*, *almost*, *mostly*, *usually*, *generally*, *rarely*, and *sometimes*. Question writers insert these hedge phrases to cover every possibility. Often an answer choice will be wrong simply because it leaves no room for exception. Be on guard for answer choices that have definitive words such as *exactly* and *always*.

SWITCHBACK WORDS

Stay alert for *switchbacks*. These are the words and phrases frequently used to alert you to shifts in thought. The most common switchback words are *but*, *although*, and *however*. Others include *nevertheless*, *on the other hand*, *even though*, *while*, *in spite of*, *despite*, *regardless of*. Switchback words are important to catch because they can change the direction of the question or an answer choice.

8

FACE VALUE

When in doubt, use common sense. Accept the situation in the problem at face value. Don't read too much into it. These problems will not require you to make wild assumptions. If you have to go beyond creativity and warp time or space in order to have an answer choice fit the question, then you should move on and consider the other answer choices. These are normal problems rooted in reality. The applicable relationship or explanation may not be readily apparent, but it is there for you to figure out. Use your common sense to interpret anything that isn't clear.

Answer Choice Strategies

ANSWER SELECTION

The most thorough way to pick an answer choice is to identify and eliminate wrong answers until only one is left, then confirm it is the correct answer. Sometimes an answer choice may immediately seem right, but be careful. The test writers will usually put more than one reasonable answer choice on each question, so take a second to read all of them and make sure that the other choices are not equally obvious. As long as you have time left, it is better to read every answer choice than to pick the first one that looks right without checking the others.

ANSWER CHOICE FAMILIES

An answer choice family consists of two (in rare cases, three) answer choices that are very similar in construction and cannot all be true at the same time. If you see two answer choices that are direct opposites or parallels, one of them is usually the correct answer. For instance, if one answer choice says that quantity x increases and another either says that quantity x decreases (opposite) or says that quantity y increases (parallel), then those answer choices would fall into the same family. An answer choice that doesn't match the construction of the answer choice family is more likely to be incorrect. Most questions will not have answer choice families, but when they do appear, you should be prepared to recognize them.

ELIMINATE ANSWERS

Eliminate answer choices as soon as you realize they are wrong, but make sure you consider all possibilities. If you are eliminating answer choices and realize that the last one you are left with is also wrong, don't panic. Start over and consider each choice again. There may be something you missed the first time that you will realize on the second pass.

AVOID FACT TRAPS

Don't be distracted by an answer choice that is factually true but doesn't answer the question. You are looking for the choice that answers the question. Stay focused on what the question is asking for so you don't accidentally pick an answer that is true but incorrect. Always go back to the question and make sure the answer choice you've selected actually answers the question and is not merely a true statement.

EXTREME STATEMENTS

In general, you should avoid answers that put forth extreme actions as standard practice or proclaim controversial ideas as established fact. An answer choice that states the "process should be used in certain situations, if…" is much more likely to be correct than one that states the "process should be discontinued completely." The first is a calm rational statement and doesn't even make a definitive, uncompromising stance, using a hedge word *if* to provide wiggle room, whereas the second choice is a radical idea and far more extreme.

BENCHMARK

As you read through the answer choices and you come across one that seems to answer the question well, mentally select that answer choice. This is not your final answer, but it's the one that will help you evaluate the other answer choices. The one that you selected is your benchmark or standard for judging each of the other answer choices. Every other answer choice must be compared to your benchmark. That choice is correct until proven otherwise by another answer choice beating it. If you find a better answer, then that one becomes your new benchmark. Once you've decided that no other choice answers the question as well as your benchmark, you have your final answer.

PREDICT THE ANSWER

Before you even start looking at the answer choices, it is often best to try to predict the answer. When you come up with the answer on your own, it is easier to avoid distractions and traps because you will know exactly what to look for. The right answer choice is unlikely to be word-for-word what you came up with, but it should be a close match. Even if you are confident that you have the right answer, you should still take the time to read each option before moving on.

General Strategies

TOUGH QUESTIONS

If you are stumped on a problem or it appears too hard or too difficult, don't waste time. Move on! Remember though, if you can quickly check for obviously incorrect answer choices, your chances of guessing correctly are greatly improved. Before you completely give up, at least try to knock out a couple of possible answers. Eliminate what you can and then guess at the remaining answer choices before moving on.

CHECK YOUR WORK

Since you will probably not know every term listed and the answer to every question, it is important that you get credit for the ones that you do know. Don't miss any questions through careless mistakes. If at all possible, try to take a second to look back over your answer selection and make sure you've selected the correct answer choice and haven't made a costly careless mistake (such as marking an answer choice that you didn't mean to mark). This quick double check should more than pay for itself in caught mistakes for the time it costs.

DON'T RUSH

It is very easy to make errors when you are in a hurry. Maintaining a fast pace in answering questions is pointless if it makes you miss questions that you would have gotten right otherwise. Test writers like to include distracting information and wrong answers that seem right. Taking a little extra time to avoid careless mistakes can make all the difference in your test score. Find a pace that allows you to be confident in the answers that you select.

KEEP MOVING

Panicking will not help you pass the test, so do your best to stay calm and keep moving. Taking deep breaths and going through the answer elimination steps you practiced can help to break through a stress barrier and keep your pace.

Final Notes

The combination of a solid foundation of content knowledge and the confidence that comes from practicing your plan for applying that knowledge is the key to maximizing your performance on test day. As your foundation of content knowledge is built up and strengthened, you'll find that the strategies included in this chapter become more and more effective in helping you quickly sift through the distractions and traps of the test to isolate the correct answer.

Now it's time to move on to the test content chapters of this book, but be sure to keep your goal in mind. As you read, think about how you will be able to apply this information on the test. If you've already seen sample questions for the test and you have an idea of the question format and style, try to come up with questions of your own that you can answer based on what you're reading. This will give you valuable practice applying your knowledge in the same ways you can expect to on test day.

Good luck and good studying!

Mathematics

Elementary Algebra and Functions

NUMBERS AND THEIR CLASSIFICATIONS

Numbers are the basic building blocks of mathematics. Specific features of numbers are identified by the following terms:

Integers – The set of whole positive and negative numbers, including zero. Integers do not include fractions $\left(\frac{1}{3}\right)$, decimals (0.56), or mixed numbers $\left(7\frac{3}{4}\right)$.

Prime number – A whole number greater than 1 that has only two factors, itself and 1; that is, a number that can be divided evenly only by 1 and itself.

Composite number – A whole number greater than 1 that has more than two different factors; in other words, any whole number that is not a prime number. For example: The composite number 8 has the factors of 1, 2, 4, and 8.

Even number – Any integer that can be divided by 2 without leaving a remainder. For example: 2, 4, 6, 8, and so on.

Odd number – Any integer that cannot be divided evenly by 2. For example: 3, 5, 7, 9, and so on.

Decimal number – a number that uses a decimal point to show the part of the number that is less than one. Example: 1.234.

Decimal point – a symbol used to separate the ones place from the tenths place in decimals or dollars from cents in currency.

Decimal place – the position of a number to the right of the decimal point. In the decimal 0.123, the 1 is in the first place to the right of the decimal point, indicating tenths; the 2 is in the second place, indicating hundredths; and the 3 is in the third place, indicating thousandths.

The **decimal**, or **base 10**, **system** is a number system that uses ten different digits (0, 1, 2, 3, 4, 5, 6, 7, 8, 9). An example of a number system that uses something other than ten digits is the binary, or base 2, number system, used by computers, which uses only the numbers 0 and 1. It is thought that the decimal system originated because people had only their 10 fingers for counting.

> **Review Video: Numbers and their Classifications**
> Visit mometrix.com/academy and enter code: 461071

Rational numbers include all integers, decimals, and fractions. Any terminating or repeating decimal number is a rational number.

> **Review Video: Rational Numbers**
> Visit mometrix.com/academy and enter code: 280645

Irrational numbers cannot be written as fractions or decimals because the number of decimal places is infinite and there is no recurring pattern of digits within the number. For example, pi (π)

13

begins with 3.141592 and continues without terminating or repeating, so pi is an irrational number.

> **Review Video: Irrational Numbers on a Number Line**
> Visit mometrix.com/academy and enter code: 433866

Real numbers are the set of all rational and irrational numbers.

> **Review Video: Negative and Positive Number Line**
> Visit mometrix.com/academy and enter code: 816439

OPERATIONS

FOUR BASIC OPERATIONS

Addition increases the value of one quantity by the value of another quantity. Example: $2 + 4 = 6$; $8 + 9 = 17$. The result is called the **sum**. With addition, the order *does not* matter. $4 + 2 = 2 + 4$.

Subtraction is the opposite operation to addition; it decreases the value of one quantity by the value of another quantity. Example: $6 - 4 = 2$; $17 - 8 = 9$. The result is called the **difference**. Note that with subtraction, the order *does* matter. $6 - 4 \neq 4 - 6$.

> **Review Video: Addition and Subtraction**
> Visit mometrix.com/academy and enter code: 521157

Multiplication can be thought of as repeated addition. One number tells how many times to add the other number to itself. Example: 3×2 (three times two) $= 2 + 2 + 2 = 6$. The result is called the **product**. With multiplication, the order *does not* matter. $2 \times 3 = 3 \times 2$ or $3 + 3 = 2 + 2 + 2$.

Division is the opposite operation to multiplication; one number tells us how many parts to divide the other number into. Example: $20 \div 4 = 5$; if 20 is split into 4 equal parts, each part is 5. The result is called the **quotient**. Note that with division, the order of the numbers *does* matter. $20 \div 4 \neq 4 \div 20$.

> **Review Video: Multiplication and Division**
> Visit mometrix.com/academy and enter code: 643326

BASIC OPERATIONS WITH SIGNED NUMBERS

When **adding signed numbers**, if the signs are the same simply add the absolute values of the addends and apply the original sign to the sum. For example, $(+4) + (+8) = +12$ and $(-4) + (-8) = -12$. When the original signs are different, take the absolute values of the addends and subtract the smaller value from the larger value, then apply the original sign of the larger value to the difference. For instance, $(+4) + (-8) = -4$ and $(-4) + (+8) = +4$.

For **subtracting signed numbers**, change the sign of the number after the minus symbol and then follow the same rules used for addition. For example, $(+4) - (+8) = (+4) + (-8) = -4$.

When **multiplying signed numbers**, the product is positive if the signs are the same. For example, $(+4) \times (+8) = +32$ and $(-4) \times (-8) = +32$. If the signs are opposite, the product is negative. For example, $(+4) \times (-8) = -32$ and $(-4) \times (+8) = -32$. When more than two factors are multiplied together, the sign of the product is determined by how many negative factors are present. If there are an odd number of negative factors then the product is negative, whereas an even number of

14

negative factors indicates a positive product. For instance, $(+4) \times (-8) \times (-2) = +64$ and $(-4) \times (-8) \times (-2) = -64$.

The rules for **dividing signed numbers** are essentially the same as those for multiplying signed numbers. If the dividend and divisor have the same sign, the quotient is positive. If the dividend and divisor have opposite signs, the quotient is negative. For example, $(-4) \div (+8) = -0.5$.

PARENTHESES

Parentheses are used to designate which operations should be done first when there are multiple operations. Example: $4 - (2 + 1) = 1$; the parentheses tell us that we must add 2 and 1, and then subtract the sum from 4, rather than subtracting 2 from 4 and then adding 1 (this would give us an answer of 3).

EXPONENTS

An exponent is a superscript number placed next to another number at the top right. It indicates how many times the base number is to be multiplied by itself. **Exponents** provide a shorthand way to write what would be a longer mathematical expression. Example: $a^2 = a \times a$; $2^4 = 2 \times 2 \times 2 \times 2$. A number with an exponent of 2 is said to be **squared**, while a number with an exponent of 3 is said to be **cubed**. The value of a number raised to an exponent is called its power. So, 8^4 is read as "8 to the 4th power," or "8 raised to the power of 4." A negative exponent is the same as the **reciprocal** of a positive exponent. Example: $a^{-2} = \frac{1}{a^2}$.

Review Video: Exponents
Visit mometrix.com/academy and enter code: 600998

The laws of exponents are as follows:

1. Any number to the power of 1 is equal to itself: $a^1 = a$.
2. The number 1 raised to any power is equal to 1: $1^n = 1$.
3. Any number raised to the power of 0 is equal to 1: $a^0 = 1$.
4. Add exponents to multiply powers of the same base number: $a^n \times a^m = a^{n+m}$.
5. Subtract exponents to divide powers of the same number; that is $a^n \div a^m = a^{n-m}$.
6. Multiply exponents to raise a power to a power: $(a^n)^m = a^{n \times m}$.
7. If multiplied or divided numbers inside parentheses are collectively raised to a power, this is the same as each individual term being raised to that power: $(a \times b)^n = a^n \times b^n$; $(a \div b)^n = a^n \div b^n$.

Note: Exponents do not have to be integers. Fractional or decimal exponents follow all the rules above as well. Example: $5^{\frac{1}{4}} \times 5^{\frac{3}{4}} = 5^{\frac{1}{4}+\frac{3}{4}} = 5^1 = 5$.

ROOTS AND SQUARES

A **root**, such as a *square root*, is another way of writing a fractional exponent. Instead of using a superscript, roots use the radical symbol ($\sqrt{}$) to indicate the operation. A radical will have a number underneath the bar, and may sometimes have a number in the upper left: $\sqrt[n]{a}$, read as "the nth root of a." The relationship between radical notation and exponent notation can be described by this equation: $\sqrt[n]{a} = a^{\frac{1}{n}}$.

The two special cases of $n = 2$ and $n = 3$ are called square roots and cube roots. If there is no number to the upper left, it is understood to be a square root ($n = 2$). Nearly all of the roots you encounter will be square roots.

A square root is the same as a number raised to the one-half power. When we say that a is the square root of b ($a = \sqrt{b}$), we mean that a multiplied by itself equals b: ($a \times a = b$).

Review Video: Roots
Visit mometrix.com/academy and enter code: 795655

A perfect square is a number that has an integer for its square root. There are 10 perfect squares from 1 to 100: 1, 4, 9, 16, 25, 36, 49, 64, 81, 100 (the squares of integers 1 through 10).

Review Video: Square Root and Perfect Square
Visit mometrix.com/academy and enter code: 648063

ORDER OF OPERATIONS

Order of Operations is a set of rules that dictates the order in which we must perform each operation in an expression so that we will evaluate it accurately. If we have an expression that includes multiple different operations, *Order of Operations* tells us which operations to do first. The most common mnemonic for *Order of Operations* is PEMDAS, or "Please Excuse My Dear Aunt Sally." PEMDAS stands for Parentheses, Exponents, Multiplication, Division, Addition, Subtraction. It is important to understand that multiplication and division have equal precedence, as do addition and subtraction, so those pairs of operations are simply worked from left to right in order.

Review Video: Order of Operations
Visit mometrix.com/academy and enter code: 259675

Example: Evaluate the expression $5 + 20 \div 4 \times (2 + 3)^2 - 6$ using the correct order of operations.

- P: Perform the operations inside the parentheses, $(2 + 3) = 5$.
- E: Simplify the exponents, $(5)^2 = 25$.
  - The equation now looks like this: $5 + 20 \div 4 \times 25 - 6$.
- MD: Perform multiplication and division from left to right, $20 \div 4 = 5$; then $5 \times 25 = 125$.
  - The equation now looks like this: $5 + 125 - 6$.
- AS: Perform addition and subtraction from left to right, $5 + 125 = 130$; then $130 - 6 = 124$.

ABSOLUTE VALUE

A number's **absolute value** can be thought of as its distance from zero on the number line. Absolute value is indicated by vertical bars on either side of a specified quantity (e.g., $|x - 5|$).

Example:

$$|3| = |-3| = 3$$

The distance between 0 and 3 on a number line is three units. Likewise, the distance between 0 and -3 is three units.

For order of operations purposes, an absolute value is treated like parentheses in that the quantity inside of it must be calculated before anything else can be done.

SCIENTIFIC NOTATION

Scientific notation is a way of writing large numbers in a shorter form. The form $a \times 10^n$ is used in scientific notation, where a is greater than or equal to 1, but less than 10, and n is the number of places the decimal must move to get from the original number to a.

Example: The number 230,400,000 is cumbersome to write. To write the value in scientific notation, place a decimal point between the first and second numbers, and include all digits through the last non-zero digit ($a = 2.304$). To find the appropriate power of 10, count the number of places the decimal point has to move ($n = 8$). The number is positive if the decimal moves to the left, and negative if it moves to the right. We can then write 230,400,000 as 2.304×10^8.

If we look instead at the number 0.00002304, we have the same value for a, but this time the decimal moves 5 places to the right ($n = -5$). Thus, 0.00002304 can be written as 2.304×10^{-5}.

Using this notation makes it simple to compare very large or very small numbers. By comparing exponents, it is easy to see that 3.28×10^4 is smaller than 1.51×10^5, because 4 is less than 5.

> **Review Video: Scientific Notation**
> Visit mometrix.com/academy and enter code: 976454

FACTORS AND MULTIPLES

The **factors** of a given number are all of the numbers that can be divided evenly into the given number. For example, the number 12 has six factors: 1, 2, 3, 4, 6, and 12. Every number has at least two factors (1 and itself). A **prime number** has *only* these two factors, but other numbers can have many factors.

A **common factor** is a factor that is shared by two or more different numbers. For example, the factors of 12 are 1, 2, 3, 4, 6, and 12, while the factors of 15 are 1, 3, 5, and 15. The *common* factors of 12 and 15 are 1 and 3.

A **prime factor** is a factor that is also a prime number. The prime factors of 12 are 2 and 3, while 15 has prime factors of 3 and 5.

A **multiple** of a given number is a number that can be obtained by multiplying that given number by a positive integer. For example, multiples of 3 include 3, 6, 9, 12, 15, and so on. Multiples of 7 include 7, 14, 21, 28, 35, and so on.

Prime factorization is the process of recording all prime factors of a given number. A factor is recorded as many times as it is used; for example, the prime factorization of 18 is $2 \times 3 \times 3$. Prime factorization is often used to find quantities such as the **least common multiple** (LCM) and the **greatest common factor** (GCF). To illustrate these concepts, we'll take the prime factorizations of 60 and 72:

$$60 = 2 \times 2 \times 3 \times 5$$

$$72 = 2 \times 2 \times 2 \times 3 \times 3$$

The **GCF** of two numbers is the largest number that is a factor of both numbers. To find the GCF of 60 and 72, find which numbers appear in both prime factorizations. Both sets include two 2's and a 3, with no other values in common. This means that the GCF of 60 and 72 is $2 \times 2 \times 3 = 12$.

The **LCM** of two numbers is the smallest number that is a multiple of both numbers. To find the LCM of 60 and 72, the initial steps are the same: we find that both sets of numbers include two 2's and a 3. We note that 60 also includes a 5 while 72 includes an additional 2 and 3. With all numbers in the prime factorization accounted for, we find that the LCM of 60 and 72 is $(2 \times 2 \times 3) \times (2 \times 3 \times 5) = 12 \times 30 = 360$.

Note: For two numbers a and b where $a < b$, note that the GCF of a and b must be less than or equal to a, while the LCM of a and b must be greater than or equal to b.

FRACTIONS, PERCENTAGES, AND RELATED CONCEPTS

FRACTIONS

A **fraction** is a number that is expressed as one integer written above another integer, with a dividing line between them $\left(\frac{x}{y}\right)$. It represents the **quotient** of the two numbers "x divided by y." It can also be thought of as x out of y equal parts.

The top number of a fraction is called the **numerator**, and it represents the number of parts under consideration. The 1 in $\frac{1}{4}$ means that 1 part out of the whole is being considered in the calculation. The bottom number of a fraction is called the **denominator**, and it represents the total number of equal parts. The 4 in $\frac{1}{4}$ means that the whole consists of 4 equal parts. A fraction cannot have a denominator of zero; this is referred to as "undefined."

Review Video: <u>Fractions</u>
Visit mometrix.com/academy and enter code: 262335

MANIPULATING FRACTIONS

Fractions can be manipulated, without changing the value of the fraction, by multiplying or dividing (but not adding or subtracting) both the numerator and denominator by the same number. If you divide both numbers by a common factor, you are **reducing** or **simplifying** the fraction. Two fractions that have the same value, but are expressed differently are known as **equivalent fractions**. For example, $\frac{2}{10}, \frac{3}{15}, \frac{4}{20}$, and $\frac{5}{25}$ are all equivalent fractions. They can also all be reduced or simplified to $\frac{1}{5}$.

COMMON DENOMINATORS

When two fractions are manipulated so that they have the same denominator, this is known as finding a **common denominator**. The number chosen to be that common denominator should be the **least common multiple** of the two original denominators. Example: $\frac{3}{4}$ and $\frac{5}{6}$; the least common multiple of 4 and 6 is 12. Manipulating to achieve the common denominator: $\frac{3}{4} = \frac{9}{12}; \frac{5}{6} = \frac{10}{12}$.

OPERATIONS WITH FRACTIONS

If two fractions have a common denominator, they can be added or subtracted simply by adding or subtracting the two numerators and retaining the same denominator. If the two fractions do not already have the same denominator, one or both of them must be manipulated so that they have a common denominator before they can be added or subtracted. Example: $\frac{1}{2} + \frac{1}{4} = \frac{2}{4} + \frac{1}{4} = \frac{3}{4}$.

Review Video: <u>Adding and Subtracting Fractions</u>
Visit mometrix.com/academy and enter code: 378080

Two fractions can be multiplied by multiplying the two numerators to find the new numerator and the two denominators to find the new denominator. Example: $\frac{1}{3} \times \frac{2}{3} = \frac{1 \times 2}{3 \times 3} = \frac{2}{9}$.

Review Video: <u>Multiplying Fractions</u>
Visit mometrix.com/academy and enter code: 638849

Two fractions can be divided by flipping the numerator and denominator of the second fraction and then proceeding as though it were a multiplication. Example: $\frac{2}{3} \div \frac{3}{4} = \frac{2}{3} \times \frac{4}{3} = \frac{8}{9}$.

Review Video: <u>Dividing Fractions</u>
Visit mometrix.com/academy and enter code: 300874

PROPER AND IMPROPER FRACTIONS

A fraction whose denominator is greater than its numerator is known as a **proper fraction**, while a fraction whose numerator is greater than its denominator is known as an **improper fraction**. Proper fractions have values less than one and improper fractions have values greater than one.

MIXED NUMBERS

A mixed number is a number that contains both an integer and a fraction. Any improper fraction can be rewritten as a mixed number.

$$\frac{8}{3} = \frac{6}{3} + \frac{2}{3} = 2 + \frac{2}{3} = 2\frac{2}{3}$$

Similarly, any mixed number can be rewritten as an improper fraction.

$$1\frac{3}{5} = 1 + \frac{3}{5} = \frac{5}{5} + \frac{3}{5} = \frac{8}{5}$$

PERCENTAGES

Percentages can be thought of as fractions that are based on a whole of 100; that is, one whole is equal to 100%. The word **percent** means "per hundred." Fractions can be expressed as percentages by finding equivalent fractions with a denominator of 100. Example: $\frac{7}{10} = \frac{70}{100} = 70\%$; $\frac{1}{4} = \frac{25}{100} = 25\%$.

> **Review Video: Percentages**
> Visit mometrix.com/academy and enter code: 141911

To express a percentage as a fraction, divide the percentage number by 100 and reduce the fraction to its simplest possible terms. Example: $60\% = \frac{60}{100} = \frac{3}{5}$; $96\% = \frac{96}{100} = \frac{24}{25}$.

Converting decimals to percentages and percentages to decimals is as simple as moving the decimal point. To convert from a decimal to a percentage, move the decimal point **two places to the right**. To convert from a percentage to a decimal, move it **two places to the left**. Example: 0.23 = 23%; 5.34 = 534%; 0.007 = 0.7%; 700% = 7.00; 86% = 0.86; 0.15% = 0.0015.

It may be helpful to remember that the percentage number will always be larger than the equivalent decimal number.

> **Review Video: Converting Decimals to Fractions and Percentages**
> Visit mometrix.com/academy and enter code: 986765

PERCENTAGE PROBLEMS

A percentage problem can be presented three main ways: (1) Find what percentage of some number another number is. Example: What percentage of 40 is 8? (2) Find what number is some percentage of a given number. Example: What number is 20% of 40? (3) Find what number another number is a given percentage of. Example: What number is 8 20% of?

The three components in all of these cases are the same: a **whole** (W), a **part** (P), and a **percentage** (%). These are related by the equation: $P = W \times \%$. This is the form of the equation you would use to solve problems of type (2). To solve types (1) and (3), you would use these two forms: $\% = \frac{P}{W}$ and $W = \frac{P}{\%}$.

The thing that frequently makes percentage problems difficult is that they are most often also word problems, so a large part of solving them is figuring out which quantities are what.

Example: In a school cafeteria, 7 students choose pizza, 9 choose hamburgers, and 4 choose tacos. Find the percentage that chooses tacos. To find the whole, you must first add all of the parts: 7 + 9 + 4 = 20. The percentage can then be found by dividing the part by the whole $\left(\% = \frac{P}{W}\right)$: $\frac{4}{20} = \frac{20}{100} = 20\%$.

RATIOS

A **ratio** is a comparison of two quantities in a particular order. Example: If there are 14 computers in a lab, and the class has 20 students, there is a student to computer ratio of 20 to 14, commonly written as 20:14. Ratios are normally reduced to their smallest whole number representation, so 20:14 would be reduced to 10:7 by dividing both sides by 2.

> **Review Video: Ratios**
> Visit mometrix.com/academy and enter code: 996914

PROPORTIONS

A **proportion** is a relationship between two quantities that dictates how one changes when the other changes. A **direct proportion** describes a relationship in which a quantity increases by a set amount for every increase in the other quantity, or decreases by that same amount for every decrease in the other quantity.

> **Review Video: Proportions**
> Visit mometrix.com/academy and enter code: 505355

INVERSE PROPORTIONS

An **inverse proportion** is a relationship in which an increase in one quantity is accompanied by a decrease in the other, or vice versa. Example: the time required for a car trip decreases as the speed increases, and increases as the speed decreases, so the time required is inversely proportional to the speed of the car.

RULES FOR MANIPULATING EQUATIONS

LIKE TERMS

Like terms are terms in an equation that have the same variable, regardless of whether or not they also have the same coefficient. This includes terms that *lack* a variable; all constants (i.e. numbers without variables) are considered like terms. If the equation involves terms with a variable raised to different powers, the like terms are those that have the variable raised to the same power.

For example, consider the equation $x^2 + 3x + 2 = 2x^2 + x - 7 + 2x$. In this equation, 2 and –7 are like terms; they are both constants. $3x$, x, and $2x$ are like terms: they all include the variable x raised to the first power. x^2 and $2x^2$ are like terms; they both include the variable x, raised to the second power. $2x$ and $2x^2$ are not like terms; although they both involve the variable x, the variable is not raised to the same power in both terms. The fact that they have the same coefficient, 2, is not relevant.

CARRYING OUT THE SAME OPERATION ON BOTH SIDES OF AN EQUATION

When solving an equation, the general procedure is to carry out a series of operations on both sides of an equation, choosing operations that will tend to simplify the equation when doing so. The reason why the same operation must be carried out on both sides of the equation is because that leaves the meaning of the equation unchanged, and yields a result that is equivalent to the original equation. This would not be the case if we carried out an operation on one side of an equation and not the other. Consider what an equation means: it is a statement that two values or expressions are equal. If we carry out the same operation on both sides of the equation—add 3 to both sides, for example—then the two sides of the equation are changed in the same way, and so remain equal. If we do that to only one side of the equation—add 3 to one side but not the other—then that wouldn't be true; if we change one side of the equation but not the other then the two sides are no longer equal.

ADVANTAGE OF COMBINING LIKE TERMS

Combining like terms refers to adding or subtracting like terms—terms with the same variable— and therefore reducing sets of like terms to a single term. The main advantage of doing this is that it simplifies the equation. Often combining like terms can be done as the first step in solving an equation, though it can also be done later, such as after distributing terms in a product.

For example, consider the equation $2(x + 3) + 3(2 + x + 3) = -4$. The 2 and the 3 in the second set of parentheses are like terms, and we can combine them, yielding $2(x + 3) + 3(x + 5) = -4$. Now we can carry out the multiplications implied by the parentheses, distributing the outer 2 and 3 accordingly: $2x + 6 + 3x + 15 = -4$. The $2x$ and the $3x$ are like terms, and we can add them together: $5x + 6 + 15 = -4$. Now, the constants 6, 15, and –4 are also like terms, and we can combine them as well: subtracting 6 and 15 from both sides of the equation, we get $5x = -4 - 6 - 15$, or $5x = -25$, which simplifies further to $x = -5$.

CANCELING TERMS ON OPPOSITE SIDES OF AN EQUATION

Two terms on opposite sides of an equation can be canceled if and only if they *exactly* match each other. They must have the same variable raised to the same power and the same coefficient. For example, in the equation $3x + 2x^2 + 6 = 2x^2 - 6$, $2x^2$ appears on both sides of the equation, and can be canceled, leaving $3x + 6 = -6$. The 6 on each side of the equation can*not* be canceled, because it is added on one side of the equation and subtracted on the other. While they cannot be canceled, however, the 6 and –6 are like terms and can be combined, yielding $3x = -12$, which simplifies further to $x = -4$.

It's also important to note that the terms to be canceled must be independent terms and cannot be part of a larger term. For example, consider the equation $2(x + 6) = 3(x + 4) + 1$. We cannot cancel the xs, because even though they match each other they are part of the larger terms $2(x + 6)$ and $3(x + 4)$. We must first distribute the 2 and 3, yielding $2x + 12 = 3x + 12 + 1$. Now we see that the terms with the x's do not match, but the 12's do, and can be canceled, leaving $2x = 3x + 1$, which simplifies to $x = -1$.

IMPORTANCE OF SIMPLIFYING ALL TERMS IN EQUATIONS

Example:

> *Seeing the equation $2x + 4 = 4x + 7$, a student divides the first terms on each side by 2, yielding $x + 4 = 2x + 7$, and then combines like terms to get $x = -3$. However, this is incorrect, as can be seen by substituting –3 into the original equation. Explain what is wrong with the student's reasoning.*

As stated, it's easy to verify that the student's solution is incorrect: $2(-3) + 4 = -2$ and $4(-3) + 7 = -5$; clearly $-2 \neq -5$. The mistake was in the first step, which illustrates a common type of error in solving equations. The student tried to simplify the two variable terms by dividing them by 2. However, it's not valid to multiply or divide only one term on each side of an equation by a number; when multiplying or dividing, the operation must be applied to *every* term in the equation. So, dividing by 2 would yield not $x + 4 = 2x + 7$, but $x + 2 = 2x + \frac{7}{2}$. While this is now valid, that fraction is inconvenient to work with, so this may not be the best first step in solving the equation. Rather, it may have been better to first combine like terms: subtracting $4x$ from both sides yields $-2x + 4 = 7$; subtracting 4 from both sides yields $-2x = 3$; and *now* we can divide both sides by -2 to get $x = -\frac{3}{2}$.

PROCESS FOR MANIPULATING EQUATIONS

ISOLATING VARIABLES

To **isolate a variable** means to manipulate the equation so that the variable appears by itself on one side of the equation, and does not appear at all on the other side. Generally, an equation or inequality is considered to be solved once the variable is isolated and the other side of the equation or inequality is simplified as much as possible. In the case of a two-variable equation or inequality, only one variable need be isolated; it will not usually be possible to simultaneously isolate both variables.

For a linear equation—an equation in which the variable only appears raised to the first power—isolating a variable can be done by first moving all the terms with the variable to one side of the equation and all other terms to the other side. (*Moving* a term really means adding the inverse of the term to both sides; when a term is *moved* to the other side of the equation its sign is flipped.) Then combine like terms on each side. Finally, divide both sides by the coefficient of the variable, if applicable. The steps need not necessarily be done in this order, but this order will always work.

EQUATIONS WITH MORE THAN ONE SOLUTION

Some types of non-linear equation, such as equations involving squares of variables, may have more than one solution. For example, the equation $x^2 = 4$ has two solutions: 2 and -2. Equations with absolute values can also have multiple solutions: $|x| = 1$ has the solutions $x = 1$ and $x = -1$.

It is also possible for a linear equation to have more than one solution, but only if the equation is true regardless of the value of the variable. In this case, the equation is considered to have infinitely many solutions, because any possible value of the variable is a solution. We know a linear equation has infinitely many solutions if when we combine like terms the variables cancel, leaving a true statement. For example, consider the equation $2(3x + 5) = x + 5(x + 2)$. Distributing, we get $6x + 10 = x + 5x + 10$; combining like terms gives $6x + 10 = 6x + 10$, and the $6x$ terms cancel to leave $10 = 10$. This is clearly true, so the original equation is true for any value of x. We could also have canceled the 10s leaving $0 = 0$, but again this is clearly true—in general if both sides of the equation match exactly, it has infinitely many solutions.

EQUATIONS WITH NO SOLUTION

Some types of non-linear equation, such as equations involving squares of variables, may have no solution. For example, the equation $x^2 = -2$ has no solutions in the real numbers, because the square of any real number must be positive. Similarly, $|x| = -1$ has no solution, because the absolute value of a number is always positive.

It is also possible for an equation to have no solution even if does not involve any powers greater than one or absolute values or other special functions. For example, the equation $2(x + 3) + x = 3x$ has no solution. We can see that if we try to solve it: first we distribute, leaving $2x + 6 + x = 3x$. But now if we try to combine all the terms with the variable, we find that they cancel: we have $3x$ on the left and $3x$ on the right, canceling to leave us with $6 = 0$. This is clearly false. In general, whenever the variable terms in an equation cancel leaving different constants on both sides, it means that the equation has no solution. (If we are left with the *same* constant on both sides, the equation has infinitely many solutions instead.)

NECESSARY STEPS FOR SOLVING EQUATIONS

EXAMPLE 1

Describe the steps necessary to solve the equation $2x + 1 - x = 4 + 3x + 7$.

The following description of the steps in solving the equation represents only one way of doing so; there are other ways to solve the equation that involve the steps being done in a different order, but if done correctly they will all yield the same answer.

Our ultimate goal is to isolate the variable, x. To that end we first move all the terms containing x to the left side of the equation, and all the constant terms to the right side. Note that when we move a term to the other side of the equation its sign changes. We are therefore now left with $2x - x - 3x = 4 + 7 - 1$.

Next, we combine the like terms on each side of the equation, adding and subtracting the terms as appropriate. This leaves us with $-2x = 10$.

At this point, we're almost done; all that remains is to divide both sides by -2 to leave the x by itself. We now have our solution, $x = -5$. We can verify that this is a correct solution by substituting it back into the original equation.

EXAMPLE 2

Describe the steps necessary to solve the equation $2(x + 5) = 7(4 - x)$.

Generally, in equations that have a sum or difference of terms multiplied by another value or expression, the first step is to multiply those terms, distributing as necessary: $2(x + 5) = 2(x) + 2(5) = 2x + 10$, and $7(4 - x) = 7(4) - 7(x) = 28 - 7x$. So, the equation becomes $2x + 10 = 28 - 7x$. We can now add $7x$ to both sides to eliminate the variable from the right-hand side: $9x + 10 = 28$. Similarly, we can subtract 10 from both sides to move all the constants to the right: $9x = 18$. Finally, we can divide both sides by 9, yielding the final answer, $x = 2$.

FEATURES OF EQUATIONS THAT REQUIRE SPECIAL TREATMENT

LINEAR EQUATIONS

A linear equation is an equation in which variables only appear by themselves: not multiplied together, not with exponents other than one, and not inside absolute value signs or any other functions. For example, the equation $x + 1 - 3x = 5 - x$ is a linear equation: while x appears multiple times, it never appears with an exponent other than one or inside a function. The two-variable equation $2x - 3y = 5 + 2x$ is also a linear equation. In contrast, the equation $x^2 - 5 = 3x$ is *not* a linear equation, because it involves the term x^2. $\sqrt{x} = 5$ is not a linear equation, because it involves a square root. $(x - 1)^2 = 4$ is not a linear equation because even though there's no exponent on the x directly, it appears as part of an expression that is squared. The two-variable equation $x + xy - y = 5$ is not a linear equation because it includes the term xy, where two variables are multiplied together.

Linear equations can always be solved (or shown to have no solution) by combining like terms and performing simple operations on both sides of the equation. Some non-linear equations can also be solved by similar methods, but others may require more advanced methods of solution, if they can be solved analytically at all.

SOLVING EQUATIONS INVOLVING ROOTS
Example:

$$2\sqrt{x + 1} - 1 = 3$$

In an equation involving roots, the first step is to isolate the term with the root, if possible, and then raise both sides of the equation to the appropriate power to eliminate it. In this case, that can be done by adding 1 to both sides, yielding $2\sqrt{x + 1} = 4$, and then dividing both sides by 2, yielding $\sqrt{x + 1} = 2$. Now square both sides, yielding $x + 1 = 4$. Finally, subtracting 1 from both sides yields $x = 3$.

Squaring both sides of an equation may, however, yield a spurious solution—a solution to the squared equation that is *not* a solution of the original equation. It's therefore necessary to plug the solution back into the original equation to make sure it works. In this case, it does: $2\sqrt{3 + 1} - 1 = 2\sqrt{4} - 1 = 2(2) - 1 = 4 - 1 = 3$.

The same procedure applies for roots other than square roots. For example, given the equation $3 + \sqrt[3]{2x} = 5$, we can first subtract 3 from both sides, yielding $\sqrt[3]{2x} = 2$ and isolating the root. Raising both sides to the third power yields $2x = 2^3$, i.e. $2x = 8$. We can now divide both sides by 2 to get $x = 4$.

SOLVING EQUATIONS WITH EXPONENTS
Example:

$$2x^3 + 17 = 5x^3 - 7 \text{ or } (x - 1)^2 - 1 = 3$$

To solve an equation involving an exponent, the first step is to isolate the variable with the exponent. We can then take the appropriate root of both sides to eliminate the exponent. For instance, for the equation $2x^3 + 17 = 5x^3 - 7$, we can subtract $5x^3$ from both sides to get $-3x^3 + 17 = -7$, and then subtract 17 from both sides to get $-3x^3 = -24$. Finally, we can divide both sides by –3 to get $x^3 = 8$. Finally, we can take the cube root of both sides to get $x = \sqrt[3]{8} = 2$.

One important but often overlooked point is that equations with an exponent greater than 1 may have more than one answer. The solution to $x^2 = 9$ isn't simply $x = 3$; it's $x = \pm 3$: that is, $x = 3$ or $x = -3$. For a slightly more complicated example, consider the equation $(x - 1)^2 - 1 = 3$. Adding one to both sides yields $(x - 1)^2 = 4$; taking the square root of both sides yields $x - 1 = 2$. We can then add 1 to both sides to get $x = 3$. However, there's a second solution: we also have the possibility that $x - 1 = -2$, in which case $x = -1$. Both $x = 3$ and $x = -1$ are valid solutions, as can be verified by substituting them both into the original equation.

SOLVING EQUATIONS WITH ABSOLUTE VALUES
When solving an equation with an absolute value, the first step is to isolate the absolute value term. We then consider the two possibilities: when the expression inside the absolute value is positive or

when it is negative. In the former case, the expression in the absolute value equals the expression on the other side of the equation; in the latter, it equals the additive inverse of that expression—the expression times negative one. We consider each case separately, and finally check for spurious solutions.

EXAMPLE

Solve $|2x - 1| + x = 5$.

We can first isolate the absolute value by moving the x to the other side: $|2x - 1| = -x + 5$. Now, we have two possibilities. First, that $2x - 1$ is positive, and hence $2x - 1 = -x + 5$. Rearranging and combining like terms yields $3x = 6$, and hence $x = 2$. The other possibility is that $2x - 1$ is negative, and hence $2x - 1 = -(-x + 5) = x - 5$. In this case, rearranging and combining like terms yields $x = -4$. Substituting $x = 2$ and $x = -4$ back into the original equation, we see that they are both valid solutions.

Note that the absolute value of a sum or difference applies to the sum or difference as a whole, not to the individual terms: in general, $|2x - 1|$ is not equal to $|2x + 1|$ or to $|2x| - 1$.

SPURIOUS SOLUTIONS

A **spurious solution** may arise when we square both sides of an equation as a step in solving it, or under certain other operations on the equation. It is a solution to the squared or otherwise modified equation that is *not* a solution of the original equation. To identify a spurious solution, it's useful when you solve an equation involving roots or absolute values to plug the solution back into the original equation to make sure it's valid.

EXAMPLE 1

Find all real solutions to the equation $1 - \sqrt{x} = 2$.

It's not hard to isolate the root: subtract one from both sides, yielding $-\sqrt{x} = 1$. Finally, multiply both sides by –1, yielding $\sqrt{x} = -1$. Squaring both sides of the equation yields $x = 1$. However, if we plug this back into the original equation, we get $1 - \sqrt{1} = 2$, which is false. Therefore $x = 1$ is a spurious solution, and the equation has no real solutions.

EXAMPLE 2

Find all real solutions to the equation $|x + 1| = 2x + 5$.

This equation has two possibilities: $x + 1 = 2x + 5$, which simplifies to $x = -4$; or $x + 1 = -(2x + 5) = -2x - 5$, which simplifies to $x = -2$. However, if we try substituting both values back into the original equation, we see that only $x = -2$ yields a true statement. $x = -4$ is a spurious solution; $x = -2$ is the only valid solution to the equation.

STEPS TO SOLVING EQUATIONS

Example:

$$-x + 2\sqrt{x + 5} + 1 = 3$$

Start by isolating the term with the root. We can do that by moving the $-x$ and the 1 to the other side, yielding $2\sqrt{x + 5} = 3 + x - 1$, or $2\sqrt{x + 5} = x + 2$. Dividing both sides of the equation by 2 would give us a fractional term that could be messy to deal with, so we won't do that for now. Instead, we square both sides of the equation; note that on the left-hand side the 2 is outside the square root sign, so we have to square it. As a result, we get $4(x + 5) = (x + 2)^2$. Expanding both sides gives us $4x + 20 = x^2 + 4x + 4$. In this case, we see that we have $4x$ on both sides, so we can cancel the $4x$ (which is what allows us to solve this equation despite the different powers of x). We now have $20 = x^2 + 4$, or $x^2 = 16$. Since the variable is raised to an even power, we need to take the positive and negative roots, so $x = \pm 4$: that is, $x = 4$ or $x = -4$. Substituting both values into the original equation, we see that $x = 4$ satisfies the equation but $x = -4$ does not; hence $x = -4$ is a spurious solution, and the only solution to the equation is $x = 4$.

DIFFERENCES IN WORKING WITH INEQUALITIES VS. EQUATIONS

FLIPPING INEQUALITY SIGNS

When given an inequality, we can always turn the entire inequality around, swapping the two sides of the inequality and changing the inequality sign. For instance, $x + 2 > 2x - 3$ is equivalent to $2x - 3 < x + 2$. Aside from that, normally the inequality does not change if we carry out the same operation on both sides of the inequality. There is, however, one principal exception: if we *multiply* or *divide* both sides of the inequality by a *negative number*, the inequality is flipped. For example, if we take the inequality $-2x < 6$ and divide both sides by -2, the inequality flips and we are left with $x > -3$. This *only* applies to multiplication and division, and only with negative numbers. Multiplying or dividing both sides by a positive number, or adding or subtracting any number regardless of sign, does not flip the inequality.

COMPOUND INEQUALITIES

A **compound inequality** is an equality that consists of two inequalities combined with *and* or *or*. The two components of a proper compound inequality must be of opposite type: that is, one must be greater than (or greater than or equal to), the other less than (or less than or equal to). For instance, "$x + 1 < 2$ or $x + 1 > 3$" is a compound inequality, as is "$2x \geq 4$ and $2x \leq 6$." An *and* inequality can be written more compactly by having one inequality on each side of the common part: "$2x \geq 1$ and $2x \leq 6$," can also be written as $1 \leq 2x \leq 6$.

In order for the compound inequality to be meaningful, the two parts of an *and* inequality must overlap; otherwise no numbers satisfy the inequality. On the other hand, if the two parts of an *or* inequality overlap, then *all* numbers satisfy the inequality and as such is usually not meaningful.

Solving a compound inequality requires solving each part separately. For example, given the compound inequality "$x + 1 < 2$ or $x + 1 > 3$," the first inequality, $x + 1 < 2$, reduces to $x < 1$, and the second part, $x + 1 > 3$, reduces to $x > 2$, so the whole compound inequality can be written as "$x < 1$ or $x > 2$." Similarly, $1 \leq 2x \leq 6$ can be solved by dividing each term by 2, yielding $\frac{1}{2} \leq x \leq 3$.

SOLVING INEQUALITIES INVOLVING ABSOLUTE VALUES

To solve an inequality involving an absolute value, first isolate the term with the absolute value. Then proceed to treat the two cases separately as with an absolute value equation, but flipping the inequality in the case where the expression in the absolute value is negative (since that essentially involves multiplying both sides by -1.) The two cases are then combined into a compound inequality; if the absolute value is on the greater side of the inequality, then it is an *or* compound inequality, if on the lesser side, then it's an *and*.

EXAMPLE

Solve $2 + |x - 1| \geq 3$.

We can isolate the absolute value term by subtracting 2 from both sides: $|x - 1| \geq 1$. Now, we're left with the two cases $x - 1 \geq 1$ or $x - 1 \leq -1$: note that in the latter, negative case, the inequality is flipped. $x - 1 \geq 1$ reduces to $x \geq 2$, and $x - 1 \leq -1$ reduces to $x \leq 0$. Since in the inequality $|x - 1| \geq 1$ the absolute value is on the greater side, the two cases combine into an *or* compound inequality, so the final, solved inequality is "$x \leq 0$ or $x \geq 2$."

SOLVING INEQUALITIES INVOLVING SQUARE ROOTS

Solving an inequality with a square root involves two parts. First, we solve the inequality as if it were an equation, isolating the square root and then squaring both sides of the equation. Second, we restrict the solution to the set of values of x for which the value inside the square root sign is non-negative.

EXAMPLE

Solve $\sqrt{x - 2} + 1 < 5$.

We can isolate the square root by subtracting 1 from both sides, yielding $\sqrt{x - 2} < 4$. Squaring both sides of the inequality yields $x - 2 < 16$, so $x < 18$.

Since we can't take the square root of a negative number, we also require the part inside the square root to be non-negative. In this case, that means $x - 2 \geq 0$. Adding 2 to both sides of the inequality yields $x \geq 2$. Our final answer is a compound inequality combining the two simple inequalities: $x \geq 2$ and $x < 18$, or $2 \leq x < 18$.

Note that we only get a compound inequality if the two simple inequalities are in opposite directions; otherwise we take the one that is more restrictive.

The same technique can be used for other even roots, such as fourth roots. It is *not*, however, used for cube roots or other odd roots—negative numbers *do* have cube roots, so the condition that the quantity inside the root sign cannot be negative does not apply.

SPECIAL CIRCUMSTANCES

Sometimes an inequality involving an absolute value or an even exponent is true for all values of x, and we don't need to do any further work to solve it. This is true if the inequality, once the absolute value or exponent term is isolated, says that term is greater than a negative number (or greater than or equal to zero). Since an absolute value or a number raised to an even exponent is *always* non-negative, this inequality is always true.

EXAMPLE 1

Analyze the inequality $2 - |x + 1| < 3$.

Subtracting 2 from both sides yields $-|x + 1| < 1$; multiplying by -1—and flipping the inequality, since we're multiplying by a negative number—yields $|x + 1| > -1$. But since the absolute value cannot be negative, it's *always* greater than –1, so this inequality is true for all values of x.

EXAMPLE 2

Analyze the inequality $2(x - 1)^2 + 7 \leq 1$.

Subtracting 7 from both sides yields $2(x - 1)^2 \leq -6$; dividing by 2 yields $(x - 1)^2 \leq -3$. But $(x - 1)^2$ must be nonnegative, and hence cannot be less than or equal to –3; this inequality has no solution.

DIFFERENCES IN WORKING WITH ONE- VS. TWO-VARIABLE EQUATIONS

CHOOSING WHICH VARIABLE TO ISOLATE IN TWO-VARIABLE EQUATIONS

Similar to methods for a one-variable equation, solving a two-variable equation involves isolating a variable: manipulating the equation so that a variable appears by itself on one side of the equation, and not at all on the other side. However, in a two-variable equation, you will usually only be able to isolate one of the variables; the other variable may appear on the other side along with constant terms, or with exponents or other functions.

Often one variable will be much more easily isolated than the other, and therefore that's the variable you should choose. If one variable appears with various exponents, and the other is only raised to the first power, the latter variable is the one to isolate: given the equation $a^2 + 2b = a^3 + b + 3$, the b only appears to the first power, whereas a appears squared and cubed, so b is the variable that can be solved for: combining like terms and isolating the b on the left side of the equation, we get $b = a^3 - a^2 + 3$.

If both variables are equally easy to isolate, then it's best to isolate the independent variable, if one is defined. If the two variables are x and y, the convention is that y is the independent variable.

KINDS OF TWO-VARIABLE EQUATIONS AND THEIR GRAPHS

While not all two-variable equations fall into these categories, there are a few kinds of two-variable equations that are particularly useful and commonly seen. Perhaps the simplest is the **linear equation**. As with a linear equation with a single variable, in a linear two-variable equation neither variable appears with an exponent greater than one, and the two variables are not multiplied together. As the name implies, the graph of a linear equation is a straight line. Another important kind of two-variable equation is a **quadratic equation**, in which one variable only appears raised to the first power but the other appears squared (and possibly to the first power as well). The graph of a quadratic equation is a parabola. We can continue with higher powers: if one variable is raised to the third power, we have a **cubic equation**, and so on.

Two-variable equations that do not involve positive integral powers include square root equations, in which one variable only appears as a square root, and reciprocal equations, or inverse variation, in which one variable appears in the denominator of a fraction. The graphs of these equations are half a parabola and a two-part curve called a hyperbola, respectively.

STEPS IN SOLVING TWO-VARIABLE EQUATIONS

Example:

$$3x + 2 + 2y = 5y - 7 + |2x - 1|$$

To solve this equation, we must isolate one of its variables on one side of the equation. In this case, the x appears under an absolute value sign, which makes it difficult to isolate. The y, on the other hand, only appears without an exponent—the equation is linear in y. We will therefore choose to isolate the y. The first step, then, is to move all the terms with y to the left side of the equation, which we can do by subtracting $5y$ from both sides:

$$3x + 2 - 3y = -7 + |2x - 1|$$

We can then move all the terms that do *not* include y to the right side of the equation, by subtracting $3x$ and 2 from both sides of the equation:

$$-3y = -3x - 9 + |2x - 1|$$

29

Finally, we can isolate the *y* by dividing both sides by –3.

$$y = x + 3 - \frac{1}{3}|2x - 1|$$

This is as far as we can simplify the equation; we cannot combine the terms inside and outside the absolute value sign. We can therefore consider the equation to be solved.

GRAPHICAL SOLUTIONS TO EQUATIONS AND INEQUALITIES

GRAPHING SIMPLE INEQUALITIES

To graph a simple inequality, we first mark on the number line the value that signifies the end point of the inequality. If the inequality is strict (involves a less than or greater than), we use a hollow circle; if it is not strict (less than or equal to or greater than or equal to), we use a solid circle. We then fill in the part of the number line that satisfies the inequality: to the left of the marked point for less than (or less than or equal to), to the right for greater than (or greater than or equal to).

<u>EXAMPLE 1</u>

Graph $x < 5$.

We would graph the inequality $x < 5$ by putting a hollow circle at 5 and filling in the part of the line to the left:

<u>EXAMPLE 2</u>

Graph $x \geq 3$.

We would graph the inequality $x \geq 3$ by putting a solid circle at 3 and filling in the part of the line to the right:

GRAPHING COMPOUND INEQUALITIES

To graph a compound inequality, we fill in both parts of the inequality for an *or* inequality, or the overlap between them for an *and* inequality. More specifically, we start by plotting the endpoints of each inequality on the number line. For an *or* inequality, we then fill in the appropriate side of the line for each inequality. Typically, the two component inequalities do not overlap, that means the shaded part is *outside* the two points. For an *and* inequality, we instead fill in the part of the line that meets both inequalities.

EXAMPLE 1

Graph "$x \leq -3$ or $x > 4$."

For the inequality "$x \leq -3$ or $x > 4$," we first put a solid circle at –3 and a hollow circle at 4. We then fill the parts of the line *outside* these circles:

EXAMPLE 2

Graph $-2 \leq x \leq 6$.

The inequality $-2 \leq x \leq 6$ is equivalent to "$x \geq -2$ and $x \leq 6$." To plot this compound inequality, we first put solid circles at –2 and 6, and then fill in the part of the line *between* these circles:

GRAPHING INEQUALITIES INCLUDING ABSOLUTE VALUES

An inequality with an absolute value can be converted to a compound inequality. To graph the inequality, first convert it to a compound inequality, and then graph that normally. If the absolute value is on the greater side of the inequality, we end up with an *or* inequality; we plot the endpoints of the inequality on the number line and fill in the part of the line *outside* those points. If the absolute value is on the smaller side of the inequality, we end up with an *and* inequality; we plot the endpoints of the inequality on the number line and fill in the part of the line *between* those points.

EXAMPLE 1

Graph $|x| < 2$.

The inequality $|x| < 2$ can be rewritten as "$x > -2$ and $x < 2$." We place hollow circles at the points –2 and 2 and fill in the part of the line between them:

EXAMPLE 2

Graph $|x + 1| \geq 4$.

The inequality $|x + 1| \geq 4$ can be rewritten as $x \geq 3$ or $x \leq -5$. We place solid circles at the points 3 and –5 and fill in the part of the line *outside* them:

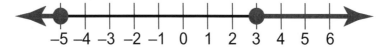

GRAPHING EQUATIONS IN TWO VARIABLES

One way of graphing an equation in two variables is to plot enough points to get an idea for its shape, and then draw the appropriate curve through those points. A point can be plotted by substituting in a value for one variable and solving for the other. If the equation is linear, we only need two points, and can then draw a straight line between them.

<u>EXAMPLE 1</u>

Graph $y = 2x - 1$.

For example, consider the equation $y = 2x - 1$. This is a linear equation—both variables only appear raised to the first power—so we only need two points. When $x = 0$, $y = 2(0) - 1 = -1$. When $x = 2$, $y = 2(2) - 1 = 3$. We can therefore choose the points $(0, -1)$ and $(2, 3)$, and draw a line between them:

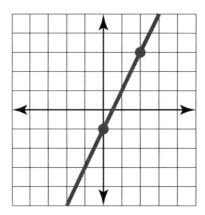

<u>EXAMPLE 2</u>

Graph $y = x^2 - 3x + 2$.

The equation $y = x^2 - 3x + 2$ is not linear, so we may need more points to get an idea of its shape. By substituting in different values of x, we find the points $(0, 2)$, $(1, 0)$, $(2, 0)$, and $(3, 2)$. That may be enough to give us an idea of the shape, though we can find more points if we're still not sure:

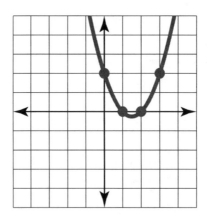

GRAPHING INEQUALITIES IN TWO VARIABLES

To graph an inequality in two variables, we first graph the border of the inequality. This means graphing the equation that we get if we replace the inequality sign with an equals sign. If the inequality is strict (> or <), we graph the border with a dashed or dotted line; if it is not strict (≥ or ≤), we use a solid line. We can then test any point not on the border to see if it satisfies the inequality. If it does, we shade in that side of the border; if not, we shade in the other side.

<u>EXAMPLE</u>

Graph $y > 2x + 2$.

To graph this inequality, we first graph the border, $y = 2x + 2$. Since it is a strict inequality, we use a dashed line.

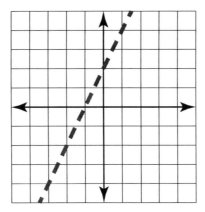

Now, we choose a test point. This can be any point not on the border; in this case, we will choose the origin, $(0, 0)$. (This makes the calculation easy and is generally a good choice unless the border passes through the origin.) Putting this into the original inequality, we get $0 > 2(0) + 2$, i.e. $0 > 2$. This is *not* true, so we shade in the side of the border that does *not* include the point $(0, 0)$:

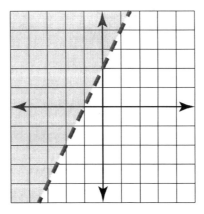

GRAPHING COMPOUND INEQUALITIES IN TWO VARIABLES

One way to graph a compound inequality in two variables is to first graph each of the component inequalities. For an *and* inequality, we then shade in only the parts where the two graphs overlap; for an *or* inequality, we shade in any region that pertains to either of the individual inequalities.

<u>EXAMPLE</u>

Graph "$y \geq x - 1$ *and* $y \leq -x$."

We first shade in the individual inequalities—in the diagram below, $y \geq x - 1$ is shown with horizontal lines, and $y \leq -x$ is shown with vertical lines.

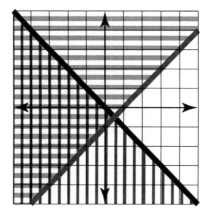

Now, since the compound inequality has an *and*, we only leave shaded the overlap—the part that pertains to *both* inequalities:

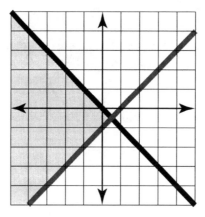

If instead the inequality had been "$y \geq x - 1$ *or* $y \leq -x$," our final graph would involve the *total* shaded area:

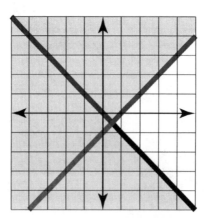

SOLVING SYSTEMS OF EQUATIONS

Systems of equations are a set of simultaneous equations that all use the same variables. A solution to a system of equations must be true for each equation in the system. **Consistent systems** are those with at least one solution. **Inconsistent systems** are systems of equations that have no solution.

SUBSTITUTION

To solve a system of linear equations by **substitution**, start with the easier equation and solve for one of the variables. Express this variable in terms of the other variable. Substitute this expression in the other equation, and solve for the other variable. The solution should be expressed in the form (x, y). Substitute the values into both of the original equations to check your answer. Consider the following problem.

Solve the system using substitution:

$$x + 6y = 15$$

$$3x - 12y = 18$$

Solving the first equation for x:

$$x = 15 - 6y$$

Substitute this value in place of x in the second equation, and solve for y:

$$3(15 - 6y) - 12y = 18$$

$$45 - 18y - 12y = 18$$

$$30y = 27$$

$$y = \frac{27}{30} = \frac{9}{10} = 0.9$$

Plug this value for y back into the first equation to solve for x:

$$x = 15 - 6(0.9) = 15 - 5.4 = 9.6$$

Check both equations if you have time:

$$9.6 + 6(0.9) = 9.6 + 5.4 = 15$$

$$3(9.6) - 12(0.9) = 28.8 - 10.8 = 18$$

Therefore, the solution is (9.6, 0.9).

ELIMINATION

To solve a system of equations using **elimination**, begin by rewriting both equations in standard form $Ax + By = C$. Check to see if the coefficients of one pair of like variables add to zero. If not, multiply one or both of the equations by a non-zero number to make one set of like variables add to zero. Add the two equations to solve for one of the variables. Substitute this value into one of the original equations to solve for the other variable. Check your work by substituting into the other equation. Next, we will solve the same problem as above, but using the addition method.

Solve the system using elimination:

$$x + 6y = 15$$

$$3x - 12y = 18$$

If we multiply the first equation by 2, we can eliminate the y terms:

$$2x + 12y = 30$$

$$3x - 12y = 18$$

Add the equations together and solve for x:

$$5x = 48$$

$$x = \frac{48}{5} = 9.6$$

Plug the value for x back in to either of the original equations and solve for y:

$$9.6 + 6y = 15$$

$$y = \frac{15 - 9.6}{6} = 0.9$$

Check both equations if you have time:

$$9.6 + 6(0.9) = 9.6 + 5.4 = 15$$

$$3(9.6) - 12(0.9) = 28.8 - 10.8 = 18$$

Therefore, the solution is $(9.6, 0.9)$.

Review Video: Substitution and Elimination for Solving Linear Systems
Visit mometrix.com/academy and enter code: 958611

Intermediate Algebra and Functions

FUNCTIONS

A **function** is an equation that has exactly one value of output variable (**dependent variable**) for each value of the input variable (**independent variable**). The set of all values for the input variable (most commonly *x*) is the *domain* of the function, and the set of all corresponding values of output variable (most commonly *y*) is the *range* of the function. When looking at a graph of an equation, the easiest way to determine if the equation is a function or not is to conduct the **vertical line test**. If a vertical line drawn through any value of *x* crosses the graph in more than one place, the equation is not a function.

In functions with the notation *f*(*x*), the value substituted for *x* in the equation is called the **argument**. The domain is the set of all values for *x* in a function. Unless otherwise given, assume the domain is the set of real numbers that will yield real numbers for the range. This is the **domain of definition**.

The **graph** of a function is the set of all ordered pairs (*x*, *y*) that satisfy the equation of the function. The points that have zero as the value for *y* are called the **roots** of the function. These are also the *x*-**intercepts**, because that is the point at which the graph crosses, or intercepts, the *x*-axis. The points that have zero as the value for *x* are the **y-intercepts** because that is where the graph crosses the *y*-axis.

Any time there are **vertical asymptotes** or holes in a graph, such that the complete graph cannot be drawn as one continuous line, a graph is said to have **discontinuities**. Examples include the graphs of hyperbolas that are functions, and the function $f(x) = \tan x$.

MANIPULATION OF FUNCTIONS

Horizontal and **vertical shift** occur when values are added to or subtracted from the *x* or *y* values, respectively.

If a constant is **added** to the *y* portion of each point, the graph shifts **up**. If a constant is **subtracted** from the *y* portion of each point, the graph shifts **down**. This is represented by the expression $f(x) \pm k$, where *k* is a constant.

If a constant is **added** to the *x* portion of each point, the graph shifts **left**. If a constant is **subtracted** from the *x* portion of each point, the graph shifts **right**. This is represented by the expression $f(x \pm k)$, where *k* is a constant.

Stretch, compression, and reflection occur when different parts of a function are multiplied by different groups of constants. If the function as a whole is multiplied by a real number constant greater than 1 ($k \times f(x)$), the graph is **stretched vertically**. If *k* in the previous equation is greater than zero but less than 1, the graph is **compressed vertically**. If *k* is less than zero, the graph is **reflected about the x-axis**, in addition to being either stretched or compressed vertically if *k* is less than or greater than -1, respectively.

If instead, just the *x*-term is multiplied by a constant greater than 1 ($f(k \times x)$), the graph is **compressed horizontally**. If *k* in the previous equation is greater than zero but less than 1, the graph is **stretched horizontally**. If *k* is less than zero, the graph is **reflected about the y-axis**, in addition to being either stretched or compressed horizontally if *k* is greater than or less than -1, respectively.

37

CLASSIFICATION OF FUNCTIONS

There are many different ways to classify functions based on their structure or behavior. Listed here are a few common classifications.

Constant functions are given by the equation $y = b$ or $f(x) = b$, where b is a real number. There is no independent variable present in the equation, so the function has a constant value for all x. The graph of a constant function is a horizontal line of slope 0 that is positioned b units from the x-axis. If b is positive, the line is above the x-axis; if b is negative, the line is below the x-axis.

Identity functions are identified by the equation $y = x$ or $f(x) = x$, where every value of y is equal to its corresponding value of x. The only zero is the point $(0, 0)$. The graph is a diagonal line with slope 1.

In **linear functions**, the value of the function changes in direct proportion to x. The rate of change, represented by the slope on its graph, is constant throughout. The standard form of a linear equation is $ax + by = c$, where a, b, and c are real numbers. As a function, this equation is commonly written as $y = mx + b$ or $f(x) = mx + b$. This is known as the slope-intercept form, because the coefficients give the slope of the graphed function (m) and its y-intercept (b). Solve the equation $mx + b = 0$ for x to get $x = -\dfrac{b}{m}$, which is the only zero of the function. The domain and range are both the set of all real numbers.

A **polynomial function** is a function with multiple terms and multiple powers of x, such as

$$f(x) = a_n x^n + a_{n-1} x^{n-1} + a_{n-2} x^{n-2} + \cdots + a_1 x + a_0$$

where n is a non-negative integer that is the highest exponent in the polynomial, and $a_n \neq 0$. The domain of a polynomial function is the set of all real numbers. If the greatest exponent in the polynomial is even, the polynomial is said to be of even degree and the range is the set of real numbers that satisfy the function. If the greatest exponent in the polynomial is odd, the polynomial is said to be odd and the range, like the domain, is the set of all real numbers.

A **quadratic function** is a polynomial function that follows the equation pattern $y = ax^2 + bx + c$, or $f(x) = ax^2 + bx + c$, where a, b, and c are real numbers and $a \neq 0$. The domain of a quadratic function is the set of all real numbers. The range is also real numbers, but only those in the subset of the domain that satisfy the equation. To determine the number of roots of a quadratic equation (values of x for which y equals 0), solve the expression $b^2 - 4ac$. If this value is positive, there are two unique real roots. If this value equals zero, there is one real root, which is a double root. If this value is less than zero, there are no real roots. The root(s) of any quadratic function can be found by plugging the values of a, b, and c into the **quadratic formula**:

$$x = \frac{-b \pm \sqrt{b^2 - 4ac}}{2a}$$

If the expression $b^2 - 4ac$ is negative, you will instead find complex roots.

> **Review Video: Using the Quadratic Formula**
> Visit mometrix.com/academy and enter code: 163102

To solve a quadratic equation by **factoring**, begin by rewriting the equation in standard form, if necessary. Factor the side with the variable then set each of the factors equal to zero and solve the resulting linear equations. Check your answers by substituting the roots you found into the original equation. If, when writing the equation in standard form, you have an equation in the form $x^2 + c = 0$ or $x^2 - c = 0$, set $x^2 = -c$ or $x^2 = c$ and take the square root of c. If $c = 0$, the only real root is zero. If c is positive, there are two real roots—the positive and negative square root values. If c is negative, there are no real roots.

Review Video: Factoring Quadratic Equations
Visit mometrix.com/academy and enter code: 336566

To solve a quadratic equation by **completing the square**, rewrite the equation so that all terms containing the variable are on the left side of the equal sign, and all the constants are on the right side of the equal sign. Make sure the coefficient of the squared term is 1. If there is a coefficient with the squared term, divide each term on both sides of the equal side by that number. Next, work with the coefficient of the single-variable term. Square half of this coefficient, and add that value to both sides. Now you can factor the left side (the side containing the variable) as the square of a binomial. $x^2 + 2ax + a^2 = C \Rightarrow (x + a)^2 = C$, where x is the variable, and a and C are constants. Take the square root of both sides and solve for the variable. Substitute the value of the variable in the original problem to check your work.

A quadratic function has a parabola for its graph. In the equation $f(x) = ax^2 + bx + c$, if a is positive, the parabola will open upward. If a is negative, the parabola will open downward. The **axis of symmetry** is a vertical line that passes through the vertex.

To determine whether or not the parabola will intersect the x-axis, check the number of real roots. An equation with two real roots will cross the x-axis twice. An equation with one real root will have its vertex on the x-axis. An equation with no real roots will not contact the x-axis.

Review Video: Domain and Range of Quadratic Functions
Visit mometrix.com/academy and enter code: 331768

A **rational function** is a function that can be constructed as a ratio of two polynomial expressions: $f(x) = \frac{p(x)}{q(x)}$, where $p(x)$ and $q(x)$ are both polynomial expressions and $q(x) \neq 0$. The **domain** is the set of all real numbers, except any values for which $q(x) = 0$. The **range** is the set of real numbers that satisfies the function when the domain is applied. When you graph a rational function, you will have vertical asymptotes wherever $q(x) = 0$. If the polynomial in the numerator is of lesser degree than the polynomial in the denominator, the x-axis will also be a horizontal asymptote. If the numerator and denominator have equal degrees, there will be a horizontal asymptote not on the x-axis. If the degree of the numerator is exactly one greater than the degree of the denominator, the graph will have an oblique, or diagonal, asymptote. The asymptote will be along the line $y = \frac{p_n}{q_{n-1}} x + \frac{p_{n-1}}{q_{n-1}}$, where p_n and q_{n-1} are the coefficients of the highest degree terms in their respective polynomials.

A **square root function** is a function that contains a radical and is in the format $f(x) = \sqrt{ax + b}$. The domain is the set of all real numbers that yields a positive radicand or a radicand equal to zero. Because square root values are assumed to be positive unless otherwise identified, the range is all real numbers from zero to infinity. To find the zero of a square root function, set the radicand equal to zero and solve for *x*. The graph of a square root function is always to the right of the zero and always above the *x*-axis.

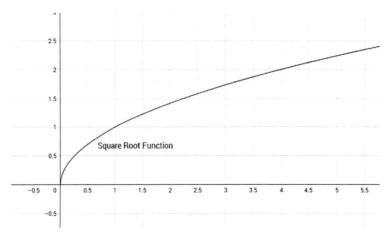

An **absolute value function** is in the format $f(x) = |ax + b|$. Like other functions, the domain is the set of all real numbers. However, because absolute value indicates positive numbers, the range is limited to positive real numbers. To find the zero of an absolute value function, set the portion inside the absolute value sign equal to zero and solve for *x*.

An absolute value function is also known as a piecewise function because it must be solved in pieces—one for if the value inside the absolute value sign is positive, and one for if the value is negative. The function can be expressed as

$$f(x) = \begin{cases} ax + b \text{ if } ax + b \geq 0 \\ -(ax + b) \text{ if } ax + b < 0 \end{cases}$$

This will allow for an accurate statement of the range.

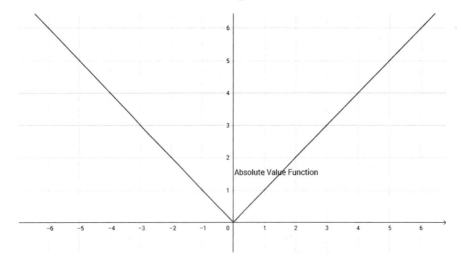

Exponential functions are equations that have the format $y = b^x$, where base $b > 0$ and $b \neq 1$. The exponential function can also be written $f(x) = b^x$.

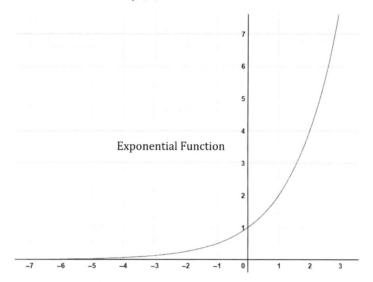

Exponential Function

Logarithmic functions are equations that have the format $y = \log_b x$ or $f(x) = \log_b x$. The base b may be any number except one; however, the most common bases for logarithms are base 10 and base e. The log base e is known the **natural logarithm**, or ln, expressed by the function $f(x) = \ln x$.

Any logarithm that does not have an assigned value of b is assumed to be base 10: $\log x = \log_{10} x$. Exponential functions and logarithmic functions are related in that one is the inverse of the other. If $f(x) = b^x$, then $f^{-1}(x) = \log_b x$. This can perhaps be expressed more clearly by the two equations: $y = b^x$ and $x = \log_b y$.

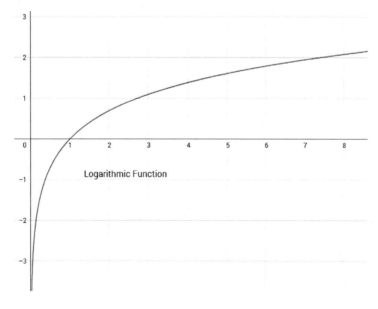

Logarithmic Function

The following properties apply to logarithmic expressions:

$$\log_b 1 = 0$$
$$\log_b b = 1$$
$$\log_b b^p = p$$
$$\log_b MN = \log_b M + \log_b N$$
$$\log_b \frac{M}{N} = \log_b M - \log_b N$$
$$\log_b M^p = p \log_b M$$

In a **one-to-one function**, each value of x has exactly one value for y (this is the definition of a function) *and* each value of y has exactly one value for x. While the vertical line test will determine if a graph is that of a function, the horizontal line test will determine if a function is a one-to-one function. If a horizontal line drawn at any value of y intersects the graph in more than one place, the graph is not that of a one-to-one function. Do not make the mistake of using the horizontal line test exclusively in determining if a graph is that of a one-to-one function. A one-to-one function must pass both the vertical line test and the horizontal line test. One-to-one functions are also **invertible functions**.

A **monotone function** is a function whose graph either constantly increases or constantly decreases. Examples include the functions $f(x) = x$, $f(x) = -x$, or $f(x) = x^3$.

An **even function** has a graph that is symmetric with respect to the y-axis and satisfies the equation $f(x) = f(-x)$. Examples include the functions $f(x) = x^2$ and $f(x) = ax^n$, where a is any real number and n is a positive even integer.

An **odd function** has a graph that is symmetric with respect to the origin and satisfies the equation $f(x) = -f(-x)$. Examples include the functions $f(x) = x^3$ and $f(x) = ax^n$, where a is any real number and n is a positive odd integer.

Algebraic functions are those that exclusively use polynomials and roots. These would include polynomial functions, rational functions, square root functions, and all combinations of these functions, such as polynomials as the radicand. These combinations may be joined by addition, subtraction, multiplication, or division, but may not include variables as exponents.

Transcendental functions are all functions that are non-algebraic. Any function that includes logarithms, trigonometric functions, variables as exponents, or any combination that includes any of these is not algebraic in nature, even if the function includes polynomials or roots.

THEOREMS RELATED TO POLYNOMIAL FUNCTIONS

According to the **Fundamental Theorem of Algebra**, every non-constant, single variable polynomial has exactly as many roots as the polynomial's highest exponent. For example, if x^4 is the largest exponent of a term, the polynomial will have exactly 4 roots. However, some of these roots may have multiplicity or be non-real numbers. For instance, in the polynomial function $f(x) = x^4 - 4x + 3$, the only real roots are 1 and -1. The root 1 has multiplicity of 2 and there is one non-real root $(-1 - \sqrt{2}i)$.

The **Remainder Theorem** is useful for determining the remainder when a polynomial is divided by a binomial. The Remainder Theorem states that if a polynomial function $f(x)$ is divided by a binomial $x - a$, where a is a real number, the remainder of the division will be the value of $f(a)$. If $f(a) = 0$, then a is a root of the polynomial.

The **Factor Theorem** is related to the Remainder Theorem and states that if $f(a) = 0$ then $(x - a)$ is a factor of the function.

According to the **Rational Root Theorem,** any rational root of a polynomial function $f(x) = a_n x^n + a_{n-1} x^{n-1} + \cdots + a_1 x + a_0$ with integer coefficients will, when reduced to its lowest terms, be a positive or negative fraction such that the numerator is a factor of a_0 and the denominator is a factor of a_n. For instance, if the polynomial function $f(x) = x^3 + 3x^2 - 4$ has any rational roots, the numerators of those roots can only be factors of 4 (1, 2, 4), and the denominators can only be factors of 1 (1). The function in this example has roots of 1 (or $\frac{1}{1}$) and -2 (or $-\frac{2}{1}$).

TYPES OF VARIABLES

Variables that vary **directly** are those that either both increase at the same rate or both decrease at the same rate. For example, in the functions $f(x) = kx$ or $f(x) = kx^n$, where k and n are positive, the value of $f(x)$ increases as the value of x increases and decreases as the value of x decreases.

Variables that vary **inversely** are those where one increases while the other decreases. For example, in the functions $f(x) = \frac{k}{x}$ or $f(x) = \frac{k}{x^n}$ where k is a positive constant, the value of y increases as the value of x decreases, and the value of y decreases as the value of x increases.

In both cases, k is **constant of variation**.

APPLYING THE BASIC OPERATIONS TO FUNCTIONS

For each of the basic functions, we will use these functions as examples: $f(x) = x^2$ and $g(x) = x$.

To find the **sum** of two functions f and g, assuming the domains are compatible, simply add the two functions together: $(f + g)(x) = f(x) + g(x) = x^2 + x$

To find the **difference** of two functions f and g, assuming the domains are compatible, simply subtract the second function from the first: $(f - g)(x) = f(x) - g(x) = x^2 - x$.

To find the **product** of two functions f and g, assuming the domains are compatible, multiply the two functions together: $(f \cdot g)(x) = f(x) \cdot g(x) = x^2 \cdot x = x^3$.

To find the **quotient** of two functions f and g, assuming the domains are compatible, divide the first function by the second: $\frac{f}{g}(x) = \frac{f(x)}{g(x)} = \frac{x^2}{x} = x \; ; x \neq 0$.

The example given in each case is fairly simple, but on a given problem, if you are looking only for the value of the sum, difference, product, or quotient of two functions at a particular x-value, it may be simpler to solve the functions individually and then perform the given operation using those values.

COMPOSITE AND INVERSE FUNCTIONS

The composite of two functions f and g, written as $(f \circ g)(x)$ simply means that the output of the second function is used as the input of the first. This can also be written as $f(g(x))$. In general, this can be solved by substituting $g(x)$ for all instances of x in $f(x)$ and simplifying. Using the example functions $f(x) = x^2 - x + 2$ and $g(x) = x + 1$, we can find that $(f \circ g)(x)$ or $f(g(x))$ is equal to $f(x + 1) = (x + 1)^2 - (x + 1) + 2$, which simplifies to $x^2 + x + 2$.

It is important to note that $(f \circ g)(x)$ is not necessarily the same as $(g \circ f)(x)$. The process is *not commutative* like addition or multiplication expressions. If $f(g(x)) = g(f(x))$, the two functions are permutable. If $f(g(x)) = g(f(x)) = x$, then the functions are **inverses** of each other.

POLYNOMIAL ALGEBRA

Equations are made up of monomials and polynomials. A **monomial** is a single variable or product of constants and variables, such as x, $2x$, or $\frac{2}{x}$. There will never be addition or subtraction symbols in a monomial. Like monomials have like variables, but they may have different coefficients. **Polynomials** are algebraic expressions which use addition and subtraction to combine two or more monomials. Two terms make a binomial, three terms make a trinomial, etc. The **degree of a monomial** is the sum of the exponents of the variables. The **degree of a polynomial** is the highest degree of any individual term.

> **Review Video: Polynomials**
> Visit mometrix.com/academy and enter code: 305005

To multiply two binomials, follow the **FOIL** method. FOIL stands for:

- First: Multiply the first term of each binomial
- Outer: Multiply the outer terms of each binomial
- Inner: Multiply the inner terms of each binomial
- Last: Multiply the last term of each binomial

Using FOIL, $(Ax + By)(Cx + Dy) = ACx^2 + ADxy + BCxy + BDy^2$.

> **Review Video: Multiplying Terms Using the FOIL Method**
> Visit mometrix.com/academy and enter code: 854792

To divide polynomials, set up a long division problem, dividing a polynomial by either a monomial or another polynomial of equal or lesser degree.

When **dividing by a monomial**, divide each term of the polynomial by the monomial.

When **dividing by a polynomial**, begin by arranging the terms of each polynomial in order of one variable. You may arrange in ascending or descending order, but be consistent with both polynomials. To get the first term of the quotient, divide the first term of the dividend by the first term of the divisor. Multiply the first term of the quotient by the entire divisor and subtract that product from the dividend. Repeat for the second and successive terms until you either get a remainder of zero or a remainder whose degree is less than the degree of the divisor. If the quotient has a remainder, write the answer as a mixed expression in the form:

$$\text{quotient} + \frac{\text{remainder}}{\text{divisor}}$$

Rational expressions are fractions with polynomials in both the numerator and the denominator; the value of the polynomial in the denominator cannot be equal to zero.

To **add or subtract** rational expressions, first find the common denominator, then rewrite each fraction as an equivalent fraction with the common denominator. Finally, add or subtract the numerators to get the numerator of the answer, and keep the common denominator as the denominator of the answer.

When **multiplying** rational expressions factor each polynomial and cancel like factors (a factor which appears in both the numerator and the denominator). Then, multiply all remaining factors in the numerator to get the numerator of the product, and multiply the remaining factors in the denominator to get the denominator of the product. Remember: cancel entire factors, not individual terms.

To **divide** rational expressions, take the reciprocal of the divisor (the rational expression you are dividing by) and multiply by the dividend.

Review Video: Simplifying Rational Polynomial Functions
Visit mometrix.com/academy and enter code: 351038

Below are patterns of some special products to remember: *perfect trinomial squares*, the *difference between two squares*, the *sum and difference of two cubes*, and *perfect cubes*.

- Perfect Trinomial Squares: $x^2 + 2xy + y^2 = (x + y)^2$ or $x^2 - 2xy + y^2 = (x - y)^2$
- Difference Between Two Squares: $x^2 - y^2 = (x + y)(x - y)$
- Sum of Two Cubes: $x^3 + y^3 = (x + y)(x^2 - xy + y^2)$
    - Note: the second factor is NOT the same as a perfect trinomial square, so do not try to factor it further.
- Difference Between Two Cubes: $x^3 - y^3 = (x - y)(x^2 + xy + y^2)$
    - Again, the second factor is NOT the same as a perfect trinomial square.
- Perfect Cubes: $x^3 + 3x^2y + 3xy^2 + y^3 = (x + y)^3$ and $x^3 - 3x^2y + 3xy^2 - y^3 = (x - y)^3$

When **factoring** a polynomial, first check for a **common monomial factor**. When the greatest common monomial factor has been factored out, look for patterns of special products: differences of two squares, the sum or difference of two cubes for binomial factors, or perfect trinomial squares for trinomial factors. If the factor is a trinomial but not a perfect trinomial square, look for a factorable form, such as one of these:

$$x^2 + (a + b)x + ab = (x + a)(x + b)$$

$$(ac)x^2 + (ad + bc)x + bd = (ax + b)(cx + d)$$

For factors with four terms, look for groups to factor. Once you have found the factors, write the original polynomial as the product of all the factors. Make sure all of the polynomial factors are prime. Monomial factors may be *prime* or *composite*. Check your work by multiplying the factors to make sure you get the original polynomial.

EQUATIONS AND GRAPHING

When algebraic functions and equations are shown graphically, they are usually shown on a **Cartesian coordinate plane**. The Cartesian coordinate plane consists of two number lines placed perpendicular to each other, and intersecting at the **zero point**, also known as the **origin**. The horizontal number line is known as the **x-axis**, with positive values to the right of the origin and negative values to the left of the origin. The vertical number line is known as the **y-axis**, with positive values above the origin and negative values below the origin. Any point on the plane can be identified by an ordered pair in the form (*x,y*), called **coordinates**. The *x*-value of the coordinate is called the **abscissa**, and the *y*-value of the coordinate is called the **ordinate**.

The two number lines divide the plane into four **quadrants**: I, II, III, and IV.

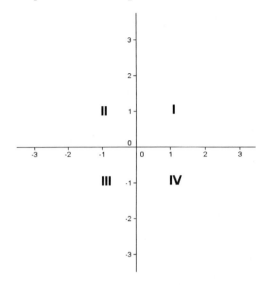

Before learning the different forms, equations can be written in, it is important to understand some terminology. A ratio of the change in the vertical distance to the change in horizontal distance is called the **slope**. On a graph with two points, (x_1, y_1) and (x_2, y_2), the slope is represented by the formula $m = \frac{y_2 - y_1}{x_2 - x_1}$; $x_1 \neq x_2$. If the value of the slope is positive, the line slopes upward from left to right. If the value of the slope is negative, the line slopes downward from left to right. If the *y*-coordinates are the same for both points, the slope is 0 and the line is a **horizontal line**. If the *x*-coordinates are the same for both points, there is no slope and the line is a **vertical line**. Two or more lines that have equal slopes are **parallel lines**. **Perpendicular lines** have slopes that are negative reciprocals of each other, such as $\frac{a}{b}$ and $\frac{-b}{a}$.

As mentioned previously, equations can be written many ways. Below is a list of the many forms equations can take.

- Standard form: $Ax + By = C$; the slope is $\frac{-A}{B}$ and the *y*-intercept is $\frac{C}{B}$
- Slope-intercept form: $y = mx + b$, where m is the slope and b is the *y*-intercept
- Point-slope form: $y - y_1 = m(x - x_1)$, where m is the slope and (x_1, y_1) is a point on the line
- Two-point form: $\frac{y - y_1}{x - x_1} = \frac{y_2 - y_1}{x_2 - x_1}$, where (x_1, y_1) and (x_2, y_2) are two points on the given line
- Intercept form: $\frac{x}{x_1} + \frac{y}{y_1} = 1$, where $(x_1, 0)$ is the point at which a line intersects the *x*-axis, and $(0, y_1)$ is the point at which the same line intersects the *y*-axis

CALCULATIONS USING POINTS

Sometimes you need to perform calculations using only points on a graph as input data. Using points, you can determine what the midpoint and distance are. If you know the equation for a line you can calculate the distance between the line and the point.

To find the **midpoint** of two points (x_1, y_1) and (x_2, y_2), average the x-coordinates to get the x-coordinate of the midpoint, and average the y-coordinates to get the y-coordinate of the midpoint:

$$\text{midpoint} = \left(\frac{x_1 + x_2}{2}, \frac{y_1 + y_2}{2}\right)$$

The **distance** between two points is the same as the length of the hypotenuse of a right triangle with the two given points as endpoints, and the two sides of the right triangle parallel to the x-axis and y-axis, respectively. The length of the segment parallel to the x-axis is the difference between the x-coordinates of the two points. The length of the segment parallel to the y-axis is the difference between the y-coordinates of the two points. Using the Pythagorean Theorem, the formula is

$$d = \sqrt{(x_2 - x_1)^2 + (y_2 - y_1)^2}$$

When a line is in the format $Ax + By + C = 0$, you can find the **distance between the line and a point** (x_1, y_1) not on the line using the formula

$$d = \frac{|Ax_1 + By_1 + C|}{\sqrt{A^2 + B^2}}$$

Review Video: <u>Distance & Midpoint for Points on the Coordinate Plane</u>
Visit mometrix.com/academy and enter code: 973653

Geometry and Measurement

LINES AND PLANES

A **point** is a fixed location in space; has no size or dimensions; commonly represented by a dot.

A **line** is a set of points that extends infinitely in two opposite directions. It has length, but no width or depth. A line can be defined by any two distinct points that it contains. A line segment is a portion of a line that has definite endpoints. A ray is a portion of a line that extends from a single point on that line in one direction along the line. It has a definite beginning, but no ending.

A **plane** is a two-dimensional flat surface defined by three non-collinear points. A plane extends an infinite distance in all directions in those two dimensions. It contains an infinite number of points, parallel lines and segments, intersecting lines and segments, as well as parallel or intersecting rays. A plane will never contain a three-dimensional figure or skew lines. Two given planes will either be parallel or they will intersect to form a line. A plane may intersect a circular conic surface, such as a cone, to form conic sections, such as the parabola, hyperbola, circle or ellipse.

Perpendicular lines are lines that intersect at right angles. They are represented by the symbol ⊥. The shortest distance from a line to a point not on the line is a perpendicular segment from the point to the line.

Parallel lines are lines in the same plane that have no points in common and never meet. Lines that are in different planes, have no points in common, and never meet are called *skew lines*.

A **bisector** is a line or line segment that divides another line segment into two equal lengths. A perpendicular bisector of a line segment is composed of points that are equidistant from the endpoints of the segment it is dividing.

Intersecting lines are lines that have exactly one point in common. Concurrent lines are multiple lines that intersect at a single point.

A **transversal** is a line that intersects at least two other lines, which may or may not be parallel to one another. A transversal that intersects parallel lines is a common occurrence in geometry.

ANGLES

An **angle** is formed when two lines or line segments meet at a common point. It may be a common starting point for a pair of segments or rays, or it may be the intersection of lines. Angles are represented by the symbol ∠.

> **Review Video: Geometric Symbols: Angles**
> Visit mometrix.com/academy and enter code: 452738

The **vertex** is the point at which two segments or rays meet to form an angle. If the angle is formed by intersecting rays, lines, and/or line segments, the vertex is the point at which four angles are formed. The pairs of angles opposite one another are called vertical angles, and their measures are equal.

- An *acute* angle is an angle with a degree measure less than 90°.
- A *right* angle is an angle with a degree measure of exactly 90°.
- An *obtuse* angle is an angle with a degree measure greater than 90° but less than 180°.
- A *straight angle* is an angle with a degree measure of exactly 180°.
- A *reflex angle* is an angle with a degree measure greater than 180° but less than 360°.
- A *full angle* is an angle with a degree measure of exactly 360°.

Two angles that have the same vertex and share a side are said to be **adjacent**. Vertical angles are not adjacent because they share a vertex but no common side.

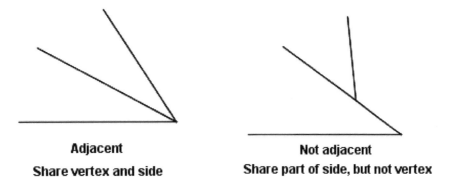

Adjacent
Share vertex and side

Not adjacent
Share part of side, but not vertex

Two angles whose sum is exactly 90° are said to be **complementary**. The two angles may or may not be adjacent. In a right triangle, the two acute angles are complementary.

Two angles whose sum is exactly 180° are said to be **supplementary**. The two angles may or may not be adjacent. Two intersecting lines always form two pairs of supplementary angles. Adjacent supplementary angles will always form a straight line.

When two parallel lines are cut by a transversal, the angles that are between the two parallel lines are **interior angles**. In the diagram below, angles 3, 4, 5, and 6 are interior angles.

When two parallel lines are cut by a transversal, the angles that are outside the parallel lines are **exterior angles**. In the diagram below, angles 1, 2, 7, and 8 are exterior angles.

When two parallel lines are cut by a transversal, the angles that are in the same position relative to the transversal and a parallel line are **corresponding angles**. The diagram below has four pairs of corresponding angles: angles 1 and 5; angles 2 and 6; angles 3 and 7; and angles 4 and 8. Corresponding angles formed by parallel lines are congruent.

When two parallel lines are cut by a transversal, the two interior angles that are on opposite sides of the transversal are called **alternate interior angles**. In the diagram below, there are two pairs of alternate interior angles: angles 3 and 6, and angles 4 and 5. Alternate interior angles formed by parallel lines are congruent.

When two parallel lines are cut by a transversal, the two exterior angles that are on opposite sides of the transversal are called **alternate exterior angles**. In the diagram below, there are two pairs of alternate exterior angles: angles 1 and 8, and angles 2 and 7. Alternate exterior angles formed by parallel lines are congruent.

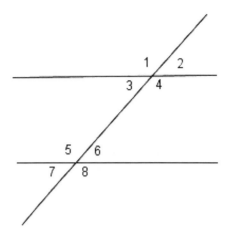

When two lines intersect, four angles are formed. The non-adjacent angles at this vertex are called **vertical angles**. Vertical angles are congruent. In the diagram, $\angle ABD \cong \angle CBE$ and $\angle ABC \cong \angle DBE$.

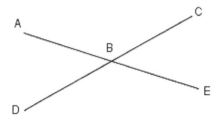

POLYGONS

Each straight line segment of a polygon is called a **side**.

A point at which two sides of a polygon intersect is called a **vertex**. In a polygon, the number of sides is always equal to the number of vertices.

A polygon with all sides congruent and all angles equal is called a **regular polygon**.

Congruent figures are geometric figures that have the same size and shape. All corresponding angles are equal, and all corresponding sides are equal. It is indicated by the symbol ≅.

 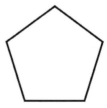

Congruent polygons

Similar figures are geometric figures that have the same shape, but do not necessarily have the same size. All corresponding angles are equal, and all corresponding sides are proportional, but they do not have to be equal. It is indicated by the symbol ~.

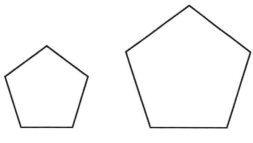

Similar polygons

Note that all congruent figures are also similar, but not all similar figures are congruent.

Review Video: Polygons, Similarity, and Congruence
Visit mometrix.com/academy and enter code: 686174

EXAMPLE 1

To determine the height of a streetlamp, Dillon decides to use his shadow. He draws the diagram below, and fills in the measurements he knows. The larger outside triangle and the smaller inner triangle are similar. What is the height of the street lamp, s?

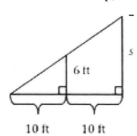

Using properties of similar triangles, Dillon can solve for s. To solve for s, set up a proportion:

$$\frac{6}{10} = \frac{s}{20}$$

$$120 = 10s$$

$$12 = s$$

The street lamp is 12 feet tall.

EXAMPLE 2

The two rectangles below are **similar**.

1. Describe the relationship between the perimeters of the two rectangles.

2. Describe the relationship between the areas of the two rectangles.

Since the two rectangles are similar, the width of the smaller rectangle can be determined. The relationship between the length of the larger and smaller rectangles is:

$$\frac{10n}{2n} = 5$$

The dimensions of the larger rectangle are five times each dimension of the smaller rectangle. The width of the smaller rectangle is:

$$5n \div 5 = n$$

1. The perimeter of the larger rectangle is: $(10n + 5n) \cdot 2 = 15n \cdot 2 = 30n$ in. The perimeter of the smaller rectangle is: $(2n + n) \cdot 2 = 3n \cdot 2 = 6n$ in. The perimeter of the larger rectangle is 5 times the perimeter of the smaller rectangle. The perimeter and side lengths of the similar rectangles have the same relationship.

2. The area of the larger rectangle is: $10n \cdot 5n = 50n^2$ in². The area of the smaller rectangle is: $2n \cdot n = 2n^2$ in². The area of the larger rectangle is 25 times the area of the smaller rectangle. The area of the larger rectangle is increased by the square of the relationship between the side lengths, or 5^2.

EXAMPLE 3

The area of a rectangle is 216 cm². Describe the area of a new rectangle if both dimensions are multiplied by a factor of $\frac{1}{3}$.

The area of a rectangle is a product of the length and width: $A = lw$. If both dimensions are multiplied by a factor of $\frac{1}{3}$, the new area would be: $A = \frac{1}{3}l \times \frac{1}{3}w = \frac{1}{9}lw$. The given area of the rectangle is 216 cm², and if both dimensions are multiplied by a factor of $\frac{1}{3}$, the new area will be multiplied by a factor of $\frac{1}{9}$:

$$\text{new } A = \frac{1}{9}(\text{original } A) = \frac{1}{9}(216) = 24 \text{ cm}^2$$

The new area is 24 cm².

Review Video: Proportional Change of Dimensions
Visit mometrix.com/academy and enter code: 186545

52

SYMMETRY

A **line of symmetry** is a line that divides a figure or object into two symmetric parts. Each symmetric half is congruent to the other. An object may have no lines of symmetry, one line of symmetry, or more than one line of symmetry.

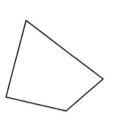 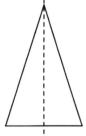 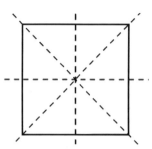

No lines of symmetry   One line of symmetry   Multiple lines of symmetry

Review Video: Symmetry
Visit mometrix.com/academy and enter code: 528106

QUADRILATERALS

A **quadrilateral** is a closed two-dimensional geometric figure composed of exactly four straight sides. The sum of the interior angles of any quadrilateral is 360°.

PARALLELOGRAM

A **parallelogram** is a quadrilateral that has exactly two pairs of opposite parallel sides. The sides that are parallel are also congruent. The opposite interior angles are always congruent, and the consecutive interior angles are supplementary. The diagonals of a parallelogram bisect each other. Each diagonal divides the parallelogram into two congruent triangles.

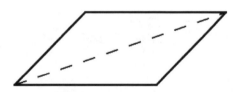

Review Video: Parallelogram
Visit mometrix.com/academy and enter code: 129981

The *area of a parallelogram* is found by the formula $A = bh$, where b is the length of the base, and h is the height. Note that the base and height correspond to the length and width in a rectangle, so this formula would apply to rectangles as well. Do not confuse the height of a parallelogram with the length of the second side. The two are only the same measure in the case of a rectangle.

The *perimeter of a parallelogram* is found by the formula $P = 2a + 2b$ or $P = 2(a + b)$, where a and b are the lengths of the two sides.

Review Video: Area and Perimeter of a Parallelogram
Visit mometrix.com/academy and enter code: 718313

TRAPEZOID

Traditionally, a **trapezoid** is a quadrilateral that has exactly one pair of parallel sides. Some math texts define trapezoid as a quadrilateral that has at least one pair of parallel sides. Because there are no rules governing the second pair of sides, there are no rules that apply to the properties of the diagonals of a trapezoid.

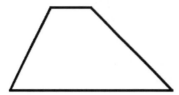

Rectangles, rhombuses, and squares are all special forms of parallelograms.

The *area of a trapezoid* is found by the formula $A = \frac{1}{2}h(b_1 + b_2)$, where h is the height (segment joining and perpendicular to the parallel bases), and b_1 and b_2 are the two parallel sides (bases). Do not use one of the other two sides as the height unless that side is also perpendicular to the parallel bases.

The *perimeter of a trapezoid* is found by the formula $P = a + b_1 + c + b_2$, where a, b_1, c, and b_2 are the four sides of the trapezoid.

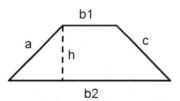

> **Review Video: Area and Perimeter of a Trapezoid**
> Visit mometrix.com/academy and enter code: 587523

RECTANGLE

A **rectangle** is a parallelogram with four right angles. All rectangles are parallelograms, but not all parallelograms are rectangles. The diagonals of a rectangle are congruent.

The *area of a rectangle* is found by the formula $A = lw$, where A is the area of the rectangle, l is the length (usually considered to be the longer side) and w is the width (usually considered to be the shorter side). The numbers for l and w are interchangeable.

The *perimeter of a rectangle* is found by the formula $P = 2l + 2w$ or $P = 2(l + w)$, where l is the length, and w is the width. It may be easier to add the length and width first and then double the result, as in the second formula.

<u>EXAMPLE</u>

Leslie decides to tile her bathroom floor with tiles that are rectangles. Each rectangle has a length of 10 inches and a width of 8 inches. Find the number of tiles needed for a floor with an area of 3600 in².

First, find the area of each tile. The area of a rectangle is: *lw*, where *l* is the length of the rectangle, and *w* is the width. The area of each tile is 10 in × 8 in = 80 in². To find the number of tiles needed, divide the total area of the floor, 3600 in², by the area of each tile:

$$3600 \text{ in}^2 \div 80 \text{ in}^2 = 45 \text{ tiles}$$

Review Video: <u>Area and Perimeter of a Rectangle</u>
Visit mometrix.com/academy and enter code: 933707

RHOMBUS

A **rhombus** is a parallelogram with four congruent sides. All rhombuses are parallelograms, but not all parallelograms are rhombuses. The diagonals of a rhombus are perpendicular to each other.

Review Video: <u>Diagonals of Parallelograms, Rectangles, and Rhombi</u>
Visit mometrix.com/academy and enter code: 320040

SQUARE

A **square** is a parallelogram with four right angles and four congruent sides. All squares are also parallelograms, rhombuses, and rectangles. The diagonals of a square are congruent and perpendicular to each other.

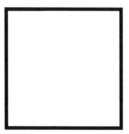

The *area of a square* is found by using the formula $A = s^2$, where and *s* is the length of one side.

The *perimeter of a square* is found by using the formula $P = 4s$, where *s* is the length of one side. Because all four sides are equal in a square, it is faster to multiply the length of one side by 4 than to add the same number four times. You could use the formulas for rectangles and get the same answer.

Review Video: <u>Area and Perimeter of a Square</u>
Visit mometrix.com/academy and enter code: 620902

TRIANGLES

An **equilateral triangle** is a triangle with three congruent sides. An equilateral triangle will also have three congruent angles, each 60°. All equilateral triangles are also acute triangles.

An **isosceles triangle** is a triangle with two congruent sides. An isosceles triangle will also have two congruent angles opposite the two congruent sides.

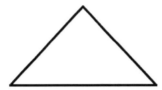

A **scalene triangle** is a triangle with no congruent sides. A scalene triangle will also have three angles of different measures. The angle with the largest measure is opposite the longest side, and the angle with the smallest measure is opposite the shortest side.

An **acute triangle** is a triangle whose three angles are all less than 90°. If two of the angles are equal, the acute triangle is also an isosceles triangle. If the three angles are all equal, the acute triangle is also an equilateral triangle.

A **right triangle** is a triangle with exactly one angle equal to 90°. All right triangles follow the Pythagorean theorem. A right triangle can never be acute or obtuse.

An **obtuse triangle** is a triangle with exactly one angle greater than 90°. The other two angles may or may not be equal. If the two remaining angles are equal, the obtuse triangle is also an isosceles triangle.

The **sum** of the measures of the interior angles of a triangle is always 180°. Therefore, a triangle can never have more than one angle greater than or equal to 90°.

Review Video: <u>Introduction to Types of Triangles</u>
Visit mometrix.com/academy and enter code: 511711

PYTHAGOREAN THEOREM

The side of a triangle opposite the right angle is called the **hypotenuse**. The other two sides are called the **legs**. The Pythagorean theorem states a relationship among the legs and hypotenuse of a right triangle: $a^2 + b^2 = c^2$, where a and b are the lengths of the legs of a right triangle, and c is the length of the hypotenuse. Note that this formula will only work with right triangles.

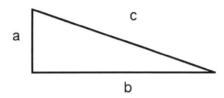

Review Video: Pythagorean Theorem
Visit mometrix.com/academy and enter code: 906576

EXAMPLE

A ladder is needed to reach a window that is 12 feet off the ground. Use the diagram below to determine the length of the ladder, x, needed to reach the window if it is placed 5 feet from the base of the building.

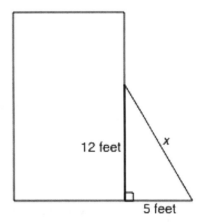

The length of the ladder, x, is the **hypotenuse** of a right triangle with **legs** 12 and 5. The third side can be found using the Pythagorean Theorem:

$$x^2 = 12^2 + 5^2$$

$$x^2 = 144 + 25 = 169$$

$$x = \sqrt{169} = 13$$

Thus, a 13-foot ladder is needed to reach the window 12 feet from the ground.

AREA AND PERIMETER FORMULAS

The *perimeter of any triangle* is found by summing the three side lengths: $P = a + b + c$. For an equilateral triangle, this is the same as $P = 3s$, where s is any side length, since all three sides are the same length.

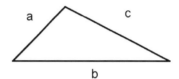

The *area of any triangle* can be found by taking half the product of one side length (base or b) and the perpendicular distance from that side to the opposite vertex (height or h). In equation form, this is $A = \frac{1}{2}bh$.

> **Review Video: Area and Perimeter of a Triangle**
> Visit mometrix.com/academy and enter code: 853779

CIRCLES

The **center** is the single point inside the circle that is **equidistant** from every point on the circle. (Point O in the diagram below.)

> **Review Video: Points of a Circle**
> Visit mometrix.com/academy and enter code: 420746

The **radius** is a line segment that joins the center of the circle and any one point on the circle. All radii of a circle are equal. (Segments OX, OY, and OZ in the diagram below.)

The **diameter** is a line segment that passes through the center of the circle and has both endpoints on the circle. The length of the diameter is exactly twice the length of the radius. (Segment XZ in the diagram below.)

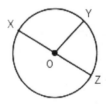

The **area of a circle** is found by the formula $A = \pi r^2$, where r is the length of the radius. If the diameter of the circle is given, remember to divide it in half to get the length of the radius before proceeding.

The **circumference** of a circle is found by the formula $C = 2\pi r$, where r is the radius. Again, remember to convert the diameter if you are given that measure rather than the radius.

> **Review Video: <u>Area and Circumference of a Circle</u>**
> Visit mometrix.com/academy and enter code: 243015
>
> **Review Video: <u>The Diameter, Radius, and Circumference of Circles</u>**
> Visit mometrix.com/academy and enter code: 448988

TRANSFORMATIONS

ROTATION, CENTER OF ROTATION, AND ANGLE OF ROTATION

A rotation is a transformation that turns a figure around a point called the **center of rotation**, which can lie anywhere in the plane. If a line is drawn from a point on a figure to the center of rotation, and another line is drawn from the center to the rotated image of that point, the angle between the two lines is the **angle of rotation**. The vertex of the angle of rotation is the center of rotation.

> **Review Video: <u>Rotation</u>**
> Visit mometrix.com/academy and enter code: 602600

REFLECTION OVER A LINE AND REFLECTION IN A POINT

A reflection of a figure **over a line** (a "flip") creates a congruent image that is the same distance from the line as the original figure but on the opposite side. The **line of reflection** is the perpendicular bisector of any line segment drawn from a point on the original figure to its reflected image (unless the point and its reflected image happen to be the same point, which happens when a figure is reflected over one of its own sides).

A reflection of a figure **in a point** is the same as the rotation of the figure 180° about that point. The image of the figure is congruent to the original figure. The **point of reflection** is the midpoint of a line segment which connects a point in the figure to its image (unless the point and its reflected image happen to be the same point, which happens when a figure is reflected in one of its own points).

> **Review Video: <u>Reflection</u>**
> Visit mometrix.com/academy and enter code: 955068

EXAMPLE

Use the coordinate plane of the given image below to reflect the image across the *y*-axis.

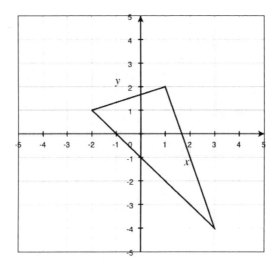

To reflect the image across the *y*-axis, replace each *x*-coordinate of the points that are the vertex of the triangle, *x*, with its negative, −*x*.

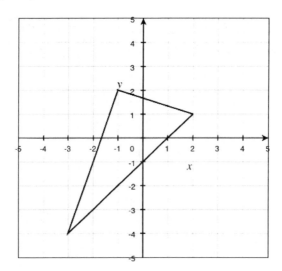

TRANSLATION

A translation is a transformation which slides a figure from one position in the plane to another position in the plane. The original figure and the translated figure have the same size, shape, and orientation.

DILATION

A dilation is a transformation which proportionally stretches or shrinks a figure by a **scale factor**. The dilated image is the same shape and orientation as the original image but a different size. A polygon and its dilated image are similar.

<u>EXAMPLE</u>

Use the coordinate plane to create a dilation of the given image below, where the dilation is the enlargement of the original image.

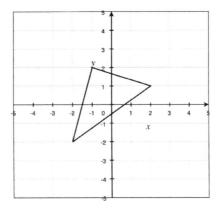

An enlargement can be found by multiplying each coordinate of the coordinate pairs located at the triangle's vertices by a constant. If the figure is enlarged by a factor of 2, the new image would be:

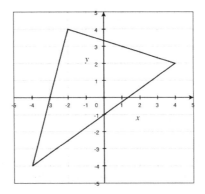

Review Video: <u>Dilation</u>
Visit mometrix.com/academy and enter code: 471630

EVIDENCE OF A TRANSFORMATION

To identify that a figure has been **rotated**, look for evidence that the figure is still face-up, but has changed its orientation.

To identify that a figure has been **reflected** across a line, look for evidence that the figure is now face-down.

To identify that a figure has been **translated**, look for evidence that a figure is still face-up and has not changed orientation; the only change is location.

To identify that a figure has been **dilated**, look for evidence that the figure has changed its size but not its orientation.

SOLIDS

The **surface area** of a solid object is the area of all sides or exterior surfaces. For objects such as prisms and pyramids, a further distinction is made between base surface area (B) and lateral surface area (LA). For a prism, the total surface area (SA) is $SA = LA + 2B$. For a pyramid or cone, the total surface area is $SA = LA + B$.

The **volume** of a sphere is given by the formula $V = \frac{4}{3}\pi r^3$, where r is the radius. The **surface area** can be found by the formula $A = 4\pi r^2$. Both quantities are generally recorded in terms of π.

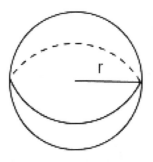

The **volume of any prism** is found by the formula $V = Bh$, where B is the area of the base, and h is the height (perpendicular distance between the bases). The **surface area** of any prism is the sum of the areas of both bases and all sides. It can be calculated as $SA = 2B + Ph$, where P is the perimeter of the base.

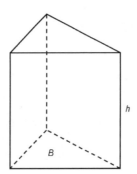

For a *rectangular prism*, the **volume** can be found by the formula $V = lwh$, where V is the volume, l is the length, w is the width, and h is the height. The **surface area** can be calculated as $SA = 2lw + 2hl + 2wh$ or $SA = 2(lw + hl + wh)$.

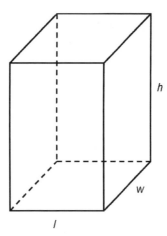

The **volume** of a cube can be found by the formula $V = s^3$, where s is the length of a side. The **surface area** of a cube is calculated as $SA = 6s^2$, where SA is the total surface area and s is the length of a side.

These formulas are the same as the ones used for the volume and surface area of a rectangular prism, but simplified since all three quantities (length, width, and height) are the same.

> **Review Video: Volume and Surface Area of a Cube**
> Visit mometrix.com/academy and enter code: 664455

The **volume** of a cylinder can be calculated by the formula $V = \pi r^2 h$, where r is the radius, and h is the height. The **surface area** of a cylinder can be found by the formula $SA = 2\pi r^2 + 2\pi rh$. The first term is the base area multiplied by two, and the second term is the perimeter of the base multiplied by the height.

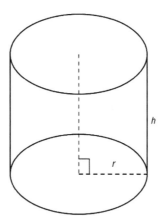

> **Review Video: Volume and Surface Area of a Right Circular Cylinder**
> Visit mometrix.com/academy and enter code: 226463

The **volume** of a pyramid is found by the formula $V = \frac{1}{3}Bh$, where B is the area of the base, and h is the height (perpendicular distance from the vertex to the base). Notice this formula is the same as $\frac{1}{3}$ times the volume of a prism. Like a prism, the base of a pyramid can be any shape.

Review Video: <u>Volume and Surface Area of a Pyramid</u>
Visit mometrix.com/academy and enter code: 621932

Finding the **surface area** of a pyramid is not as simple as the other shapes we've looked at thus far. If the pyramid is a right pyramid, meaning the base is a regular polygon and the vertex is directly over the center of that polygon, the surface area can be calculated as $SA = B + \frac{1}{2}Ph_s$, where P is the perimeter of the base, and h_s is the slant height (distance from the vertex to the midpoint of one side of the base). If the pyramid is irregular, the area of each triangle side must be calculated individually and then summed, along with the base.

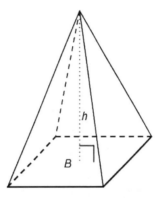

The **volume** of a cone is found by the formula $V = \frac{1}{3}\pi r^2 h$, where r is the radius, and h is the height. Notice this is the same as $\frac{1}{3}$ times the volume of a cylinder. The **surface area** can be calculated as $SA = \pi r^2 + \pi rs$, where s is the slant height. The slant height can be calculated using the Pythagorean Thereom to be $\sqrt{r^2 + h^2}$, so the surface area formula can also be written as $SA = \pi r^2 + \pi r\sqrt{r^2 + h^2}$.

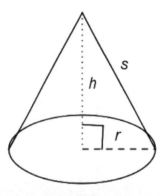

Review Video: <u>Volume and Surface Area of a Right Circular Cone</u>
Visit mometrix.com/academy and enter code: 573574

VOLUME EXAMPLES

EXAMPLE 1

Draw an object with a volume described by the formula $V = lwh$ in^2.

This formula is used to find the volume of a **rectangular prism** of length, l, width, w, and height, h, all in inches.

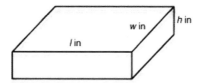

EXAMPLE 2

Draw an object with a volume described by the formula $V = \frac{1}{3}lwh$ in^2.

This formula is used to find the volume of a **rectangular pyramid**, whose base is a rectangle of length, l, and width, w. The pyramid has a height given by h, and all side lengths are in inches.

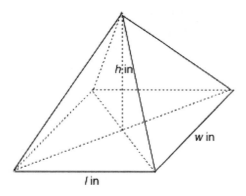

EXAMPLE 3

Draw an object with a volume described by the formula $V = \frac{4}{3}\pi r^3$ cm^3.

This formula is used to find the volume of a **sphere** with radius, r, in centimeters.

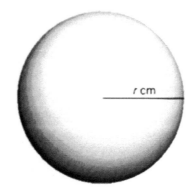

Example 4

The two rectangular prisms below are **similar**.

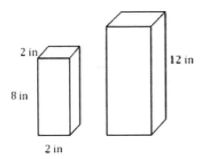

Part 1: Describe the relationship between the dimensions of the two prisms.

Using the given heights, the relationship between the dimensions of the two prisms, as a proportion, is: $\frac{\text{height of smaller}}{\text{height of larger}} = \frac{8}{12} = \frac{2}{3}$.

Part 2: Describe the relationship between the volumes of the two prisms.

The volume of the smaller prism is: $(2)(2)(8) = 32$ in³. To find the volume of the larger prism, first find the length and width of the larger prism. Because the length and width of the smaller prism are equal, the length and width of the larger prism are also equal. Use the proportion relating the dimensions to find one of the measurements, for example the length, of the larger prism:

$$\frac{2}{3} = \frac{2}{x}$$

$$2x = 6$$

$$x = 3$$

The length and width of the larger prism is 3 inches. Find the volume of the larger prism: $(3)(3)(12) = 108$ in³. The relationship between the two volumes, as a proportion, is:

$$\frac{\text{volume of smaller}}{\text{volume of larger}} = \frac{32}{108} = \frac{8}{27}$$

This relationship can also be determined by using the ratio of the dimensions. The ratio of the volumes of two three-dimensional shapes is the cube of the ratio of their dimensions:

$$\left(\frac{2}{3}\right)^3 = \frac{8}{27}$$

SURFACE AREA EXAMPLES

EXAMPLE 1

Find the surface area of the figure below. Each triangular face is congruent, and the base is a square.

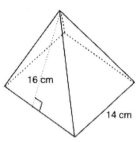

16 cm

14 cm

The surface area is the sum of the areas of the faces. The area of the base, which is given as a square, will be the side length squared:

$$a = s^2 = 14^2 = 196 \text{ cm}^2$$

The area of one of the triangular faces will be one half times the height and base of the triangle. The base of the triangle will be one of the sides of the square.

$$a = \frac{1}{2}bh = \frac{1}{2}(14)(16) = 112 \text{ cm}^2$$

There are four triangular faces, so the surface area will be four times the area of the triangular face plus the area of the square base.

$$SA = 4(\text{triangular face area}) + \text{square face area} = 4(112) + 196 = 448 + 196 = 644 \text{ cm}^2$$

EXAMPLE 2

Sophia is covering a rectangular prism-shaped couch cushion with fabric. She will be covering all sides of the cushion. The cushion is 4 inches high, 20 inches wide, and 32 inches deep. Determine the area of the fabric needed to cover the cushion.

Drawing a diagram may be helpful. Label the dimensions as given in the problem.

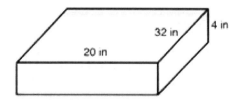

32 in   4 in

20 in

To find the area of fabric needed, find the surface area of the cushion. Sum the areas of each face of the rectangle prism. Opposite faces will have an equal area. The front/back faces of the prism have an area of $20 \times 4 = 80 \text{ in}^2$. The left/right side faces of the prism have an area of $32 \times 4 = 128 \text{ in}^2$. The top/bottom faces of the prism have an area of $20 \times 32 = 640 \text{ in}^2$.

The total surface area of the prism, or area of the fabric needed to cover the cushion, is

$$80 \text{ in}^2 + 80 \text{ in}^2 + 128 \text{ in}^2 + 128 \text{ in}^2 + 640 \text{ in}^2 + 640 \text{ in}^2 = 1696 \text{ in}^2$$

Data Analysis, Statistics, and Probability

FREQUENCY TABLES

Frequency tables show how frequently each unique value appears in the set. A **relative frequency table** is one that shows the proportions of each unique value compared to the entire set. Relative frequencies are given as percentages; however, the total percentage for a relative frequency table will not necessarily equal 100 percent due to rounding. An example of a frequency table with relative frequencies is shown below.

Favorite Color	Frequency	Relative Frequency
Blue	4	13%
Red	7	22%
Purple	3	9%
Green	6	19%
Cyan	12	38%

TWO-WAY FREQUENCY TABLES

A **two-way frequency table** is a table showing the counts of data sets matching two categorical variables, one running horizontally on the table and the other vertically. For example, suppose we count the number of books on a bookshelf and categorize them according to whether they're hardbacks or paperbacks and whether they're fiction or nonfiction. We could end up with the following two-way frequency table:

	Hardbacks	Paperbacks	Total
Fiction	30	45	75
Nonfiction	35	25	60
Total	65	70	135

JOINT RELATIVE FREQUENCIES

The **joint relative frequencies** are the fractions of items that match a particular combination of values of the variables. The number of matching items can be read directly from the table by just finding the cell in the corresponding row and column; to find the relative frequency just divide by the total from the lower right. For example, in the above frequency table, the relative frequency of non-fiction paperbacks is 25/135—the number in the cell in the Paperbacks column and the Nonfiction row, divided by the total number of books—which can be reduced to 5/27.

MARGINAL RELATIVE FREQUENCIES

The **marginal relative frequencies** are the fractions of items that match a particular value of one variable. The number of matching items can be read directly from the table from the totals on the right side or the bottom, by finding the row or column corresponding to the category in question. Then to find the relative frequency, divide by the total from the lower right. For example, suppose an ice cream parlor surveys a number of customers asking them if they prefer chocolate or vanilla and whether they prefer ice cream in a cone or a bowl. We could end up with the following two-way frequency table:

	Chocolate	Vanilla	Total
Cone	50	42	92
Bowl	45	30	75
Total	95	72	167

In the above frequency table, the marginal relative frequency of people who prefer their ice cream in a cone is 92/167—the total in the Cone row, divided by the overall total. The marginal relative frequency of people who prefer chocolate is 95/167—the total in the Chocolate column, divided by the overall total.

<u>CONDITIONAL RELATIVE FREQUENCIES</u>

The **conditional relative frequencies** are the fractions of items that match particular values of one variable, given that they match particular values of the other. The numerator of the ratio can be read directly from the cell of the row and column that matches the appropriate values of both variables; the denominator is the total on the bottom or right that matches the given value. For example, suppose a café tracks whether each of its customers on a given day orders regular coffee or decaf, and with or without cream. We could end up with the following two-way frequency table:

	With Cream	Without Cream	Total
Regular	62	45	107
Decaf	24	27	51
Total	86	72	158

Now, suppose we want to know how many people who ordered regular coffee ordered it with cream. The numerator is the number of people who ordered regular coffee with cream, which is 62. The denominator is the total number of people who ordered regular coffee, which is 107. Thus, this conditional relative frequency is 62/107.

<u>IDENTIFYING TRENDS</u>

A **trend** simply refers to a pattern in the data—any observation of which frequencies are larger than others. For example, suppose a magazine tallies the submissions it receives, recording whether each is from a man or a woman and whether it was sent by mail or by e-mail. We could end up with the following two-way frequency table:

	Mail	E-mail	Total
Men	30	62	92
Women	45	55	100
Total	75	117	192

Among the trends evident in this table are:

- Both men and women are more likely to send submissions by e-mail than by mail. (The number in the "e-mail" column is larger in both rows than the number in the "mail" column.)
- Most submissions sent by mail are from women; most submissions sent by e-mail are from men. (The "mail" column has a larger number in the "women" row, the "e-mail" in the "men" row.)
- Slightly more submissions are sent overall by women than by men. (The total in the "women" row is larger than the total in the "men" row.)

OTHER TYPES OF GRAPHS

PICTOGRAPHS

A **pictograph** is a graph, generally in the horizontal orientation, that uses pictures or symbols to represent the data. Each pictograph must have a key that defines the picture or symbol and gives the quantity each picture or symbol represents. Pictures or symbols on a pictograph are not always shown as whole elements. In this case, the fraction of the picture or symbol shown represents the same fraction of the quantity a whole picture or symbol stands for. For example, a row with $3\frac{1}{2}$ ears of corn, where each ear of corn represents 100 stalks of corn in a field, would equal $3\frac{1}{2} \cdot 100 = 350$ stalks of corn in the field.

PIE CHARTS

Pie charts, also known as **circle graphs**, provide a visual depiction of the relationship of each type of data compared to the whole set of data. The circle graph is divided into sections by drawing radii to create central angles whose percentage of the circle is equal to the individual data's percentage of the whole set. Each 1% of data is equal to 3.6° in the circle graph. Therefore, data represented by a 90° section of the circle graph makes up 25% of the whole. When complete, a circle graph often looks like a pie cut into uneven wedges. The pie chart below shows the data from the frequency table referenced earlier where people were asked their favorite color.

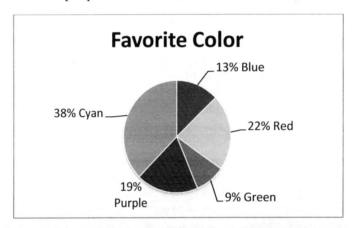

Favorite Color

Review Video: **Pie Chart**
Visit mometrix.com/academy and enter code: 895285

LINE GRAPHS

Line graphs have one or more lines of varying styles (solid or broken) to show the different values for a set of data. The individual data are represented as ordered pairs, much like on a Cartesian plane. In this case, the x- and y- axes are defined in terms of their units, such as dollars or time. The individual plotted points are joined by line segments to show whether the value of the data is increasing (line sloping upward), decreasing (line sloping downward) or staying the same (horizontal line). Multiple sets of data can be graphed on the same line graph to give an easy visual comparison. An example of this would be graphing achievement test scores for different groups of students over the same time period to see which group had the greatest increase or decrease in performance from year-to-year (as shown below).

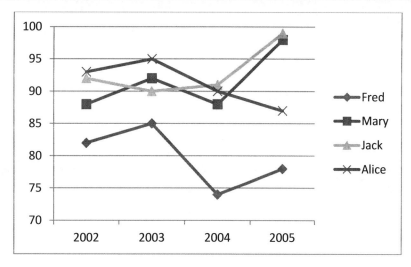

Review Video: Line Graphs
Visit mometrix.com/academy and enter code: 480147

SCATTER PLOTS

A **scatter plot**, also known as a **dot plot**, has plotted points that are NOT connected by line segments. In this graph, the horizontal axis lists the different possible values for the data, and the vertical axis lists the number of times the individual value occurs. A single dot is graphed for each value to show the number of times it occurs. This graph is more closely related to a bar graph than a line graph. Do not connect the dots in a line plot or it will misrepresent the data.

Review Video: Line Plot
Visit mometrix.com/academy and enter code: 754610

BAR GRAPHS

A **bar graph** is one of the few graphs that can be drawn correctly in two different configurations – both horizontally and vertically. A bar graph is similar to a line plot in the way the data is organized on the graph. Both axes must have their categories defined for the graph to be useful. Rather than placing a single dot to mark the point of the data's value, a bar, or thick line, is drawn from zero to the exact value of the data, whether it is a number, percentage, or other numerical value. Longer bar lengths correspond to greater data values. To read a bar graph, read the labels for the axes to find the units being reported. Then look where the bars end in relation to the scale given on the corresponding axis and determine the associated value. The bar chart below represents the responses from our favorite color survey.

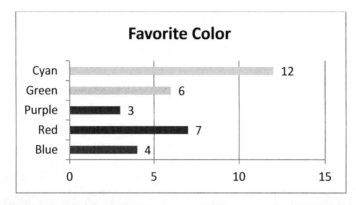

HISTOGRAMS

At first glance, a **histogram** looks like a vertical bar graph. The difference is that a bar graph has a separate bar for each piece of data and a histogram has one continuous bar for each **range** of data. For example, a histogram may have one bar for the range 0–9, one bar for 10–19, etc. While a bar graph has numerical values on one axis, a histogram has numerical values on both axes. Each range is of equal size, and they are ordered left to right from lowest to highest. The height of each column on a histogram represents the number of data values within that range. Below is an example of histogram. Note that most histograms will not have the particular values listed within the bars, but they are included here for graphical illustration of what each bar height means.

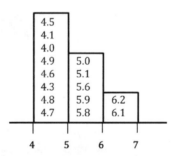

STEM-AND-LEAF PLOTS

A **stem-and-leaf plot** is useful for depicting groups of data that fall into a range of values. Each piece of data is separated into two parts: the stem and the leaf. Each stem is listed in the left-most column from smallest to largest, descending. Each leaf that has the common stem is listed in that stem's row from smallest to largest.

For example, in a set of two-digit numbers, the digit in the tens place is the **stem**, and the digit in the ones place is the **leaf**. With a stem-and-leaf plot, you can easily see which subset of numbers (10s, 20s, 30s, etc.) is the largest. This information is also readily available by looking at a histogram, but a stem-and-leaf plot also allows you to look closer and see exactly which values fall in that range. The stem-and-leaf plot below is assembled from a set of 16 test scores.

Test Scores									
7	4	8							
8	2	5	7	8	8				
9	0	0	1	2	2	3	5	8	9

MEASURES OF CENTRAL TENDENCY

A **measure of central tendency** is a statistical value that gives a general tendency for the center of a group of data. There are three measures of central tendency commonly used in statistics that we will discuss here: **mean**, **median**, and **mode**. Each one is calculated in a different way and gives a slightly different perspective on the data set.

Measures of central tendency are useful when understood and used in an appropriate manner, but they are **not a substitute** for understanding what is going on with the data set as a whole. The idea that a single value, whether mean, median, or mode (or even all of them together), can give you a complete and accurate picture of an entire data set is faulty thinking.

MEAN

The **statistical mean** of a group of data is the same as the arithmetic average of that group. To find the mean of a set of data, first convert each value to the same units, if necessary. Then find the sum of all the values, and count the total number of data values, making sure you take into consideration each individual value. If a value appears more than once, count it more than once. Divide the sum of the values by the total number of values and apply the units, if any. Note that the mean does not have to be one of the data values in the set, and may not divide evenly.

$$\text{mean} = \frac{\text{sum of data values}}{\text{quantity of data values}}$$

The mean of the data set {88, 72, 61, 90, 97, 94, 90, 63, 69, 89} would be the sum of the 10 numbers divided by 10:

$$\frac{88 + 72 + 61 + 90 + 97 + 94 + 90 + 63 + 69 + 89}{10} = \frac{813}{10} = 81.3$$

While the mean is relatively easy to calculate and averages are understood by most people, the mean can be very misleading if used as the sole measure of central tendency. If the data set has **outliers** (data values that are unusually high or unusually low compared to the rest of the data values), the mean can be very distorted, especially if the data set has a small number of values. If **unusually high** values are countered with **unusually low** values, the mean is not affected as much. For example, if five of twenty students in a class get a 100 on a test, but the other 15 students have an average of 60 on the same test, the class average would appear as 70. It is usually a good idea to look at more measures than just the mean.

MEDIAN

The **statistical median** is the value in the middle of the set of data. To find the median, list all data values in order from smallest to largest or from largest to smallest. Any value that is repeated in the set must be listed the number of times it appears. If there are an odd number of data values, the median is the value in the middle of the list. If there is an even number of data values, the median is the arithmetic mean (average) of the two middle values.

When the individual values in a set of data are evenly dispersed, the median is a useful tool. However, if a data set consists of a group of high numbers and a group of low numbers, then the median will be a high number (if there are more high numbers) or a low number (if there are more low numbers), and not something in between.

MODE

The **statistical mode** is the data value that occurs the most number of times in the data set. It is possible to have exactly one mode, more than one mode, or no mode. To find the mode of a set of data, arrange the data like you do to find the median (all values in order, listing all multiples of data values). Count the number of times each value appears in the data set. If all values appear an equal number of times, there is no mode. If one value appears more than any other value, that value is the mode. If two or more values appear the same number of times, but there are other values that appear fewer times and no values that appear more times, all of those values are the modes.

The main disadvantage of the mode is that the values of the other data in the set have no bearing on the mode. The mode may be the largest value, the smallest value, or a value anywhere in between in the set. The mode only tells which value or values, if any, occurred the most number of times. It does not give any suggestions about the remaining values in the set.

> **Review Video: Mean, Median, and Mode**
> Visit mometrix.com/academy and enter code: 286207

PROBABILITY

Probability is the branch of statistics that deals with the likelihood of something taking place. One classic example is a coin toss. There are only two possible results: heads or tails. The likelihood, or probability, that the coin will land as heads is 1 out of 2 $\left(\frac{1}{2}, 0.5, 50\%\right)$. Tails has the same probability as heads. Another common example is a 6-sided die roll. There are six possible results from rolling a single die, each with an equal chance of happening, so the probability of any given number coming up is 1 out of 6.

The probability of an outcome occurring can often be determined mathematically. If each possible outcome is equally likely to take place, the probability of a specific outcome, A, occurring can be calculated with the following equation:

$$P(A) = \frac{\text{Number of acceptable outcomes}}{\text{Number of possible outcomes}}$$

The total number of acceptable outcomes must be less than or equal to the total number of possible outcomes. If the two are equal, then the outcome is certain to occur and the probability is 1. If the number of acceptable outcomes is zero, then the outcome is impossible and the probability is 0.

Reading

Literary Analysis

SETTING AND TIME FRAME

A literary text has both a setting and time frame. A **setting** is the place in which the story as a whole is set. The **time frame** is the period in which the story is set. This may refer to the historical period the story takes place in or if the story takes place over a single day. Both setting and time frame are relevant to a text's meaning because they help the reader place the story in time and space. An author uses setting and time frame to anchor a text, create a mood, and enhance its meaning; helping a reader understand why a character acts the way he does, or why certain events in the story are important. The setting impacts the **plot** and character **motivations**, while the time frame helps place the story in **chronological context**.

EXAMPLE

Read the following excerpt from The Adventures of Huckleberry Finn by Mark Twain and analyze the relevance of setting to the text's meaning:

> We said there warn't no home like a raft, after all. Other places do seem so cramped up and smothery, but a raft don't. You feel mighty free and easy and comfortable on a raft.

This excerpt from *The Adventures of Huckleberry Finn* by Mark Twain reveals information about the **setting** of the book. By understanding that the main character, Huckleberry Finn, lives on a raft, the reader can place the story on a river, in this case, the Mississippi River in the South before the Civil War. The information about the setting also gives the reader clues about the **character** of Huck Finn: he clearly values independence and freedom and he likes the outdoors. The information about the setting in the quote helps the reader to better understand the rest of the text.

THEME

The theme of a passage is what the reader learns from the text or the passage. It is the lesson or **moral** contained in the passage. It also is a unifying idea that is used throughout the text; it can take the form of a common setting, idea, symbol, design, or recurring event. A passage can have two or more themes that convey its overall idea. The theme or themes of a passage are often based on **universal themes**. They can frequently be expressed using well-known sayings about life, society, or human nature, such as "Hard work pays off" or "Good triumphs over evil." Themes are not usually stated **explicitly**. The reader must figure them out by carefully reading the passage. Themes are often the reason why passages are written; they give a passage unity and meaning. Themes are created through **plot development**. The events of a story help shape the themes of a passage.

> **Review Video: Theme**
> Visit mometrix.com/academy and enter code: 732074

75

<u>EXAMPLE</u>

Explain why "Take care of what you care about" accurately describes the theme of the following excerpt.

> Luca collected baseball cards, but he wasn't very careful with them. He left them around the house. His dog liked to chew. Luca and his friend Bart were looking at his collection. Then they went outside. When Luca got home, he saw his dog chewing on his cards. They were ruined.

This excerpt tells the story of a boy who is careless with his baseball cards and leaves them lying around. His dog ends up chewing them and ruining them. The lesson is that if you care about something, you need to take care of it. This is the point of the story. The **theme** is the lesson that a story teaches. Some stories have more than one theme, but this is not really true of this excerpt. The reader needs to figure out the theme based on what happens in the story. Sometimes, as in the case of fables, the theme is stated directly in the text. However, this is not usually the case.

CONFLICT

Read the following paragraph and discuss the type of conflict present:

> Timothy was shocked out of sleep by the appearance of a bear just outside his tent. After panicking for a moment, he remembered some advice he had read in preparation for this trip: he should make noise so the bear would not be startled. As Timothy started to hum and sing, the bear wandered away.

There are three main types of conflict in literature: **man versus man**, man versus nature, and **man versus self**. This paragraph is an example of man versus nature. Timothy is in conflict with the bear. Even though no physical conflict like an attack exists, Timothy is pitted against the bear. Timothy uses his knowledge to "defeat" the bear and keep himself safe. The solution to the conflict is that Timothy makes noise, the bear wanders away, and Timothy is safe.

> **Review Video: <u>Conflict</u>**
> Visit mometrix.com/academy and enter code: 559550

CONFLICT RESOLUTION

The way the conflict is **resolved** depends on the type of conflict. The plot of any book starts with the lead up to the conflict, then the conflict itself, and finally the solution, or **resolution**, to the conflict. In *man versus man* conflicts, the conflict is often resolved by two parties coming to some sort of agreement or by one party triumphing over the party. In *man versus nature* conflicts, the conflict is often resolved by man coming to some realization about some aspect of nature. In *man versus self* conflicts, the conflict is often resolved by the character growing or coming to an understanding about part of himself.

SYNTAX AND WORD CHOICE

Authors use words and **syntax**, or sentence structure, to make their texts unique, convey their own writing style, and sometimes to make a point or emphasis. They know that word choice and syntax contribute to the reader's understanding of the text as well as to the tone and mood of a text.

ALLUSION

An allusion is an uncited but recognizable reference to something else. Authors use language to make allusions to places, events, artwork, and other books in order to make their own text richer.

For example, an author may allude to a very important text in order to make his own text seem more important. Martin Luther King, Jr. started his "I Have a Dream" speech by saying "Five score years ago..." This is a clear allusion to President Abraham Lincoln's "Gettysburg Address" and served to remind people of the significance of the event. An author may allude to a place to ground his text or make a cultural reference to make readers feel included. There are many reasons that authors make allusions.

COMIC RELIEF

Comic relief is the use of comedy by an author to break up a dramatic or tragic scene and infuse it with a bit of **lightheartedness**. In William Shakespeare's *Hamlet*, two gravediggers digging the grave for Ophelia share a joke while they work. The death and burial of Ophelia are tragic moments that directly follow each other. Shakespeare uses an instance of comedy to break up the tragedy and give his audience a bit of a break from the tragic drama. Authors sometimes use comic relief so that their work will be less depressing; other times they use it to create irony or contrast between the darkness of the situation and the lightness of the joke. Often, authors will use comedy to parallel what is happening in the tragic scenes.

Main Idea and Supporting Details

UNDERSTANDING A PASSAGE

One of the most important skills in reading comprehension is the identification of **topics** and **main ideas.** There is a subtle difference between these two features. The topic is the subject of a text (i.e., what the text is all about). The main idea, on the other hand, is the most important point being made by the author. The topic is usually expressed in a few words at the most while the main idea often needs a full sentence to be completely defined. As an example, a short passage might have the topic of penguins and the main idea could be written as *Penguins are different from other birds in many ways*. In most nonfiction writing, the topic and the main idea will be **stated directly** and often appear in a sentence at the very beginning or end of the text. When being tested on an understanding of the author's topic, you may be able to skim the passage for the general idea, by reading only the first sentence of each paragraph. A body paragraph's first sentence is often—but not always—the main **topic sentence** which gives you a summary of the content in the paragraph.

However, there are cases in which the reader must figure out an **unstated** topic or main idea. In these instances, you must read every sentence of the text and try to come up with an overarching idea that is supported by each of those sentences.

Note: The main idea should not be confused with the thesis statement. While the main idea gives a brief, general summary of a text, the thesis statement provides a specific perspective on an issue that the author supports with evidence.

> **Review Video: Topics and Main Ideas**
> Visit mometrix.com/academy and enter code: 407801

Supporting details provide evidence and backing for the main point. In order to show that a main idea is correct, or valid, authors add details that prove their point. All texts contain details, but they are only classified as supporting details when they serve to reinforce some larger point. Supporting details are most commonly found in informative and persuasive texts. In some cases, they will be clearly indicated with terms like *for example* or *for instance*, or they will be enumerated with terms like *first*, *second*, and *last*. However, you need to be prepared for texts that do not contain those indicators. As a reader, you should consider whether the author's supporting details really back up his or her main point. Supporting details can be factual and correct, yet they may not be **relevant** to the author's point. Conversely, supporting details can seem pertinent, but they can be ineffective because they are based on opinion or assertions that cannot be proven.

> **Review Video: Supporting Details**
> Visit mometrix.com/academy and enter code: 396297

An example of a main idea is: *Giraffes live in the Serengeti of Africa.* A supporting detail about giraffes could be: *A giraffe in this region benefits from a long neck by reaching twigs and leaves on tall trees.* The main idea gives the general idea that the text is about giraffes. The supporting detail gives a specific fact about how the giraffes eat.

EVALUATING A PASSAGE

When reading informational texts, there is importance in understanding the logical conclusion of the author's ideas. **Identifying a logical conclusion** can help you determine whether you agree with the writer or not. Coming to this conclusion is much like making an inference: the approach requires you to combine the information given by the text with what you already know in order to make a logical conclusion. If the author intended the reader to draw a certain conclusion, then you can expect the author's argumentation and detail to be leading in that direction.

One way to approach the task of drawing conclusions is to make brief **notes** of all the points made by the author. When the notes are arranged on paper, they may clarify the logical conclusion. Another way to approach conclusions is to consider whether the reasoning of the author raises any pertinent questions. Sometimes you will be able to draw several conclusions from a passage. On occasion these will be conclusions that were never imagined by the author. Therefore, be aware that these conclusions must be **supported directly by the text**.

> **Review Video: Identifying Logical Conclusions**
> Visit mometrix.com/academy and enter code: 281653

A reader should always be drawing conclusions from the text. Sometimes conclusions are **implied** from written information, and other times the information is **stated directly** within the passage. One should always aim to draw conclusions from information stated within a passage, rather than to draw them from mere implications. At times an author may provide some information and then describe a counterargument. Readers should be alert for direct statements that are subsequently rejected or weakened by the author. Furthermore, you should always read through the entire passage before drawing conclusions. Many readers are trained to expect the author's conclusions at either the beginning or the end of the passage, but many texts do not adhere to this format.

Drawing conclusions from information implied within a passage requires confidence on the part of the reader. **Implications** are things that the author does not state directly, but readers can assume based on what the author does say. Consider the following passage: *I stepped outside and opened my umbrella. By the time I got to work, the cuffs of my pants were soaked.* The author never states that it is raining, but this fact is clearly implied. Conclusions based on implication must be well supported by the text. In order to draw a solid conclusion, readers should have **multiple pieces of evidence**. If readers have only one piece, they must be assured that there is no other possible explanation than their conclusion. A good reader will be able to draw many conclusions from information implied by the text, which will be a great help on the exam.

As an aid to drawing conclusions, **outlining** the information contained in the passage should be a familiar skill to readers. An effective outline will reveal the structure of the passage and will lead to solid conclusions. An effective outline will have a title that refers to the basic subject of the text though the title does not need not restate the main idea. In most outlines, the main idea will be the first major section. Each major idea of the passage will be established as the head of a category. For instance, the most common outline format calls for the main ideas of the passage to be indicated with Roman numerals. In an effective outline of this kind, each of the main ideas will be represented by a Roman numeral and none of the Roman numerals will designate minor details or secondary ideas. Moreover, all supporting ideas and details should be placed in the appropriate place on the outline. An outline does not need to include every detail listed in the text, but the outline should feature all of those that are central to the argument or message. Each of these details should be listed under the appropriate main idea.

Ideas from a text can also be organized using **graphic organizers**. A graphic organizer is a way to simplify information and take key points from the text. A graphic organizer such as a timeline may have an event listed for a corresponding date on the timeline while an outline may have an event listed under a key point that occurs in the text. Each reader needs to create the type of graphic organizer that works the best for him or her in terms of being able to recall information from a story. Examples include a *spider-map*, which takes a main idea from the story and places it in a

bubble with supporting points branching off the main idea. An *outline* is useful for diagramming the main and supporting points of the entire story, and a *Venn diagram* classifies information as separate or overlapping.

Review Video: <u>Graphic Organizers</u>
Visit mometrix.com/academy and enter code: 665513

A helpful tool is the ability to **summarize** the information that you have read in a paragraph or passage format. This process is similar to creating an effective outline. First, a summary should accurately define the main idea of the passage though the summary does not need to explain this main idea in exhaustive detail. The summary should continue by laying out the most important supporting details or arguments from the passage. All of the significant supporting details should be included, and none of the details included should be irrelevant or insignificant. Also, the summary should accurately report all of these details. Too often, the desire for brevity in a summary leads to the sacrifice of clarity or accuracy. Summaries are often difficult to read because they omit all of the graceful language, digressions, and asides that distinguish great writing. However, an effective summary should contain much the same message as the original text.

Paraphrasing is another method that the reader can use to aid in comprehension. When paraphrasing, one puts what they have read into their words by rephrasing what the author has written, or one "translates" all of what the author shared into their words by including as many details as they can.

Inferences in a Text or Texts

MAKING INFERENCES

An inference is a conclusion that a reader can make based on the facts and other information in a passage or a story. An inference is based both on what is *found in a passage or a story* and what is *known from personal experience*. For instance, a story may say that a character is frightened and that he can hear the sounds of howling in the distance. Based on both what is in the text and personal knowledge, it might be a logical conclusion that the character is frightened because he hears the sound of wolves. A good inference is supported by the information in a passage. Inferences are different from **explicit information**, which is clearly stated in a passage. Inferences are not stated in a passage. A reader must put the information together to come up with a logical conclusion.

Read the excerpt and decide why Jana finally relaxed.

> Jana loved her job, but the work was very demanding. She had trouble relaxing. She called a friend, but she still thought about work. She ordered a pizza, but eating it did not help. Then her kitten jumped on her lap and began to purr. Jana leaned back and began to hum a little tune. She felt better.

You can draw the conclusion that Jana relaxes because her kitten jumped on her lap. The kitten purred, and Jana leaned back and hummed a tune. Then, she felt better. The excerpt does not explicitly say that this is the reason why she was able to relax. The text leaves the matter unclear, but the reader can infer or make a "best guess" that this is the reason she is relaxing. This is a logical conclusion based on the information in the passage. It is the best conclusion a reader can make based on the information he or she has read. Inferences are based on the information in a passage, but they are not directly stated in the passage.

> **Review Video: Inference**
> Visit mometrix.com/academy and enter code: 379203

Test-taking tip: While being tested on your ability to make correct inferences, you must look for **contextual clues**. An answer can be *true* but not *correct*. The contextual clues will help you find the answer that is the **best answer** out of the given choices. Be careful in your reading to understand the context in which a phrase is stated. When asked for the implied meaning of a statement made in the passage, you should immediately locate the statement and read the **context** in which the statement was made. Also, look for an answer choice that has a similar phrase to the statement in question.

MAKING PREDICTIONS

When reading a good passage, readers are moved to engage actively in the text. One part of being an active reader involves making predictions. A **prediction** is a guess about what will happen next. Readers constantly make predictions based on what they have read and what they already know. Consider the following sentence: *Staring at the computer screen in shock, Kim blindly reached over for the brimming glass of water on the shelf to her side.* The sentence suggests that Kim is agitated, and that she is not looking at the glass that she is going to pick up. So, a reader might predict that Kim is going to knock over the glass. Of course, not every prediction will be accurate: perhaps Kim will pick the glass up cleanly. Nevertheless, the author has certainly created the expectation that the

water might be spilled. Predictions are always subject to revision as the reader acquires more information.

Test-taking tip: To respond to questions requiring future predictions, your answers should be based on evidence of past or present behavior.

DRAWING CONCLUSIONS

A common type of inference that a reader has to make is **drawing a conclusion**. The reader makes this conclusion based on the information provided within a text. Certain facts are included to help a reader come to a specific conclusion. For example, a story may open with a man trudging through the snow on a cold winter day, dragging a sled behind him. The reader can logically **infer** from the setting of the story that the man is wearing heavy winter clothes in order to stay warm. Information is implied based on the setting of a story, which is why **setting** is an important element of the text. If the same man in the example was trudging down a beach on a hot summer day, dragging a surf board behind him, the reader would assume that the man is not wearing heavy clothes. The reader makes inferences based on their own experiences and the information presented to them in the story.

Test-taking tip: When asked for a *conclusion* that may be drawn, look for critical "hedge" phrases, such as *likely*, *may*, *can*, *will often*, among many others. When you are being tested on this knowledge, remember the question that writers insert into these hedge phrases to cover every possibility. Often an answer will be wrong simply because there is no room for exception. Extreme positive or negative answers (such as always or never) are usually not correct. The reader **should not** use any outside knowledge that is not gathered directly or reasonably inferred from the passage. Correct answers can be derived straight from the passage.

EXAMPLE

Read the following sentence and draw a conclusion based upon the information presented:

> "You know the reason Mother proposed not having any presents this Christmas was because it is going to be a hard winter for everyone; and she thinks we ought not to spend money for pleasure, when our men are suffering so in the army." (from *Little Women* by Louisa May Alcott)

Based on the information in the sentence, the reader can conclude, or **infer**, that the men are away at war while the women are still at home. The pronoun *our* gives a clue to the reader that the character is speaking about men she knows. In addition, the reader can assume that the character is speaking to a brother or sister, since the term Mother is used by the character while speaking to another person. The reader can also come to the conclusion that the characters celebrate Christmas, since it is mentioned in the **context** of the sentence. In the sentence, the Mother is presented as an unselfish character who is opinionated and thinks about the wellbeing of other people.

COMPARING TWO STORIES

When presented with two different stories, there will be **similarities** and **differences** between the two. A reader needs to make a list or other graphic organizer of the points presented in each story. Once the reader has written down the main point and supporting points for each story, the two sets of ideas can be compared. The reader can then present each idea and show how it is the same or different in the other story. This is called **comparing and contrasting ideas**.

The reader can compare ideas by stating, for example: "In Story 1, the author believes that humankind will one day land on Mars, whereas in Story 2, the author believes that Mars is too far away for humans to ever step foot on." Note that the two viewpoints are different in each story that the reader is comparing. A reader may state that: "Both stories discussed the likelihood of humankind landing on Mars." This statement shows how the viewpoint presented in both stories is based on the same topic, rather than how each viewpoint is different. The reader will complete a comparison of two stories with a conclusion.

Author's Use of Language

ORGANIZATION OF THE TEXT

The way a text is organized can help readers to understand the author's intent and his or her conclusions. There are various ways to organize a text, and each one has a purpose and use. Usually, authors will organize information logically in a passage so the reader can follow and locate the information within the text. However, since not all passages are written with the same logical structure, you need to be familiar with several different types of passage structure.

CHRONOLOGICAL

When using **chronological** order, the author presents information in the order that it happened. For example, biographies are typically written in chronological order. The subject's birth and childhood are presented first, followed by their adult life, and lastly the events leading up to the person's death.

CAUSE AND EFFECT

One of the most common text structures is **cause and effect**. A cause is an act or event that makes something happen, and an effect is the thing that happens as a result of the cause. A cause-and-effect relationship is not always explicit, but there are some terms in English that signal causes, such as *since*, *because*, and *due to*. Furthermore, terms that signal effects include *consequently, therefore, this lead(s) to*. As an example, consider the sentence *Because the sky was clear, Ron did not bring an umbrella*. The cause is the clear sky, and the effect is that Ron did not bring an umbrella. However, readers may find that sometimes the cause-and-effect relationship will not be clearly noted. For instance, the sentence *He was late and missed the meeting* does not contain any signaling words, but the sentence still contains a cause (he was late) and an effect (he missed the meeting).

Be aware of the possibility for a single cause to have multiple effects (e.g., *Single cause*: Because you left your homework on the table, your dog engulfs the assignment. *Multiple effects*: As a result, you receive a failing grade; your parents do not allow you to visit your friends; you miss out on the new movie and meeting a potential significant other).

Also, the possibility of a single effect to have multiple causes (e.g., *Single effect*: Alan has a fever. *Multiple causes*: An unexpected cold front came through the area, and Alan forgot to take his multi-vitamin to avoid being sick.) Additionally, an effect can in turn be the cause of another effect, in what is known as a cause-and-effect chain. (e.g., As a result of her disdain for procrastination, Lynn prepared for her exam. This led to her passing her test with high marks. Hence, her resume was accepted and her application was approved.)

Persuasive essays, in which an author tries to make a convincing argument and change the minds of readers, usually include cause-and-effect relationships. However, these relationships should not always be taken at face value. Frequently, an author will assume a cause or take an effect for granted. To read a persuasive essay effectively, readers need to judge the cause-and-effect relationships that the author is presenting. For instance, imagine an author wrote the following: *The parking deck has been unprofitable because people would prefer to ride their bikes*. The relationship is clear: the cause is that people prefer to ride their bikes, and the effect is that the parking deck has been unprofitable. However, readers should consider whether this argument is conclusive. Perhaps there are other reasons for the failure of the parking deck: a down economy, excessive fees, etc. Too often, authors present causal relationships as if they are fact rather than opinion. Readers should be on the alert for these dubious claims.

PROBLEM-SOLUTION

Some nonfiction texts are organized to **present a problem** followed by a solution. For this type of text, the problem is often explained before the solution is offered. In some cases, as when the problem is well known, the solution may be introduced briefly at the beginning. Other passages may focus on the solution, and the problem will be referenced only occasionally. Some texts will outline multiple solutions to a problem, leaving readers to choose among them. If the author has an interest or an allegiance to one solution, he or she may fail to mention or describe accurately some of the other solutions. Readers should be careful of the author's agenda when reading a problem-solution text. Only by understanding the author's perspective and interests can one develop a proper judgment of the proposed solution.

COMPARE AND CONTRAST

Many texts follow the **compare-and-contrast** model in which the similarities and differences between two ideas or things are explored. Analysis of the similarities between ideas is called comparison. In an ideal comparison, the author places ideas or things in an equivalent structure (i.e., the author presents the ideas in the same way). If an author wants to show the similarities between cricket and baseball, then he or she may do so by summarizing the equipment and rules for each game. Be mindful of the similarities as they appear in the passage and take note of any differences that are mentioned. Often, these small differences will only reinforce the more general similarity.

> **Review Video: <u>Compare and Contrast</u>**
> Visit mometrix.com/academy and enter code: 798319

Thinking critically about ideas and conclusions can seem like a daunting task. One way to ease this task is to understand the basic elements of ideas and writing techniques. Looking at the way different ideas relate to each other can be a good way for readers to begin their analysis. For instance, sometimes authors will write about two ideas that are in opposition to each other. Or one author will provide his or her ideas on a topic, and another author may respond in opposition. The analysis of these opposing ideas is known as **contrast**. Contrast is often marred by the author's obvious partiality to one of the ideas. A discerning reader will be put off by an author who does not engage in a fair fight. In an analysis of opposing ideas, both ideas should be presented in clear and reasonable terms. If the author does prefer a side, you need to read carefully to determine the areas where the author shows or avoids this preference. In an analysis of opposing ideas, you should proceed through the passage by marking the major differences point by point with an eye that is looking for an explanation of each side's view. For instance, in an analysis of capitalism and communism, there is an importance in outlining each side's view on labor, markets, prices, personal responsibility, etc. Additionally, as you read through the passages, you should note whether the opposing views present each side in a similar manner.

SEQUENCE

Readers must be able to identify a text's **sequence**, or the order in which things happen. Often, when the sequence is very important to the author, the text is indicated with signal words like *first*, *then*, *next*, and *last*. However, a sequence can be merely implied and must be noted by the reader. Consider the sentence *He walked through the garden and gave water and fertilizer to the plants.* Clearly, the man did not walk through the garden before he collected water and fertilizer for the plants. So, the implied sequence is that he first collected water, then he collected fertilizer, next he walked through the garden, and last he gave water or fertilizer as necessary to the plants. Texts do not always proceed in an orderly sequence from first to last. Sometimes they begin at the end and

start over at the beginning. As a reader, you can enhance your understanding of the passage by taking brief notes to clarify the sequence.

TRANSITIONS

Transitional words and phrases are devices that guide readers through a text. You are no doubt familiar with the common transitions, though you may never have considered how they operate. Some transitional phrases (*after, before, during, in the middle of*) give information about time. Some indicate that an example is about to be given (*for example, in fact, for instance*). Writers use them to compare (*also, likewise*) and contrast (*however, but, yet*). Transitional words and phrases can suggest addition (*and, also, furthermore, moreover*) and logical relationships (*if, then, therefore, as a result, since*). Finally, transitional words and phrases can separate the steps in a process (*first, second, last*).

> **Review Video: <u>Transitional Words and Phrases</u>**
> Visit mometrix.com/academy and enter code: 197796

POINT OF VIEW

Another element that impacts a text is the author's point of view. The **point of view** of a text is the perspective from which a passage is told. An author will always have a point of view about a story before he or she draws up a plot line. The author will know what events they want to take place, how they want the characters to interact, and how they want the story to resolve. An author will also have an opinion on the topic or series of events which is presented in the story that is based on their prior experience and beliefs.

The two main points of view that authors use, especially in a work of fiction, are first person and third person. If the narrator of the story is also the main character, or *protagonist*, the text is written in first-person point of view. In first person, the author writes from the perspective of *I*. Third-person point of view is probably the most common that authors use in their passages. Using third person, authors refer to each character by using *he* or *she*. In third-person omniscient, the narrator is not a character in the story and tells the story of all of the characters at the same time.

> **Review Video: <u>Point of View</u>**
> Visit mometrix.com/academy and enter code: 383336

PURPOSES FOR WRITING

In order to be an effective reader, one must pay attention to the author's **position** and purpose. Even those texts that seem objective and impartial, like textbooks, have a position and bias. Readers need to take these positions into account when considering the author's message. When an author uses emotional language or clearly favors one side of an argument, his or her position is clear. However, the author's position may be evident not only in what he or she writes, but also in what he or she doesn't write. In a normal setting, a reader would want to review some other texts on the same topic in order to develop a view of the author's position. If this was not possible, then you would want to acquire some background about the author. However, since you are in the middle of an exam and the only source of information is the text, you should look for language and argumentation that seems to indicate a particular stance on the subject.

> **Review Video: <u>Author's Position</u>**
> Visit mometrix.com/academy and enter code: 827954

Usually, identifying the **purpose** of an author is easier than identifying his or her position. In most cases, the author has no interest in hiding his or her purpose. A text that is meant to entertain, for instance, should be written to please the reader. Most narratives, or stories, are written to entertain, though they may also inform or persuade. Informative texts are easy to identify, while the most difficult purpose of a text to identify is persuasion because the author has an interest in making this purpose hard to detect. When a reader discovers that the author is trying to persuade, he or she should be skeptical of the argument. For this reason, persuasive texts often try to establish an entertaining tone and hope to amuse the reader into agreement. On the other hand, an informative tone may be implemented to create an appearance of authority and objectivity.

An author's purpose is evident often in the organization of the text (e.g., section headings in bold font points to an informative text). However, you may not have such organization available to you in your exam. Instead, if the author makes his or her main idea clear from the beginning, then the likely purpose of the text is to inform. If the author begins by making a claim and provides various arguments to support that claim, then the purpose is probably to persuade. If the author tells a story or seems to want the attention of the reader more than to push a particular point or deliver information, then his or her purpose is most likely to entertain. As a reader, you must judge authors on how well they accomplish their purpose. In other words, you need to consider the type of passage (e.g., technical, persuasive, etc.) that the author has written and if the author has followed the requirements of the passage type.

> **Review Video: Purpose of an Author**
> Visit mometrix.com/academy and enter code: 497555

EVALUATING AN ARGUMENT

Argumentative and persuasive passages take a stand on a debatable issue, seek to explore all sides of the issue, and find the best possible solution. Argumentative and persuasive passages should not be combative or abusive. The word *argument* may remind you of two or more people shouting at each other and walking away in anger. However, an argumentative or persuasive passage should be a calm and reasonable presentation of an author's ideas for others to consider. When an author writes reasonable arguments, his or her goal is not to win or have the last word. Instead, authors want to reveal current understanding of the question at hand and suggest a solution to a problem. The purpose of argument and persuasion in a free society is to reach the best solution.

EVIDENCE

The term **text evidence** refers to information that supports a main point or minor points and can help lead the reader to a conclusion. Information used as text evidence is precise, descriptive, and factual. A main point is often followed by supporting details that provide evidence to back up a claim. For example, a passage may include the claim that winter occurs during opposite months in the Northern and Southern hemispheres. Text evidence based on this claim may include countries where winter occurs in opposite months along with reasons that winter occurs at different times of the year in separate hemispheres (due to the tilt of the Earth as it rotates around the sun).

> **Review Video: Text Evidence**
> Visit mometrix.com/academy and enter code: 486236

Evidence needs to be provided that supports the thesis and additional arguments. Most arguments must be supported by facts or statistics. Facts are something that is known with certainty and have been verified by several independent individuals. Examples and illustrations add an emotional component to arguments. With this component, you persuade readers in ways that facts and statistics cannot. The emotional component is effective when used with objective information that can be confirmed.

CREDIBILITY

The text used to support an argument can be the argument's downfall if the text is not credible. A text is **credible**, or believable, when the author is knowledgeable and objective, or unbiased. The author's motivations for writing the text play a critical role in determining the credibility of the text and must be evaluated when assessing that credibility. Reports written about the ozone layer by an environmental scientist and a hairdresser will have a different level of credibility.

APPEAL TO EMOTION

Sometimes, authors will appeal to the reader's emotion in an attempt to persuade or to distract the reader from the weakness of the argument. For instance, the author may try to inspire the pity of the reader by delivering a heart-rending story. An author also might use the bandwagon approach, in which he suggests that his opinion is correct because it is held by the majority. Some authors resort to name-calling, in which insults and harsh words are delivered to the opponent in an attempt to distract. In advertising, a common appeal is the celebrity testimonial, in which a famous person endorses a product. Of course, the fact that a famous person likes something should not really mean anything to the reader. These and other emotional appeals are usually evidence of poor reasoning and a weak argument.

> **Review Video: Appeal to Emotion**
> Visit mometrix.com/academy and enter code: 163442

COUNTER ARGUMENTS

When authors give both sides to the argument, they build trust with their readers. As a reader, you should start with an undecided or neutral position. If an author presents only his or her side to the argument, then you will need to be concerned at best.

Building common ground with neutral or opposed readers can be appealing to skeptical readers. Sharing values with undecided readers can allow people to switch positions without giving up what they feel is important. For people who may oppose a position, they need to feel that they can change their minds without betraying who they are as a person. This appeal to having an open mind can be a powerful tool in arguing a position without antagonizing other views. Objections can be countered on a point-by-point basis or in a summary paragraph. Be mindful of how an author points out flaws in counter arguments. If they are unfair to the other side of the argument, then you should lose trust with the author.

OPINIONS, FACTS, AND FALLACIES

Critical thinking skills are mastered through understanding various types of writing and the different purposes of authors in writing their passages. Every author writes for a purpose. When you understand their purpose and how they accomplish their goal, you will be able to analyze their writing and determine whether or not you agree with their conclusions.

Readers must always be conscious of the distinction between fact and opinion. A **fact** can be subjected to analysis and can be either proved or disproved. An **opinion**, on the other hand, is the author's personal thoughts or feelings which may not be alterable by research or evidence. If the author writes that the distance from New York City to Boston is about two hundred miles, then he or she is stating a fact. If the author writes that New York City is too crowded, then he or she is giving an opinion because there is no objective standard for "too crowded." Opinions are often supported by facts. For instance, the author might cite the population density of New York City as compared to that of other major American cities as evidence of an overcrowded population. An opinion supported by fact tends to be more convincing. On the other hand, when authors support their opinions with other opinions, readers should not be persuaded by the argument to any degree.

When you have an argumentative passage, you need to be sure that facts are presented to the reader from reliable sources. An opinion is what the author thinks about a given topic. An opinion is not common knowledge or proven by expert sources, instead the information is the personal beliefs and thoughts of the author. To distinguish between fact and opinion, a reader needs to consider the type of source that is presenting information, the information that backs-up a claim, and the author's motivation to have a certain point-of-view on a given topic. For example, if a panel of scientists has conducted multiple studies on the effectiveness of taking a certain vitamin, then the results are more likely to be factual than a company that is selling a vitamin and claims that taking the vitamin can produce positive effects. The company is motivated to sell their product, and the scientists are using the scientific method to prove a theory. Remember: if you find sentences that contain phrases such as "I think…", then the statement is an opinion.

> **Review Video: Fact or Opinion**
> Visit mometrix.com/academy and enter code: 870899

In their attempts to persuade, writers often make mistakes in their thinking patterns and writing choices. These patterns and choices are important to understand so you can make an informed decision. Every author has a point-of-view, but authors demonstrate a bias when they ignore reasonable counterarguments or distort opposing viewpoints. A bias is evident whenever the author is unfair or inaccurate in his or her presentation. Bias may be intentional or unintentional, and readers should be skeptical of the author's argument. Remember that a biased author may still be correct; however, the author will be correct in spite of his or her bias, not because of the bias.

A **stereotype** is a bias applied specifically to a group or place. Stereotyping is considered to be particularly abhorrent because the practice promotes negative generalizations about people. Readers should be very cautious of authors who stereotype in their writing. These faulty assumptions typically reveal the author's ignorance and lack of curiosity.

> **Review Video: Bias and Stereotype**
> Visit mometrix.com/academy and enter code: 644829

DENOTATIVE VS. CONNOTATIVE MEANING

The **denotative** meaning of a word is the literal meaning. The **connotative** meaning goes beyond the denotative meaning to include the emotional reaction that a word may invoke. The connotative meaning often takes the denotative meaning a step further due to associations which the reader makes with the denotative meaning. Readers can differentiate between the denotative and connotative meanings by first recognizing how authors use each meaning. Most non-fiction, for example, is fact-based and authors do not use flowery, figurative language. The reader can assume that the writer is using the denotative meaning of words. In fiction, the author may use the connotative meaning. Readers can determine whether the author is using the denotative or connotative meaning of a word by implementing context clues.

> **Review Video: Denotation and Connotation**
> Visit mometrix.com/academy and enter code: 310092

CONTEXT CLUES

Readers of all levels will encounter words that they have either never seen or encountered on a limited basis. The best way to define a word in **context** is to look for nearby words that can assist in learning the meaning of the word. For instance, unfamiliar nouns are often accompanied by examples that provide a definition. Consider the following sentence: *Dave arrived at the party in hilarious garb: a leopard-print shirt, buckskin trousers, and high heels.* If a reader was unfamiliar with the meaning of garb, he or she could read the examples (i.e., a leopard-print shirt, buckskin trousers, and high heels) and quickly determine that the word means *clothing.* Examples will not always be this obvious. Consider this sentence: *Parsley, lemon, and flowers were just a few of items he used as garnishes.* Here, the word *garnishes* is exemplified by parsley, lemon, and flowers. Readers who have eaten in a few restaurants will probably be able to identify a garnish as something used to decorate a plate.

> **Review Video: Context**
> Visit mometrix.com/academy and enter code: 613660

In addition to looking at the context of a passage, readers can use contrasts to define an unfamiliar word in context. In many sentences, the author will not describe the unfamiliar word directly; instead, he or she will describe the opposite of the unfamiliar word. Thus, you are provided with some information that will bring you closer to defining the word. Consider the following example: *Despite his intelligence, Hector's low brow and bad posture made him look obtuse.* The author writes that Hector's appearance does not convey intelligence. Therefore, *obtuse* must mean unintelligent. Here is another example: *Despite the horrible weather, we were beatific about our trip to Alaska.* The word *despite* indicates that the speaker's feelings were at odds with the weather. Since the weather is described as *horrible*, then *beatific* must mean something positive.

In some cases, there will be very few contextual clues to help a reader define the meaning of an unfamiliar word. When this happens, one strategy that readers may employ is **substitution**. A good reader will brainstorm some possible synonyms for the given word, and he or she will substitute these words into the sentence. If the sentence and the surrounding passage continue to make sense, then the substitution has revealed at least some information about the unfamiliar word. Consider the sentence: *Frank's admonition rang in her ears as she climbed the mountain.* A reader unfamiliar with *admonition* might come up with some substitutions like *vow, promise, advice, complaint,* or *compliment.* All of these words make general sense of the sentence though their meanings are diverse. The process has suggested; however, that an admonition is some sort of message. The substitution strategy is rarely able to pinpoint a precise definition, but this process can be effective as a last resort.

Occasionally, you will be able to define an unfamiliar word by looking at the descriptive words in the context. Consider the following sentence: *Fred dragged the recalcitrant boy kicking and screaming up the stairs.* The words *dragged, kicking,* and *screaming* all suggest that the boy does not want to go up the stairs. The reader may assume that *recalcitrant* means something like unwilling or protesting. In this example, an unfamiliar adjective was identified.

Additionally, using description to define an unfamiliar noun is a common practice compared to unfamiliar adjectives, as in this sentence: *Don's wrinkled frown and constantly shaking fist identified him as a curmudgeon of the first order.* Don is described as having a *wrinkled frown and constantly shaking fist* suggesting that a *curmudgeon* must be a grumpy man. Contrasts do not always provide detailed information about the unfamiliar word, but they at least give the reader some clues.

When a word has more than one meaning, readers can have difficulty with determining how the word is being used in a given sentence. For instance, the verb *cleave*, can mean either *join* or *separate*. When readers come upon this word, they will have to select the definition that makes the most sense. Consider the following sentence: *Hermione's knife cleaved the bread cleanly.* Since, a knife cannot join bread together, the word must indicate separation. A slightly more difficult example would be the sentence: *The birds cleaved to one another as they flew from the oak tree.* Immediately, the presence of the words *to one another* should suggest that in this sentence *cleave* is being used to mean *join*. Discovering the intent of a word with multiple meanings requires the same tricks as defining an unknown word: look for contextual clues and evaluate the substituted words.

SYNONYMS AND ANTONYMS

When you understand how words relate to each other, you will discover more in a passage. This is explained by understanding **synonyms** (e.g., words that mean the same thing) and **antonyms** (e.g., words that mean the opposite of one another). As an example, *dry* and *arid* are synonyms, and *dry* and *wet* are antonyms.

There are many pairs of words in English that can be considered synonyms, despite having slightly different definitions. For instance, the words *friendly* and *collegial* can both be used to describe a warm interpersonal relationship, and one would be correct to call them synonyms. However, *collegial* (kin to *colleague*) is often used in reference to professional or academic relationships, and *friendly* has no such connotation.

If the difference between the two words is too great, then they should not be called synonyms. *Hot* and *warm* are not synonyms because their meanings are too distinct. A good way to determine whether two words are synonyms is to substitute one word for the other word and verify that the meaning of the sentence has not changed. Substituting *warm* for *hot* in a sentence would convey a different meaning. Although warm and hot may seem close in meaning, warm generally means that the temperature is moderate, and hot generally means that the temperature is excessively high.

Antonyms are words with opposite meanings. *Light* and *dark*, *up* and *down*, *right* and *left*, *good* and *bad*: these are all sets of antonyms. Be careful to distinguish between antonyms and pairs of words that are simply different. *Black* and *gray*, for instance, are not antonyms because gray is not the opposite of black. *Black* and *white*, on the other hand, are antonyms.

Not every word has an antonym. For instance, many nouns do not: What would be the antonym of *chair*? During your exam, the questions related to antonyms are more likely to concern adjectives. You will recall that adjectives are words that describe a noun. Some common adjectives include *purple*, *fast*, *skinny*, and *sweet*. From those four adjectives, *purple* is the item that lacks a group of obvious antonyms.

> **Review Video: Synonyms and Antonyms**
> Visit mometrix.com/academy and enter code: 105612

Writing

Foundations of Grammar

THE EIGHT PARTS OF SPEECH

NOUNS

When you talk about a person, place, thing, or idea, you are talking about **nouns**. The two main types of nouns are **common** and **proper** nouns. Also, nouns can be abstract (i.e., general) or concrete (i.e., specific).

Common nouns are the class or group of people, places, and things (Note: Do not capitalize common nouns). Examples of common nouns:

> *People*: boy, girl, worker, manager
>
> *Places*: school, bank, library, home
>
> *Things*: dog, cat, truck, car

Proper nouns are the names of a specific person, place, or thing (Note: Capitalize all proper nouns). Examples of proper nouns:

> *People*: Abraham Lincoln, George Washington, Martin Luther King, Jr.
>
> *Places*: Los Angeles, California / New York / Asia
>
> *Things*: Statue of Liberty, Earth*, Lincoln Memorial

> *Note: When you talk about the planet that we live on, you capitalize *Earth*. When you mean the dirt, rocks, or land, you lowercase *earth*.

General nouns are the names of conditions or ideas. **Specific nouns** name people, places, and things that are understood by using your senses.

General nouns:

> *Condition*: beauty, strength
>
> *Idea*: truth, peace

Specific nouns:

> *People*: baby, friend, father
>
> *Places*: town, park, city hall
>
> *Things*: rainbow, cough, apple, silk, gasoline

Collective nouns are the names for a person, place, or thing that may act as a whole. The following are examples of collective nouns: *class, company, dozen, group, herd, team,* and *public*.

PRONOUNS

Pronouns are words that are used to stand in for a noun. A pronoun may be classified as personal, intensive, relative, interrogative, demonstrative, indefinite, and reciprocal.

Personal: *Nominative* is the case for nouns and pronouns that are the subject of a sentence. *Objective* is the case for nouns and pronouns that are an object in a sentence. *Possessive* is the case for nouns and pronouns that show possession or ownership.

SINGULAR

	Nominative	Objective	Possessive
First Person	I	me	my, mine
Second Person	you	you	your, yours
Third Person	he, she, it	him, her, it	his, her, hers, its

PLURAL

	Nominative	Objective	Possessive
First Person	we	us	our, ours
Second Person	you	you	your, yours
Third Person	they	them	their, theirs

Intensive: I myself, you yourself, he himself, she herself, the (thing) itself, we ourselves, you yourselves, they themselves

Relative: which, who, whom, whose

Interrogative: what, which, who, whom, whose

Demonstrative: this, that, these, those

Indefinite: all, any, each, everyone, either/neither, one, some, several

Reciprocal: each other, one another

> **Review Video: Nouns and Pronouns**
> Visit mometrix.com/academy and enter code: 312073

VERBS

If you want to write a sentence, then you need a verb in your sentence. Without a verb, you have no sentence. The verb of a sentence explains action or being. In other words, the verb shows the subject's movement or the movement that has been done to the subject.

TRANSITIVE AND INTRANSITIVE VERBS

A transitive verb is a verb whose action (e.g., drive, run, jump) points to a receiver (e.g., car, dog, kangaroo). Intransitive verbs do not point to a receiver of an action. In other words, the action of the verb does not point to a subject or object.

Transitive: He plays the piano. | The piano was played by him.

Intransitive: He plays. | John writes well.

A dictionary will let you know whether a verb is transitive or intransitive. Some verbs can be transitive and intransitive.

ACTION VERBS AND LINKING VERBS

An action verb is a verb that shows what the subject is doing in a sentence. In other words, an action verb shows action. A sentence can be complete with one word: an action verb. Linking verbs are intransitive verbs that show a condition (i.e., the subject is described but does no action).

Linking verbs link the subject of a sentence to a noun or pronoun, or they link a subject with an adjective. You always need a verb if you want a complete sentence. However, linking verbs are not able to complete a sentence.

Common linking verbs include *appear, be, become, feel, grow, look, seem, smell, sound,* and *taste*. However, any verb that shows a condition and has a noun, pronoun, or adjective that describes the subject of a sentence is a linking verb.

Action: He sings. | Run! | Go! | I talk with him every day. | She reads.

Linking:

Incorrect: I am.

Correct: I am John. | I smell roses. | I feel tired.

Note: Some verbs are followed by words that look like prepositions, but they are a part of the verb and a part of the verb's meaning. These are known as phrasal verbs and examples include *call off, look up,* and *drop off*.

VOICE

Transitive verbs come in active or passive voice. If the subject does an action or receives the action of the verb, then you will know whether a verb is active or passive. When the subject of the sentence is doing the action, the verb is **active voice**. When the subject receives the action, the verb is **passive voice**.

Active: Jon drew the picture. (The subject *Jon* is doing the action of *drawing a picture*.)

Passive: The picture is drawn by Jon. (The subject *picture* is receiving the action from Jon.)

VERB TENSES

A verb tense shows the different form of a verb to point to the time of an action. The present and past tense are shown by changing the verb's form. An action in the present *I talk* can change form for the past: *I talked*. However, for the other tenses, an auxiliary (i.e., helping) verb is needed to show the change in form. These helping verbs include *am, are, is | have, has, had | was, were, will* (or *shall*).

Present: I talk	Present perfect: I have talked
Past: I talked	Past perfect: I had talked
Future: I will talk	Future perfect: I will have talked

Present: The action happens at the current time.

Example: He *walks* to the store every morning.

To show that something is happening right now, use the progressive present tense: I *am walking*.

Past: The action happened in the past.

> Example: He *walked* to the store an hour ago.

Future: The action is going to happen later.

> Example: I *will walk* to the store tomorrow.

Present perfect: The action started in the past and continues into the present.

> Example: I *have walked* to the store three times today.

Past perfect: The second action happened in the past. The first action came before the second.

> Example: Before I walked to the store (Action 2), I *had walked* to the library (Action 1).

Future perfect: An action that uses the past and the future. In other words, the action is complete before a future moment.

> Example: When she comes for the supplies (future moment), I *will have walked* to the store (action completed in the past).

CONJUGATING VERBS

When you need to change the form of a verb, you are **conjugating** a verb. The key parts of a verb are first person singular, present tense (dream); first person singular, past tense (dreamed); and the past participle (dreamed). Note: the past participle needs a helping verb to make a verb tense. For example, I *have dreamed* of this day. | I *am dreaming* of this day.

Present Tense: Active Voice

	Singular	Plural
First Person	I dream	We dream
Second Person	You dream	You dream
Third Person	He, she, it dreams	They dream

MOOD

There are three moods in English: the indicative, the imperative, and the subjunctive.

The **indicative mood** is used for facts, opinions, and questions.

> Fact: You can do this.

> Opinion: I think that you can do this.

> Question: Do you know that you can do this?

The **imperative** is used for orders or requests.

> Order: You are going to do this!

> Request: Will you do this for me?

The **subjunctive mood** is for wishes and statements that go against fact.

> Wish: I wish that I were going to do this.

> Statement against fact: If I were you, I would do this. (This goes against fact because I am not you. You have the chance to do this, and I do not have the chance.)

The mood that causes trouble for most people is the subjunctive mood. If you have trouble with any of the moods, then be sure to practice.

ADJECTIVES

An adjective is a word that is used to modify a noun or pronoun. An adjective answers a question: *Which one? What kind of?* or *How many?* Usually, adjectives come before the words that they modify, but they may also come after a linking verb.

> Which one? The *third* suit is my favorite.

> What kind? This suit is *navy blue.*

> How many? Can I look over the *four* neckties for the suit?

ARTICLES

Articles are adjectives that are used to mark nouns. There are only three: the **definite** (i.e., limited or fixed amount) article *the*, and the **indefinite** (i.e., no limit or fixed amount) articles *a* and *an.* Note: *An* comes before words that start with a vowel sound (i.e., vowels include *a, e, i, o, u,* and *y*). For example, "Are you going to get an **u**mbrella?"

> **Definite**: I lost *the* bottle that belongs to me.

> **Indefinite**: Does anyone have *a* bottle to share?

COMPARISON WITH ADJECTIVES

Some adjectives are relative and other adjectives are absolute. Adjectives that are **relative** can show the comparison between things. Adjectives that are **absolute** can show comparison. However, they show comparison in a different way. Let's say that you are reading two books. You think that one book is perfect, and the other book is not exactly perfect. It is not possible for the book to be more perfect than the other. Either you think that the book is perfect, or you think that the book is not perfect.

The adjectives that are relative will show the different **degrees** of something or someone to something else or someone else. The three degrees of adjectives include positive, comparative, and superlative.

The **positive** degree is the normal form of an adjective.

> Example: This work is *difficult.* | She is *smart.*

The **comparative** degree compares one person or thing to another person or thing.

> Example: This work is *more difficult* than your work. | She is *smarter* than me.

The **superlative** degree compares more than two people or things.

Example: This is the *most difficult* work of my life. | She is the *smartest* lady in school.

ADVERBS

An adverb is a word that is used to **modify** a verb, adjective, or another adverb. Usually, adverbs answer one of these questions: *When?*, *Where?*, *How?*, and *Why?* . The negatives *not* and *never* are known as adverbs. Adverbs that modify adjectives or other adverbs **strengthen** or **weaken** the words that they modify.

Examples:

He walks quickly through the crowd.

The water flows smoothly on the rocks.

Note: While many adverbs end in *-ly*, you need to remember that not all adverbs end in *-ly*. Also, some words that end in *-ly* are adjectives, not adverbs. Some examples include: *early, friendly, holy, lonely, silly*, and *ugly*. To know if a word that ends in *-ly* is an adjective or adverb, you need to check your dictionary.

Examples:

He is *never* angry.

You talk *too* loudly.

COMPARISON WITH ADVERBS

The rules for comparing adverbs are the same as the rules for adjectives.

The **positive** degree is the standard form of an adverb.

Example: He arrives soon. | She speaks softly to her friends.

The **comparative** degree compares one person or thing to another person or thing.

Example: He arrives sooner than Sarah. | She speaks more softly than him.

The **superlative** degree compares more than two people or things.

Example: He arrives soonest of the group. | She speaks most softly of any of her friends.

PREPOSITIONS

A preposition is a word placed before a noun or pronoun that shows the relationship between an object and another word in the sentence.

Common prepositions:

about	before	during	on	under
after	beneath	for	over	until
against	between	from	past	up
among	beyond	in	through	with
around	by	of	to	within
at	down	off	toward	without

Examples:

The napkin is *in* the drawer.

The Earth rotates *around* the Sun.

The needle is *beneath* the haystack.

Can you find me *among* the words?

Review Video: What is a Preposition?
Visit mometrix.com/academy and enter code: 946763

CONJUNCTIONS

Conjunctions join words, phrases, or clauses, and they show the connection between the joined pieces. **Coordinating** conjunctions connect equal parts of sentences. **Correlative** conjunctions show the connection between pairs. **Subordinating** conjunctions join subordinate (i.e., dependent) clauses with independent clauses.

COORDINATING CONJUNCTIONS

The coordinating conjunctions include: *and, but, yet, or, nor, for,* and *so*

Examples:

The rock was small, but it was heavy.

She drove in the night, and he drove in the day.

CORRELATIVE CONJUNCTIONS

The correlative conjunctions are: *either...or | neither...nor | not only...but also*

Examples:

Either you are coming *or* you are staying.

He ran *not only* three miles *but also* swam 200 yards.

Review Video: Coordinating and Correlative Conjunctions
Visit mometrix.com/academy and enter code: 390329

SUBORDINATING CONJUNCTIONS

Common subordinating conjunctions include:

after	since	whenever
although	so that	where
because	unless	wherever
before	until	whether
in order that	when	while

Examples:

I am hungry *because* I did not eat breakfast.

He went home *when* everyone left.

> **Review Video: Subordinating Conjunctions**
> Visit mometrix.com/academy and enter code: 958913

INTERJECTIONS

An interjection is a word for **exclamation** (i.e., great amount of feeling) that is used alone or as a piece to a sentence. Often, they are used at the beginning of a sentence for an **introduction**. Sometimes, they can be used in the middle of a sentence to show a **change** in thought or attitude.

Common Interjections: Hey! | Oh, | Ouch! | Please! | Wow!

Agreement and Sentence Structure

SUBJECTS AND PREDICATES

SUBJECTS

Every sentence has two things: a subject and a verb. The **subject** of a sentence names who or what the sentence is all about. The subject may be directly stated in a sentence, or the subject may be the implied *you*.

The **complete subject** includes the simple subject and all of its modifiers. To find the complete subject, ask *Who* or *What* and insert the verb to complete the question. The answer is the complete subject. To find the **simple subject**, remove all of the modifiers (adjectives, prepositional phrases, etc.) in the complete subject. Being able to locate the subject of a sentence helps with many problems, such as those involving sentence fragments and subject-verb agreement.

Examples:

The small red car is the one that he wants for Christmas.

(The complete subject is *the small red car.*)

The young artist is coming over for dinner.

(The complete subject is *the young artist.*)

> **Review Video: Subjects**
> Visit mometrix.com/academy and enter code: 444771

In **imperative** sentences, the verb's subject is understood (e.g., [You] Run to the store), but not actually present in the sentence. Normally, the subject comes before the verb. However, the subject comes after the verb in sentences that begin with *There are* or *There was.*

Direct:

John knows the way to the park.

(Who knows the way to the park? Answer: John)

The cookies need ten more minutes.

(What needs ten minutes? Answer: The cookies)

By five o' clock, Bill will need to leave.

(Who needs to leave? Answer: Bill)

Remember: The subject can come after the verb.

There are five letters on the table for him.

(What is on the table? Answer: Five letters)

There were coffee and doughnuts in the house.

(What was in the house? Answer: Coffee and doughnuts)

Implied:

Go to the post office for me.

(Who is going to the post office? Answer: You are.)

Come and sit with me, please?

(Who needs to come and sit? Answer: You do.)

PREDICATES

In a sentence, you always have a predicate and a subject. The subject tells what the sentence is about, and the **predicate** explains or describes the subject.

Think about the sentence: *He sings*. In this sentence, we have a subject (He) and a predicate (sings). This is all that is needed for a sentence to be complete. Would we like more information? Of course, we would like to know more. However, if this all the information that you are given, you have a complete sentence.

Now, let's look at another sentence:

John and Jane sing on Tuesday nights at the dance hall.

What is the subject of this sentence?

Answer: John and Jane.

What is the predicate of this sentence?

Answer: Everything else in the sentence (sing on Tuesday nights at the dance hall).

SUBJECT-VERB AGREEMENT

Verbs **agree** with their subjects in number. In other words, *singular* subjects need *singular* verbs. *Plural* subjects need *plural* verbs. Singular is for one person, place, or thing. Plural is for more than one person, place, or thing. Subjects and verbs must also agree in person: first, second, or third. The present tense ending -*s* is used on a verb if its subject is third person singular; otherwise, the verb takes no ending.

> **Review Video: Subject Verb Agreement**
> Visit mometrix.com/academy and enter code: 479190

NUMBER AGREEMENT EXAMPLES:

Single Subject and Verb: *Dan calls home.*

(Dan is one person. So, the singular verb *calls* is needed.)

Plural Subject and Verb: *Dan and Bob call home.*

(More than one person needs the plural verb *call*.)

PERSON AGREEMENT EXAMPLES:

First Person: I *am* walking.

Second Person: You *are* walking.

Third Person: He *is* walking.

COMPLICATIONS WITH SUBJECT-VERB AGREEMENT

WORDS BETWEEN SUBJECT AND VERB

Words that come between the simple subject and the verb may serve as an effective distraction, but they have no bearing on subject-verb agreement.

Examples:

The joy of my life returns home tonight.

(**Singular Subject**: joy. **Singular Verb**: returns)

The phrase *of my life* does not influence the verb *returns*.

The question that still remains unanswered is "Who are you?"

(**Singular Subject**: question. **Singular Verb**: is)

Don't let the phrase "*that still remains…*" trouble you. The subject *question* goes with *is*.

COMPOUND SUBJECTS

A compound subject is formed when two or more nouns joined by *and*, *or*, or *nor* jointly act as the subject of the sentence.

JOINED BY AND

When a compound subject is joined by *and*, it is treated as a plural subject and requires a plural verb.

Examples:

You and Jon are invited to come to my house.

(**Plural Subject**: You and Jon. **Plural Verb**: are)

The pencil and paper belong to me.

(**Plural Subject**: pencil and paper. **Plural Verb**: belong)

JOINED BY OR/NOR

For a compound subject joined by *or* or *nor*, the verb must agree in number with the part of the subject that is closest to the verb (italicized in the examples below).

Examples:

Today or *tomorrow is* the day.

(**Subject**: Today / tomorrow. **Verb**: is)

Stan or *Phil wants* to read the book.

(**Subject**: Stan / Phil. **Verb**: wants)

Neither the books nor the *pen is* on the desk.

(**Subject**: Books / Pen. **Verb**: is)

Either the blanket or *pillows arrive* this afternoon.

(**Subject**: Blanket / Pillows. **Verb**: arrive)

INDEFINITE PRONOUNS AS SUBJECT

An indefinite pronoun is a pronoun that does not refer to a specific noun. Indefinite pronouns may be only singular, be only plural, or change depending on how they are used.

ALWAYS SINGULAR

Pronouns such as *each*, *either*, *everybody*, *anybody*, *somebody*, and *nobody* are always singular.

Examples:

Each of the runners *has* a different bib number.

(**Singular Subject**: Each. **Singular Verb**: has)

Is either of you ready for the game?

(**Singular Subject**: Either. **Singular Verb**: is)

Note: The words *each* and *either* can also be used as adjectives (e.g., *each* person is unique). When one of these adjectives modifies the subject of a sentence, it is always a singular subject.

Everybody grows a day older every day.

(**Singular Subject**: Everybody. **Singular Verb**: grows)

Anybody is welcome to bring a tent.

(**Singular Subject**: Anybody. **Singular Verb**: is)

ALWAYS PLURAL

Pronouns such as *both*, *several*, and *many* are always plural.

Examples:

Both of the siblings *were* too tired to argue.

(**Plural Subject**: Both. **Plural Verb**: were)

Many have tried, but none have succeeded.

(**Plural Subject**: Many. **Plural Verb**: have tried)

DEPEND ON CONTEXT

Pronouns such as *some, any, all, none, more,* and *most* can be either singular or plural depending on what they are representing in the context of the sentence.

Examples:

> *All* of my dog's food *was* still there in his bowl
>
> (**Singular Subject**: All. **Singular Verb**: was)
>
> By the end of the night, *all* of my guests *were* already excited about coming to my next party.
>
> (**Plural Subject**: All. **Plural Verb**: were)

OTHER CASES INVOLVING PLURAL OR IRREGULAR FORM

Some nouns are **singular in meaning but plural in form**: news, mathematics, physics, and economics.

> The *news is* coming on now.
>
> *Mathematics is* my favorite class.

Some nouns are plural in form and meaning, and have **no singular equivalent**: scissors and pants.

> Do these *pants come* with a shirt?
>
> The *scissors are* for my project.

Mathematical operations are **irregular** in their construction, but are normally considered to be **singular in meaning**.

> *One plus one is* two.
>
> *Three times three is* nine.

Note: Look to your **dictionary** for help when you aren't sure whether a noun with a plural form has a singular or plural meaning.

COMPLEMENTS

A complement is a noun, pronoun, or adjective that is used to give more information about the subject or verb in the sentence.

DIRECT OBJECTS

A direct object is a noun or pronoun that takes or receives the **action** of a verb. (Remember: a complete sentence does not need a direct object, so not all sentences will have them. A sentence needs only a subject and a verb.) When you are looking for a direct object, find the verb and ask *who* or *what*.

Examples:

I took the blanket. (Who or what did I take? *The blanket*)

Jane read books. (Who or what does Jane read? *Books*)

INDIRECT OBJECTS

An indirect object is a word or group of words that show how an action had an **influence** on someone or something. If there is an indirect object in a sentence, then you always have a direct object in the sentence. When you are looking for the indirect object, find the verb and ask *to/for whom or what.*

Examples:

We taught the old dog a new trick.

(To/For Whom or What was taught? *The old dog*)

I gave them a math lesson.

(To/For Whom or What was given? *Them*)

PREDICATE NOMINATIVES AND PREDICATE ADJECTIVES

As we looked at previously, verbs may be classified as either action verbs or linking verbs. A linking verb is so named because it links the subject to words in the predicate that describe or define the subject. These words are called predicate nominatives (if nouns or pronouns) or predicate adjectives (if adjectives).

Examples:

My father is a *lawyer.*

(Father is the **subject**. Lawyer is the **predicate nominative**.)

Your mother is *patient.*

(Mother is the **subject**. Patient is the **predicate adjective**.)

PRONOUN USAGE

The **antecedent** is the noun that has been replaced by a pronoun. A pronoun and its antecedent **agree** when they have the same number (singular or plural) and gender (male, female, or neuter).

Examples:

Singular agreement: *John* came into town, and *he* played for us.

(The word *he* replaces *John*.)

Plural agreement: *John and Rick* came into town, and *they* played for us.

(The word *they* replaces *John and Rick*.)

To determine which is the correct pronoun to use in a compound subject or object, try each pronoun **alone** in place of the compound in the sentence. Your knowledge of pronouns will tell you which one is correct.

Example:

Bob and (I, me) will be going.

Test: (1) *I will be going* or (2) *Me will be going*. The second choice cannot be correct because *me* cannot be used as the subject of a sentence. Instead, *me* is used as an object.

Answer: Bob and I will be going.

When a pronoun is used with a noun immediately following (as in "we boys"), try the sentence **without the added noun**.

Example:

(We/Us) boys played football last year.

Test: (1) *We played football last year* or (2) *Us played football last year*. Again, the second choice cannot be correct because *us* cannot be used as a subject of a sentence. Instead, *us* is used as an object.

Answer: We boys played football last year.

> **Review Video: Pronoun Usage**
> Visit mometrix.com/academy and enter code: 666500

A pronoun should point clearly to the **antecedent**. Here is how a pronoun reference can be unhelpful if it is not directly stated or puzzling.

Unhelpful: Ron and Jim went to the store, and *he* bought soda.

(Who bought soda? Ron or Jim?)

Helpful: Jim went to the store, and *he* bought soda.

(The sentence is clear. Jim bought the soda.)

Some pronouns change their form by their placement in a sentence. A pronoun that is a subject in a sentence comes in the **subjective case**. Pronouns that serve as objects appear in the **objective case**. Finally, the pronouns that are used as possessives appear in the **possessive case**.

Examples:

Subjective case: *He* is coming to the show.

(The pronoun *He* is the subject of the sentence.)

Objective case: Josh drove *him* to the airport.

(The pronoun *him* is the object of the sentence.)

Possessive case: The flowers are *mine*.

(The pronoun *mine* shows ownership of the flowers.)

The word *who* is a subjective-case pronoun that can be used as a **subject**. The word *whom* is an objective-case pronoun that can be used as an **object**. The words *who* and *whom* are common in subordinate clauses or in questions.

Examples:

Subject: He knows who wants to come.

(*Who* is the subject of the verb *wants*.)

Object: He knows the man whom we want at the party.

(*Whom* is the object of *we want*.)

CLAUSES

A clause is a group of words that contains both a subject and a predicate (verb). There are two types of clauses: independent and dependent. An **independent clause** contains a complete thought, while a **dependent (or subordinate) clause** does not. A dependent clause includes a subject and a verb, and may also contain objects or complements, but it cannot stand as a complete thought without being joined to an independent clause. Dependent clauses function within sentences as adjectives, adverbs, or nouns.

Example:

Independent Clause: I am running

Dependent Clause: because I want to stay in shape

The clause *I am running* is an independent clause: it has a subject and a verb, and it gives a complete thought. The clause *because I want to stay in shape* is a dependent clause: it has a subject and a verb, but it does not express a complete thought. It adds detail to the independent clause to which it is attached.

Combined: I am running because I want to stay in shape.

> **Review Video: Clauses**
> Visit mometrix.com/academy and enter code: 940170

TYPES OF DEPENDENT CLAUSES

ADJECTIVE CLAUSES

An **adjective clause** is a dependent clause that modifies a noun or a pronoun. Adjective clauses begin with a relative pronoun (*who, whose, whom, which,* and *that*) or a relative adverb (*where, when,* and *why*).

Also, adjective clauses come after the noun that the clause needs to explain or rename. This is done to have a clear connection to the independent clause.

Examples:

> I learned the reason *why I won the award*.

> This is the place *where I started my first job*.

An adjective clause can be an essential or nonessential clause. An essential clause is very important to the sentence. **Essential clauses** explain or define a person or thing. **Nonessential clauses** give more information about a person or thing but are not necessary to define them. Nonessential clauses are set off with commas while essential clauses are not.

Examples:

> **Essential**: A person *who works hard at first* can often rest later in life.

> **Nonessential**: Neil Armstrong, *who walked on the moon*, is my hero.

ADVERB CLAUSES

An **adverb clause** is a dependent clause that modifies a verb, adjective, or adverb. In sentences with multiple dependent clauses, adverb clauses are usually placed immediately before or after the independent clause. An adverb clause is introduced with words such as *after, although, as, before, because, if, since, so, unless, when, where*, and *while*.

Examples:

> *When you walked outside*, I called the manager.

> I will go with you *unless you want to stay*.

NOUN CLAUSES

A **noun clause** is a dependent clause that can be used as a subject, object, or complement. Noun clauses begin with words such as *how, that, what, whether, which, who*, and *why*. These words can also come with an adjective clause. Unless the noun clause is being used as the subject of the sentence, it should come after the verb of the independent clause.

Examples:

> The real mystery is *how you avoided serious injury*.

> *What you learn from each other* depends on your honesty with others.

SUBORDINATION

When two related ideas are not of equal importance, the ideal way to combine them is to make the more important idea an independent clause, and the less important idea a dependent or subordinate clause. This is called **subordination**.

Example:

> **Separate ideas**: The team had a perfect regular season. The team lost the championship.

> **Subordinated**: Despite having a perfect regular season, *the team lost the championship*.

PHRASES

A phrase is a group of words that functions as a single part of speech, usually a noun, adjective, or adverb. A phrase is not a complete thought, but it adds **detail** or **explanation** to a sentence, or **renames** something within the sentence.

PREPOSITIONAL PHRASES

One of the most common types of phrases is the prepositional phrase. A **prepositional phrase** begins with a preposition and ends with a noun or pronoun that is the object of the preposition. Normally, the prepositional phrase functions as an **adjective** or an **adverb** within the sentence.

Examples:

The picnic is *on the blanket*.

I am sick *with a fever* today.

Among the many flowers, John found a four-leaf clover.

VERBAL PHRASES

A verbal is a word or phrase that is formed from a verb but does not function as a verb. Depending on its particular form, it may be used as a noun, adjective, or adverb. A verbal does **not** replace a verb in a sentence.

Examples:

Correct: *Walk* a mile daily.

(*Walk* is the verb of this sentence. The subject is the implied *you*.)

Incorrect: *To walk* a mile.

(*To walk* is a type of verbal. This is not a sentence since there is no functional verb)

There are three types of verbals: **participles**, **gerunds**, and **infinitives**. Each type of verbal has a corresponding **phrase** that consists of the verbal itself along with any complements or modifiers.

PARTICIPLES

A **participle** is a type of verbal that always functions as an adjective. The present participle always ends with *-ing*. Past participles end with *-d, -ed, -n,* or *-t.*

Examples: Verb: *dance* | Present Participle: *dancing* | Past Participle: *danced*

Participial phrases most often come right before or right after the noun or pronoun that they modify.

Examples:

Shipwrecked on an island, the boys started to fish for food.

Having been seated for five hours, we got out of the car to stretch our legs.

Praised for their work, the group accepted the first-place trophy.

GERUNDS

A **gerund** is a type of verbal that always functions as a noun. Like present participles, gerunds always end with *-ing*, but they can be easily distinguished from one another by the part of speech they represent (participles always function as adjectives). Since a gerund or gerund phrase always functions as a noun, it can be used as the subject of a sentence, the predicate nominative, or the object of a verb or preposition.

Examples:

We want to be known for *teaching the poor*. (Object of preposition)

Coaching this team is the best job of my life. (Subject)

We like *practicing our songs* in the basement. (Object of verb)

INFINITIVES

An **infinitive** is a type of verbal that can function as a noun, an adjective, or an adverb. An infinitive is made of the word *to* + the basic form of the verb. As with all other types of verbal phrases, an infinitive phrase includes the verbal itself and all of its complements or modifiers.

Examples:

To join the team is my goal in life. (Noun)

The animals have enough food *to eat for the night*. (Adjective)

People lift weights *to exercise their muscles*. (Adverb)

APPOSITIVE PHRASES

An **appositive** is a word or phrase that is used to explain or rename nouns or pronouns. Noun phrases, gerund phrases, and infinitive phrases can all be used as appositives.

Examples:

Terriers, *hunters at heart*, have been dressed up to look like lap dogs.

(The noun phrase *hunters at heart* renames the noun *terriers*.)

His plan, *to save and invest his money*, was proven as a safe approach.

(The infinitive phrase explains what the plan is.)

Appositive phrases can be **essential** or **nonessential**. An appositive phrase is essential if the person, place, or thing being described or renamed is too general for its meaning to be understood without the appositive.

Examples:

Essential: Two Founding Fathers George Washington and Thomas Jefferson served as presidents.

Nonessential: George Washington and Thomas Jefferson, two Founding Fathers, served as presidents.

ABSOLUTE PHRASES

An absolute phrase is a phrase that consists of **a noun followed by a participle**. An absolute phrase provides **context** to what is being described in the sentence, but it does not modify or explain any particular word; it is essentially independent.

Examples:

The alarm ringing, he pushed the snooze button.

The music paused, she continued to dance through the crowd.

Note: Absolute phrases can be confusing, so don't be discouraged if you have a difficult time with them.

PARALLELISM

When multiple items or ideas are presented in a sentence in series, such as in a list, the items or ideas must be stated in grammatically equivalent ways. In other words, if one idea is stated in gerund form, the second cannot be stated in infinitive form. For example, to write, *I enjoy reading and to study* would be incorrect. An infinitive and a gerund are not equivalent. Instead, you should write *I enjoy reading and studying*. In lists of more than two, it can be harder to keep straight, but all items in a list must be parallel.

Example:

Incorrect: He stopped at the office, grocery store, and the pharmacy before heading home.

The first and third items in the list of places include the article *the*, so the second item needs it as well.

Correct: He stopped at the office, *the* grocery store, and the pharmacy before heading home.

Example:

Incorrect: While vacationing in Europe, she went biking, skiing, and climbed mountains.

The first and second items in the list are gerunds, so the third item must be as well.

Correct: While vacationing in Europe, she went biking, skiing, and *mountain climbing*.

SENTENCE PURPOSE

There are four types of sentences: declarative, imperative, interrogative, and exclamatory.

A **declarative** sentence states a fact and ends with a period.

Example: *The football game starts at seven o'clock.*

An **imperative** sentence tells someone to do something and generally ends with a period. (An urgent command might end with an exclamation point instead.)

Example: *Don't forget to buy your ticket.*

An **interrogative** sentence asks a question and ends with a question mark.

Example: *Are you going to the game on Friday?*

111

An **exclamatory** sentence shows strong emotion and ends with an exclamation point.

Example: *I can't believe we won the game!*

SENTENCE STRUCTURE

Sentences are classified by structure based on the type and number of clauses present. The four classifications of sentence structure are the following:

Simple: A simple sentence has one independent clause with no dependent clauses. A simple sentence may have **compound elements** (i.e., compound subject or verb).

Examples:

<u>Judy</u> *watered* the lawn. (single <u>subject</u>, single *verb*)

<u>Judy and Alan</u> *watered* the lawn. (compound <u>subject</u>, single *verb*)

<u>Judy</u> *watered* the lawn and *pulled* weeds. (single <u>subject</u>, compound *verb*)

<u>Judy and Alan</u> *watered* the lawn and *pulled* weeds. (compound <u>subject</u>, compound *verb*)

Compound: A compound sentence has two or more <u>independent clauses</u> with no dependent clauses. Usually, the independent clauses are joined with a comma and a coordinating conjunction or with a semicolon.

Examples:

<u>The time has come</u>, and <u>we are ready</u>.

<u>I woke up at dawn</u>; <u>the sun was just coming up</u>.

Complex: A complex sentence has one <u>independent clause</u> and at least one *dependent clause*.

Examples:

Although he had the flu, <u>Harry went to work</u>.

<u>Marcia got married</u> *after she finished college*.

Compound-Complex: A compound-complex sentence has at least two <u>independent clauses</u> and at least one *dependent clause*.

Examples:

<u>John is my friend</u> *who went to India*, and <u>he brought back souvenirs</u>.

<u>You may not realize this</u>, but <u>we heard the music</u> *that you played last night*.

> **Review Video: <u>Sentence Structure</u>**
> Visit mometrix.com/academy and enter code: 700478

SENTENCE FRAGMENTS

Usually when the term *sentence fragment* comes up, it is because you have to decide whether or not a group of words is a complete sentence, and if it's not a complete sentence, you're about to have to fix it. Recall that a group of words must contain at least one **independent clause** in order to be considered a sentence. If it doesn't contain even one independent clause, it would be called a **sentence fragment**. (If it contains two or more independent clauses that are not joined correctly, it would be called a run-on sentence.)

The process to use for **repairing** a sentence fragment depends on what type of fragment it is. If the fragment is a dependent clause, it can sometimes be as simple as removing a subordinating word (e.g., when, because, if) from the beginning of the fragment. Alternatively, a dependent clause can be incorporated into a closely related neighboring sentence. If the fragment is missing some required part, like a subject or a verb, the fix might be as simple as adding it in.

Examples:

> **Fragment**: Because he wanted to sail the Mediterranean.

> **Removed subordinating word**: He wanted to sail the Mediterranean.

> **Combined with another sentence**: Because he wanted to sail the Mediterranean, he booked a Greek island cruise.

RUN-ON SENTENCES

Run-on sentences consist of multiple independent clauses that have not been joined together properly. Run-on sentences can be corrected in several different ways:

Join clauses properly: This can be done with a comma and coordinating conjunction, with a semicolon, or with a colon or dash if the second clause is explaining something in the first.

Example:

> **Incorrect**: I went on the trip, we visited lots of castles.

> **Corrected**: I went on the trip, and we visited lots of castles.

Split into separate sentences: This correction is most effective when the independent clauses are very long or when they are not closely related.

Example:

> **Incorrect**: The drive to New York takes ten hours, my uncle lives in Boston.

> **Corrected**: The drive to New York takes ten hours. My uncle lives in Boston.

Make one clause dependent: This is the easiest way to make the sentence correct and more interesting at the same time. It's often as simple as adding a subordinating word between the two clauses

Example:

> **Incorrect**: I finally made it to the store and I bought some eggs.

> **Corrected**: When I finally made it to the store, I bought some eggs.

Reduce to one clause with a compound verb: If both clauses have the same subject, remove the subject from the second clause, and you now have just one clause with a compound verb.

Example:

Incorrect: The drive to New York takes ten hours, it makes me very tired.

Corrected: The drive to New York takes ten hours and makes me very tired.

Note: While these are the simplest ways to correct a run-on sentence, often the best way is to completely reorganize the thoughts in the sentence and rewrite it.

> **Review Video: Fragments and Run-on Sentences**
> Visit mometrix.com/academy and enter code: 541989

DANGLING AND MISPLACED MODIFIERS

DANGLING MODIFIERS

A dangling modifier is a dependent clause or verbal phrase that does not have a **clear logical connection** to a word in the sentence.

Example:

Dangling: *Reading each magazine article*, the stories caught my attention.

The word *stories* cannot be modified by *Reading each magazine article*. People can read, but stories cannot read. Therefore, the subject of the sentence must be a person.

Corrected: Reading each magazine article, *I* was entertained by the stories.

Example:

Dangling: Ever since childhood, my grandparents have visited me for Christmas.

The speaker in this sentence can't have been visited by her grandparents when *they* were children, since she wouldn't have been born yet. Either the modifier should be **clarified** or the sentence should be **rearranged** to specify whose childhood is being referenced.

Clarified: Ever since I was a child, my grandparents have visited for Christmas.

Rearranged: Ever since childhood, I have enjoyed my grandparents visiting for Christmas.

MISPLACED MODIFIERS

Because modifiers are grammatically versatile, they can be put in many different places within the structure of a sentence. The danger of this versatility is that a modifier can accidentally be placed where it is modifying the wrong word or where it is not clear which word it is modifying.

Example:

Misplaced: She read the book to a crowd *that was filled with beautiful pictures*.

The book was filled with beautiful pictures, not the crowd.

Corrected: She read the book *that was filled with beautiful pictures* to a crowd.

Example:

> **Ambiguous**: Derek saw a bus nearly hit a man *on his way to work.*
>
> Was Derek on his way to work? Or was the other man?
>
> **Derek**: *On his way to work*, Derek saw a bus nearly hit a man.
>
> **The other man**: Derek saw a bus nearly hit a man *who was on his way to work.*

SPLIT INFINITIVES

A split infinitive occurs when a modifying word comes between the word *to* and the verb that pairs with *to*.

> Example: To *clearly* explain vs. *To explain* clearly | To *softly* sing vs. *To sing* softly

Though considered improper by some, split infinitives may provide better clarity and simplicity in some cases than the alternatives. As such, avoiding them should not be considered a universal rule.

DOUBLE NEGATIVES

Standard English allows **two negatives** only when a **positive** meaning is intended. For example, *The team was not displeased with their performance.* Double negatives to emphasize negation are not used in standard English.

Negative modifiers (e.g., never, no, and not) should not be paired with other negative modifiers or negative words (e.g., none, nobody, nothing, or neither). The modifiers *hardly, barely*, and *scarcely* are considered negatives in standard English, so they should not be used with other negatives.

Punctuation

END PUNCTUATION

PERIODS

Use a period to end all sentences except direct questions, exclamations.

DECLARATIVE SENTENCE

A declarative sentence gives information or makes a statement.

>   Examples: I can fly a kite. | The plane left two hours ago.

IMPERATIVE SENTENCE

An imperative sentence gives an order or command.

>   Examples: You are coming with me. | Bring me that note.

PERIODS FOR ABBREVIATIONS

>   Examples: 3 P.M. | 2 A.M. | Mr. Jones | Mrs. Stevens | Dr. Smith | Bill Jr. | Pennsylvania Ave.

Note: an abbreviation is a shortened form of a word or phrase.

QUESTION MARKS

Question marks should be used following a direct question. A polite request can be followed by a period instead of a question mark.

>   **Direct Question**: What is for lunch today? | How are you? | Why is that the answer?

>   **Polite Requests**: Can you please send me the item tomorrow. | Will you please walk with me on the track.

EXCLAMATION MARKS

Exclamation marks are used after a word group or sentence that shows much feeling or has special importance. Exclamation marks should not be overused. They are saved for proper **exclamatory interjections**.

>   Example: We're going to the finals! | You have a beautiful car! | That's crazy!

COMMAS

The comma is a punctuation mark that can help you understand connections in a sentence. Not every sentence needs a comma. However, if a sentence needs a comma, you need to put it in the right place. A comma in the wrong place (or an absent comma) will make a sentence's meaning unclear. These are some of the rules for commas:

1. Use a comma **before a coordinating conjunction** joining independent clauses
    Example: Bob caught three fish, and I caught two fish.

2. Use a comma after an introductory phrase or an adverbial clause

    Examples:

    > *After the final out,* we went to a restaurant to celebrate.
    > *Studying the stars,* I was surprised at the beauty of the sky.

3. Use a comma between items in a series.

    Example: I will bring the turkey, the pie, and the coffee.

4. Use a comma **between coordinate adjectives** not joined with *and*

    Incorrect: The kind, brown dog followed me home.
    Correct: The *kind, loyal* dog followed me home.
    Not all adjectives are **coordinate** (i.e., equal or parallel). There are two simple ways to know if your adjectives are coordinate. One, you can join the adjectives with *and*: *The kind and loyal dog.* Two, you can change the order of the adjectives: *The loyal, kind dog.*

5. Use commas for **interjections** and **after *yes* and *no*** responses

    Examples:

    > **Interjection**: Oh, I had no idea. | Wow, you know how to play this game.
    > **Yes and No**: *Yes,* I heard you. | *No,* I cannot come tomorrow.

6. Use commas to separate nonessential modifiers and nonessential appositives

    Examples:

    > **Nonessential Modifier**: John Frank, who is coaching the team, was promoted today.
    > **Nonessential Appositive**: Thomas Edison, an American inventor, was born in Ohio.

7. Use commas to set off nouns of direct address, interrogative tags, and contrast

    Examples:

    > **Direct Address**: You, *John,* are my only hope in this moment.
    > **Interrogative Tag**: This is the last time, *correct*?
    > **Contrast**: You are my friend, *not my enemy.*

8. Use commas with dates, addresses, geographical names, and titles

    Examples:

    > **Date**: *July 4, 1776,* is an important date to remember.
    > **Address**: He is meeting me at *456 Delaware Avenue, Washington, D.C.,* tomorrow morning.
    > **Geographical Name**: *Paris, France,* is my favorite city.
    > **Title**: John Smith, *Ph. D.,* will be visiting your class today.

9. Use commas to **separate expressions like *he said* and *she said*** if they come between a sentence of a quote

    Examples:

    > "I want you to know," he began, "that I always wanted the best for you."
    > "You can start," Jane said, "with an apology."

> **Review Video: Commas**
> Visit mometrix.com/academy and enter code: 786797

SEMICOLONS

The semicolon is used to connect major sentence pieces of equal value. Some rules for semicolons include:

1. Use a semicolon **between closely connected independent clauses** that are not connected with a coordinating conjunction.

   Examples:

   > She is outside; we are inside.
   > You are right; we should go with your plan.

2. Use a semicolon **between independent clauses linked with a transitional word.**

   Examples:

   > I think that we can agree on this; *however,* I am not sure about my friends.
   > You are looking in the wrong places; *therefore,* you will not find what you need.

3. Use a semicolon **between items in a series that has internal punctuation.**

   Example: I have visited New York, New York; Augusta, Maine; and Baltimore, Maryland.

> **Review Video: Semicolon Usage**
> Visit mometrix.com/academy and enter code: 370605

COLONS

The colon is used to call attention to the words that follow it. A colon must come after a **complete independent clause**. The rules for colons are as follows:

1. Use a colon after an independent clause to **make a list**

   Example: I want to learn many languages: Spanish, German, and Italian.

2. Use a colon for **explanations** or to **give a quote**

   Examples:

   > **Quote**: He started with an idea: "We are able to do more than we imagine."
   > **Explanation**: There is one thing that stands out on your resume: responsibility.

3. Use a colon **after the greeting in a formal letter**, to **show hours and minutes**, and to **separate a title and subtitle**

   Examples:

   > **Greeting in a formal letter**: Dear Sir: | To Whom It May Concern:
   > **Time**: It is 3:14 P.M.
   > **Title**: The essay is titled "America: A Short Introduction to a Modern Country"

PARENTHESES

Parentheses are used for additional information. Also, they can be used to put labels for letters or numbers in a series. Parentheses should be not be used very often. If they are overused, parentheses can be a distraction instead of a help.

Examples:

> **Extra Information**: The rattlesnake (see Image 2) is a dangerous snake of North and South America.

> **Series**: Include in the email (1) your name, (2) your address, and (3) your question for the author.

QUOTATION MARKS

Use quotation marks to close off **direct quotations** of a person's spoken or written words. Do not use quotation marks around indirect quotations. An indirect quotation gives someone's message without using the person's exact words. Use **single quotation marks** to close off a quotation inside a quotation.

> **Direct Quote**: Nancy said, "I am waiting for Henry to arrive."

> **Indirect Quote**: Henry said that he is going to be late to the meeting.

> **Quote inside a Quote**: The teacher asked, "Has everyone read 'The Gift of the Magi'?"

Quotation marks should be used around the titles of **short works**: newspaper and magazine articles, poems, short stories, songs, television episodes, radio programs, and subdivisions of books or web sites.

Examples:

> "Rip van Winkle" (short story by Washington Irving)

> "O Captain! My Captain!" (poem by Walt Whitman)

Although it is not standard usage, quotation marks are sometimes used to highlight **irony**, or the use of words to mean something other than their dictionary definition. This type of usage should be employed sparingly, if at all.

Examples:

> The boss warned Frank that he was walking on "thin ice."

> (Frank is not walking on real ice. Instead, Frank is being warned to avoid mistakes.)

> The teacher thanked the young man for his "honesty."

> (In this example, the quotation marks around *honesty* show that the teacher does not believe the young man's explanation.)

> **Review Video: Quotation Marks**
> Visit mometrix.com/academy and enter code: 884918

Periods and commas are put **inside** quotation marks. Colons and semicolons are put **outside** the quotation marks. Question marks and exclamation points are placed inside quotation marks when they are part of a quote. When the question or exclamation mark goes with the whole sentence, the mark is left outside of the quotation marks.

Examples:

Period and comma: We read "The Gift of the Magi," "The Skylight Room," and "The Cactus."

Semicolon: They watched "The Nutcracker"; then, they went home.

Exclamation mark that is a part of a quote: The crowd cheered, "Victory!"

Question mark that goes with the whole sentence: Is your favorite short story "The Tell-Tale Heart"?

APOSTROPHES

An apostrophe is used to show **possession** or the **deletion of letters in contractions**. An apostrophe is not needed with the possessive pronouns *his, hers, its, ours, theirs, whose,* and *yours.*

Singular Nouns: David's car | a book's theme | my brother's board game

Plural Nouns with -*s*: the scissors' handle | boys' basketball

Plural Nouns without -*s*: Men's department | the people's adventure

HYPHENS

Hyphens are used to **separate compound words**. Use hyphens in the following cases:

1. **Compound numbers** between 21 and 99 when written out in words
   Example: This team needs *twenty-five* points to win the game.

2. **Written-out fractions** that are used as **adjectives**
   Correct: The recipe says that we need a *three-fourths* cup of butter.
   Incorrect: *One-fourth* of the road is under construction.

3. Compound words used as **adjectives that come before a noun**
   Correct: The *well-fed* dog took a nap.
   Incorrect: The dog was *well-fed* for his nap.

4. Compound words that would be **hard to read** or **easily confused with other words**
   Examples: Semi-irresponsible | Anti-itch | Re-sort

Note: This is not a complete set of the rules for hyphens. A dictionary is the best tool for knowing if a compound word needs a hyphen.

Dashes

Dashes are used to show a **break** or a **change in thought** in a sentence or to act as parentheses in a sentence. When typing, use two hyphens to make a dash. Do not put a space before or after the dash. The following are the rules for dashes:

1. To set off **parenthetical statements** or an **appositive with internal punctuation**

   Example: The three trees—oak, pine, and magnolia—are coming on a truck tomorrow.

2. To show a **break or change in tone or thought**

   Example: The first question—how silly of me—does not have a correct answer.

Ellipsis Marks

The ellipsis mark has three periods (…) to show when **words have been removed** from a quotation. If a full sentence or more is removed from a quoted passage, you need to use four periods to show the removed text and the end punctuation mark. The ellipsis mark should not be used at the beginning of a quotation. The ellipsis mark should also not be used at the end of a quotation unless some words have been deleted from the end of the final sentence.

Example:

"Then he picked up the groceries…paid for them…later he went home."

Brackets

There are two main reasons to use brackets:

1. When **placing parentheses inside of parentheses**

   Example: The hero of this story, Paul Revere (a silversmith and industrialist [see Ch. 4]), rode through towns of Massachusetts to warn of advancing British troops.

2. When adding **clarification or detail** to a quotation that is **not part of the quotation**
   Example:

   The father explained, "My children are planning to attend my alma mater [State University]."

Common Errors

WORD CONFUSION

WHICH, THAT, AND WHO

Which is used for things only.

> Example: John's dog, *which was called Max,* is large and fierce.

That is used for people or things.

> Example: Is this the only book *that Louis L'Amour wrote?*

> Example: Is Louis L'Amour the author *that wrote Western novels?*

Who is used for people only.

> Example: Mozart was the composer *who wrote those operas.*

HOMOPHONES

Homophones are words that sound alike (or similar), but they have different **spellings** and **definitions**.

TO, TOO, AND TWO

To can be an adverb or a preposition for showing direction, purpose, and relationship. See your dictionary for the many other ways use *to* in a sentence.

> Examples: I went to the store. | I want to go with you.

Too is an adverb that means *also, as well, very, or more than enough.*

> Examples: I can walk a mile too. | You have eaten too much.

Two is the second number in the series of numbers (e.g., one (1), two, (2), three (3)...)

> Example: You have two minutes left.

THERE, THEIR, AND THEY'RE

There can be an adjective, adverb, or pronoun. Often, *there* is used to show a place or to start a sentence.

> Examples: I went there yesterday. | There is something in his pocket.

Their is a pronoun that is used to show ownership.

> Examples: He is their father. | This is their fourth apology this week.

They're is a contraction of *they are.*

> Example: Did you know that they're in town?

KNEW AND NEW

Knew is the past tense of *know*.

>Example: I knew the answer.

New is an adjective that means something is current, has not been used, or modern.

>Example: This is my new phone.

THEN AND THAN

Then is an adverb that indicates sequence or order:

>Example: I'm going to run to the library and then come home.

Than is special-purpose word used only for comparisons:

>Example: Susie likes chips better than candy.

ITS AND IT'S

Its is a pronoun that shows ownership.

>Example: The guitar is in its case.

It's is a contraction of *it is*.

>Example: It's an honor and a privilege to meet you.

Note: The *h* in honor is silent, so the sound of the vowel *o* must have the article *an*.

YOUR AND YOU'RE

Your is a pronoun that shows ownership.

>Example: This is your moment to shine.

You're is a contraction of *you are*.

>Example: Yes, you're correct.

AFFECT AND EFFECT

There are two main reasons that **affect** and **effect** are so often confused: 1) both words can be used as either a noun or a verb, and 2) unlike most homophones, their usage and meanings arc closely related to each other. Here is a quick rundown of the four usage options:

Affect (n): feeling, emotion, or mood that is displayed

>Example: The patient had a flat *affect*. (i.e., his face showed little or no emotion)

Affect (v): to alter, to change, to influence

>Example: The sunshine *affects* the plant's growth.

Effect (n): a result, a consequence

>Example: What *effect* will this weather have on our schedule?

Effect (v): to bring about, to cause to be

> Example: These new rules will *effect* order in the office.

The noun form of *affect* is rarely used outside of technical medical descriptions, so if a noun form is needed on the test, you can safely select *effect*. The verb form of *effect* is not as rare as the noun form of *affect*, but it's still not all that likely to show up on your test. If you need a verb and you can't decide which to use based on the definitions, choosing *affect* is your best bet.

HOMOGRAPHS

Homographs are words that share the same spelling, and they have multiple meanings. To figure out which meaning is being used, you should be looking for context clues. The context clues give hints to the meaning of the word. For example, the word *spot* has many meanings. It can mean "a place" or "a stain or blot." In the sentence "After my lunch, I saw a spot on my shirt," the word *spot* means "a stain or blot." The context clues of "After my lunch..." and "on my shirt" guide you to this decision.

BANK

> (noun): an establishment where money is held for savings or lending

> (verb): to collect or pile up

CONTENT

> (noun): the topics that will be addressed within a book

> (adjective): pleased or satisfied

FINE

> (noun): an amount of money that acts a penalty for an offense

> (adjective): very small or thin

INCENSE

> (noun): a material that is burned in religious settings and makes a pleasant aroma

> (verb): to frustrate or anger

LEAD

> (noun): the first or highest position

> (verb): to direct a person or group of followers

OBJECT

> (noun): a lifeless item that can be held and observed

> (verb): to disagree

PRODUCE

> (noun): fruits and vegetables

> (verb): to make or create something

REFUSE

(noun): garbage or debris that has been thrown away

(verb): to not allow

SUBJECT

(noun): an area of study

(verb): to force or subdue

TEAR

(noun): a fluid secreted by the eyes

(verb): to separate or pull apart

Essay Revision and Sentence Logic

RHETORICAL DEVICES

There are many types of language devices that authors use to convey their meaning in a descriptive way. Understanding these concepts will help you understand what you read. These types of devices are called **figurative language**—language that goes beyond the literal meaning of a word or phrase. **Descriptive language** specifically evokes imagery in the reader's mind to make a story come alive. **Exaggeration** is a type of figurative language in which an author carries an idea beyond the truth in order to emphasize something. A **simile** is a type of figurative language that compares two things that are not actually alike, using words such as *like* and *as*. A **metaphor** takes the comparison one step further by fully equating the two things rather than just saying they are similar.

A **figure-of-speech** is a word or phrase that departs from straightforward, literal language. Figures-of-speech are often used and crafted for emphasis, freshness of expression, or clarity. However, clarity of a passage may suffer from use of these devices. As an example of the figurative use of a word, consider the sentence: *I am going to crown you.* The author may mean:

- I am going to place a literal crown on your head.
- I am going to symbolically exalt you to the place of kingship.
- I am going to punch you in the head with my clenched fist.
- I am going to put a second checker piece on top of your checker piece to signify that it has become a king.

> **Review Video: <u>Figure of Speech</u>**
> Visit mometrix.com/academy and enter code: 111295

A **metaphor** is a type of figurative language in which the writer equates something with another thing that is not particularly similar. For instance, *the bird was an arrow arcing through the sky*. In this sentence, the arrow is serving as a metaphor for the bird. The point of a metaphor is to encourage the reader to consider the item being described in a *different way*. Let's continue with this metaphor for a bird: you are asked to envision the bird's flight as being similar to the arc of an arrow. So, you imagine the flight to be swift and bending. Metaphors are a way for the author to describe an item *without being direct and obvious*. This literary device is a lyrical and suggestive way of providing information. Note that the reference for a metaphor will not always be mentioned explicitly by the author. Consider the following description of a forest in winter: *Swaying skeletons reached for the sky and groaned as the wind blew through them.* In this example, the author is using *skeletons* as a metaphor for leafless trees. This metaphor creates a spooky tone while inspiring the reader's imagination.

> **Review Video: <u>Metaphor</u>**
> Visit mometrix.com/academy and enter code: 133295

A **simile** is a figurative expression that is similar to a metaphor, but the expression uses a distancing word: *like* or *as*. Examples include phrases such as *the sun was like an orange, eager as a beaver*, and *nimble as a mountain goat*. Because a simile includes *like* or *as*, the device creates more space between the description and the thing being described than does a metaphor. If an author says that *a house was like a shoebox*, then the tone is different than the author saying that the house

was a shoebox. Authors will choose between a metaphor and a simile depending on their intended tone.

Another type of figurative language is **personification**. This is the description of a nonhuman thing as if the item were **human**. Literally, the word means the process of making something into a person. The general intent of personification is to describe things in a manner that will be comprehensible to readers. When an author states that a tree *groans* in the wind, he or she does not mean that the tree is emitting a low, pained sound from a mouth. Instead, the author means that the tree is making a noise similar to a human groan. Of course, this personification establishes a tone of sadness or suffering. A different tone would be established if the author said that the tree was *swaying* or *dancing*.

LEVEL OF FORMALITY

The relationship between writer and reader is important in choosing a **level of formality** as most writing requires some degree of formality. **Formal writing** is for addressing a superior in a school or work environment. Business letters, textbooks, and newspapers use a moderate to high level of formality. **Informal writing** is appropriate for private letters, personal e-mails, and business correspondence between close associates.

For your exam, you will want to be aware of informal and formal writing. One way that this can be accomplished is to watch for shifts in point of view in the essay. For example, unless writers are using a personal example, they will rarely refer to themselves (e.g., "*I* think that *my* point is very clear.") to avoid being informal when they need to be formal.

Also, be mindful of an author who addresses his or her audience **directly** in their writing (e.g., "Readers, *like you*, will understand this argument.") as this can be a sign of informal writing. Good writers understand the need to be consistent with their level of formality. Shifts in levels of formality or point of view can confuse readers and cause them to discount the message.

CLICHÉS

Clichés are phrases that have been **overused** to the point that the phrase has no importance or has lost the original meaning. The phrases have no originality and add very little to a passage. Therefore, most writers will avoid the use of clichés. Another option is to make changes to a cliché so that it is not predictable and empty of meaning.

Examples:

When life gives you lemons, make lemonade.

Every cloud has a silver lining.

JARGON

Jargon is a **specialized vocabulary** that is used among members of a trade or profession. Since jargon is understood by only a small audience, writers will use jargon in passages that will only be read by a specialized audience. For example, medical jargon should be used in a medical journal but not in a New York Times article. Jargon includes exaggerated language that tries to impress rather than inform. Sentences filled with jargon are not precise and difficult to understand.

Examples:

> "He is going to *toenail* these frames for us." (Toenail is construction jargon for nailing at an angle.)

> "They brought in a *kip* of material today." (Kip refers to 1000 pounds in architecture and engineering.)

SLANG

Slang is an **informal** and sometimes private language that is understood by some individuals. Slang has some usefulness, but the language can have a small audience. So, most formal writing will not include this kind of language.

Examples:

> "Yes, the event was a blast!" (In this sentence, *blast* means that the event was a great experience.)

> "That attempt was an epic fail." (By *epic fail*, the speaker means that his or her attempt was not a success.)

COLLOQUIALISM

A colloquialism is a word or phrase that is found in informal writing. Unlike slang, **colloquial language** will be familiar to a greater range of people. Colloquial language can include some slang, but these are limited to contractions for the most part.

Examples:

> "Can *y'all* come back another time?" (Y'all is a contraction of "you all" which has become a colloquialism.)

> "Will you stop him from building this *castle in the air*?" (A "castle in the air" is an improbable or unlikely event.)

TONE

Tone may be defined as the writer's **attitude** toward the topic, and to the audience. This attitude is reflected in the language used in the writing. The tone of a work should be **appropriate to the topic** and to the intended audience. Some texts should not contain slang or jargon, although these may be fine in a different piece. Tone can range from humorous to serious and all levels in between. It may be more or less formal, depending on the purpose of the writing and its intended audience. All these nuances in tone can flavor the entire writing and should be kept in mind as the work evolves.

WORD SELECTION

A writer's choice of words is a **signature** of their style. Careful thought about the use of words can improve a piece of writing. A passage can be an exciting piece to read when attention is given to the use of vivid or specific nouns rather than general ones. When using an active verb, one should be sure that the verb is used in the active voice instead of the passive voice. Verbs are in the active

voice when the subject is the one doing the action. A verb is in the passive voice when the subject is the recipient of an action.

Example:

General: His kindness will never be forgotten.

Specific: His thoughtful gifts and bear hugs will never be forgotten.

Attention should also be given to the kind of verbs that are used in sentences. Active verbs (e.g., run, swim) should be about an action. Whenever possible, an **active verb should replace a linking verb** to provide clear examples for arguments and to strengthen a passage overall.

Example:

Passive: The winners were called to the stage by the judges.

Active: The judges called the winners to the stage.

> **Review Video: Word Usage**
> Visit mometrix.com/academy and enter code: 197863

CONCISENESS

Conciseness is writing what you need to get your message across in the fewest words possible. Planning is important in writing concise messages. If you have in mind what you need to write beforehand, it will be easier to make a message short and to the point. Do not state the obvious.

Revising is also important. After the message is written, make sure you have short sentences. When reviewing the information, imagine a conversation taking place, and concise writing will likely result.

TRANSITIONS

Transitions are bridges between what has been read and what is about to be read. Transitions smooth the reader's path between sentences and inform the reader of major connections to new ideas forthcoming in the text. Transitional phrases should be used with care, selecting the appropriate phrase for a transition. Tone is another important consideration in using transitional phrases, varying the tone for different audiences. For example, in a scholarly essay, *in summary* would be preferable to the more informal *in short*.

When working with transitional words and phrases, writers usually find a natural flow that indicates when a transition is needed. In reading a draft of the text, it should become apparent where the flow is uneven or rough. At this point, the writer can add transitional elements during the revision process. Revising can also afford an opportunity to delete transitional devices that seem heavy handed or unnecessary.

TYPES OF TRANSITIONS

Appropriate transition words help clarify the relationships between sentences and paragraphs, and they create a much more cohesive essay. Below are listed several categories of transitions that you will need to be familiar with along with some associated transition words:

- **Logical Continuation**: therefore, as such, for this reason, thus, consequently, as a result
- **Extended Argument**: moreover, furthermore, also
- **Example or Illustration**: for instance, for example
- **Comparison**: similarly, likewise, in like manner
- **Contrast**: however, nevertheless, by contrast
- **Restatement or Clarification**: in other words, to put it another way
- **Generalization or General Application**: in broad terms, broadly speaking, in general

Review Video: <u>Transitions</u>
Visit mometrix.com/academy and enter code: 707563

Essay Writing

INTRODUCTION

The purpose of the introduction is to capture the reader's attention and announce the essay's main idea. Normally, the introduction contains 50-80 words, or 3-5 sentences. An introduction can begin with an interesting quote, a question, or a strong opinion—something that will **engage** the reader's interest and prompt them to keep reading. If you are writing your essay to a specific prompt, your introduction should include a **restatement or summarization** of the prompt so that the reader will have some context for your essay. Finally, your introduction should briefly state your **thesis or main idea**: the primary thing you hope to communicate to the reader through your essay. Don't try to include all of the details and nuances of your thesis, or all of your reasons for it, in the introduction. That's what the rest of the essay is for!

THESIS STATEMENT

The thesis is the main idea of the essay. A temporary thesis should be established early in the writing process because it will serve to keep the writer focused as ideas develop. This temporary thesis is subject to change as you continue to write.

The temporary thesis has two parts: a topic (i.e., the focus of your essay based on the prompt) and a comment. The comment makes an important point about the topic. A temporary thesis should be interesting and specific. Also, you need to limit the topic to a manageable scope. These three criteria are useful tools to measure the effectiveness of any temporary thesis:

- Does the focus of my essay have enough interest to hold an audience?
- Is the focus of my essay specific enough to generate interest?
- Is the focus of my essay manageable for the time limit? Too broad? Too narrow?

The thesis should be a generalization rather than a fact because the thesis prepares readers for facts and details that support the thesis. The process of bringing the thesis into sharp focus may help in outlining major sections of the work. Once the thesis and introduction are complete, you can address the body of the work.

> **Review Video: Thesis Statements**
> Visit mometrix.com/academy and enter code: 691033

SUPPORTING THE THESIS

Throughout your essay, the thesis should be explained clearly and supported adequately by additional arguments. The thesis sentence needs to contain a clear statement of the purpose of your essay and a comment about the thesis. With the thesis statement, you have an opportunity to state what is noteworthy of this particular treatment of the prompt. Each sentence and paragraph should build on and support the thesis.

When you respond to the prompt, use parts of the passage to support your argument or defend your position. With supporting evidence from the passage, you strengthen your argument because readers can see your attention to the entire passage and your response to the details and facts within the passage. You can use facts, details, statistics, and direct quotations from the passage to uphold your position. Be sure to point out which information comes from the original passage and base your argument around that evidence.

PARAGRAPHS

After the introduction of a passage, a series of body paragraphs will carry a message through to the conclusion. A paragraph should be unified around a main point. Normally, a good topic sentence summarizes the paragraph's main point. A topic sentence is a general sentence that gives an introduction to the paragraph.

The sentences that follow are a support to the topic sentence. However, the topic sentence can come as the final sentence to the paragraph if the earlier sentences give a clear explanation of the topic sentence. Overall, the paragraphs need to stay true to the main point. This means that any unnecessary sentences that do not advance the main point should be removed.

The main point of a paragraph requires adequate development (i.e., a substantial paragraph that covers the main point). A paragraph of two or three sentences does not cover a main point. This is true when the main point of the paragraph gives strong support to the argument of the thesis. An occasional short paragraph is fine as a transitional device. However, a well-developed argument will have paragraphs with more than a few sentences.

METHODS OF DEVELOPING PARAGRAPHS

A common method of development with paragraphs can be done with **examples**. These examples are the supporting details to the main idea of a paragraph or a passage. When authors write about something that their audience may not understand, they can provide an example to show their point. When authors write about something that is not easily accepted, they can give examples to prove their point.

Illustrations are extended examples that require several sentences. Well selected illustrations can be a great way for authors to develop a point that may not be familiar to their audience.

Analogies make comparisons between items that appear to have nothing in common. Analogies are employed by writers to provoke fresh thoughts about a subject. These comparisons may be used to explain the unfamiliar, to clarify an abstract point, or to argue a point. Although analogies are effective literary devices, they should be used carefully in arguments. Two things may be alike in some respects but completely different in others.

Cause and effect is an excellent device used when the cause and effect are accepted as true. One way that authors can use cause and effect is to state the effect in the topic sentence of a paragraph and add the causes in the body of the paragraph. With this method, an author's paragraphs can have structure which always strengthens writing.

TYPES OF PARAGRAPHS

A **paragraph of narration** tells a story or a part of a story. Normally, the sentences are arranged in chronological order (i.e., the order that the events happened). However, flashbacks (i.e., beginning the story at an earlier time) can be included.

A **descriptive paragraph** makes a verbal portrait of a person, place, or thing. When specific details are used that appeal to one or more of the senses (i.e., sight, sound, smell, taste, and touch), authors give readers a sense of being present in the moment.

A **process paragraph** is related to time order (i.e., First, you open the bottle. Second, you pour the liquid, etc.). Usually, this describes a process or teaches readers how to perform a process.

Comparing two things draws attention to their similarities and indicates a number of differences. When authors contrast, they focus only on differences. Both comparisons and contrasts may be used point-by-point or in following paragraphs.

Reasons for starting a new paragraph include:

1. To mark off the introduction and concluding paragraphs
2. To signal a shift to a new idea or topic
3. To indicate an important shift in time or place
4. To explain a point in additional detail
5. To highlight a comparison, contrast, or cause and effect relationship

PARAGRAPH LENGTH

Most readers find that their comfort level for a paragraph is between 100 and 200 words. Shorter paragraphs cause too much starting and stopping, and give a choppy effect. Paragraphs that are too long often test the attention span of readers. Two notable exceptions to this rule exist. In scientific or scholarly papers, longer paragraphs suggest seriousness and depth. In journalistic writing, constraints are placed on paragraph size by the narrow columns in a newspaper format.

The first and last paragraphs of a text will usually be the introduction and conclusion. These special-purpose paragraphs are likely to be shorter than paragraphs in the body of the work. Paragraphs in the body of the essay follow the subject's outline; one paragraph per point in short essays and a group of paragraphs per point in longer works. Some ideas require more development than others, so it is good for a writer to remain flexible. A paragraph of excessive length may be divided, and shorter ones may be combined.

COHERENT PARAGRAPHS

A smooth flow of sentences and paragraphs without gaps, shifts, or bumps will lead to paragraph coherence. Ties between old and new information can be smoothed by several methods:

- Linking ideas clearly, from the topic sentence to the body of the paragraph, is essential for a smooth transition. The topic sentence states the main point, and this should be followed by specific details, examples, and illustrations that support the topic sentence. The support may be direct or indirect. In indirect support, the illustrations and examples may support a sentence that in turn supports the topic directly.
- The repetition of key words adds coherence to a paragraph. To avoid dull language, variations of the key words may be used.
- Parallel structures are often used within sentences to emphasize the similarity of ideas and connect sentences giving similar information.
- Maintaining a consistent verb tense throughout the paragraph helps. Shifting tenses affects the smooth flow of words and can disrupt the coherence of the paragraph.

TSI Practice Test #1

Math

1. If $x + y > 0$ when $x > y$, which of the following cannot be true?

    A. $x = 3$ and $y = 0$
    B. $x = -3$ and $y = 0$
    C. $x = -4$ and $y = -3$
    D. $x = 3$ and $y = -3$

Question 2 is based on the following table.

Hours	1	2	3
Cost	$3.60	$7.20	$10.80

2. The table shows the cost of renting a bicycle for 1, 2, or 3 hours. Which of the following equations best represents the data, if C represents the cost and h represents the time (in hours) of the rental?

    A. $C = 3.60h$
    B. $C = h + 3.60$
    C. $C = 3.60h + 10.80$
    D. $C = \frac{10.80}{h}$

3. Rafael has a business selling computers. He buys computers from the manufacturer for $450 each and sells them for $800. Each month, he must also pay fixed costs of $3000 for rent and utilities at his store. If he sells n computers in a month, which of the following equations can be used to calculate his monthly profit?

    A. $P = n(800 - 450 - 3000)$
    B. $P = 3000 \cdot n(800 - 450)$
    C. $P = n(800 - 450) - 3000$
    D. $P = n(800 - 450) + 3000$

4. If $-\frac{1}{3}x + 7 = 4$, what is the value for $\frac{1}{3}x + 3$?

    A. 3
    B. 6
    C. 9
    D. 12

5. Jack and Kevin play in a basketball game. If the ratio of points scored by Jack to points scored by Kevin is 4 to 3, which of the following could NOT be the total number of points scored by the two boys?

    A. 14
    B. 16
    C. 28
    D. 35

6. How many 3-inch segments can a 4.5-yard line be divided into?

    A. 45

    B. 54

    C. 64

    D. 84

7. Which of the following expressions is equivalent to $(a + b)(a - b)$?

    A. $a^2 - b^2$

    B. $(a + b)^2$

    C. $(a - b)^2$

    D. $ab(a - b)$

8. If $2^4 = 4^x$, then $x =$

    A. 2

    B. 4

    C. 6

    D. 8

9. Simplify the following expression: $(2x^2 + 3x + 2) - (x^2 + 2x - 3)$

    A. $x^2 + x + 5$

    B. $x^2 + x - 1$

    C. $x^2 + 5x + 5$

    D. $x^2 + 5x - 1$

10. Which of the following is equivalent to $\left(\sqrt[3]{x^4}\right)^5$?

    A. $x^{\frac{12}{5}}$

    B. $x^{\frac{15}{4}}$

    C. $x^{\frac{20}{3}}$

    D. x^{60}

Question 11 is based on the following figure (figure may not be to scale).

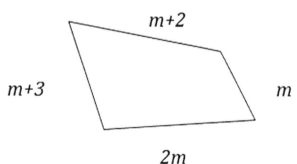

11. The figure shows an irregular quadrilateral and the lengths of its individual sides. Which of the following equations best represents the perimeter of the quadrilateral?

    A. $2m^4 + 5$

    B. $4m + 5$

    C. $5m + 5$

    D. $4m^2 + 5$

135

12. Which of the following could be a graph of the function $y = \frac{1}{x}$?

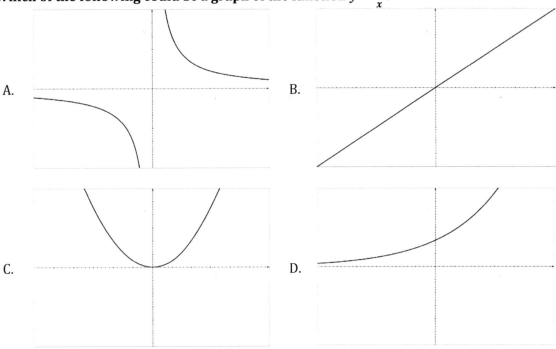

A.

B.

C.

D.

13. Which of the following statements is true?
    A. Perpendicular lines have opposite slopes
    B. Perpendicular lines have the same slopes
    C. Perpendicular lines have reciprocal slopes
    D. Perpendicular lines have opposite reciprocal slopes

Question 14 is based upon the following figure (figure may not be to scale):

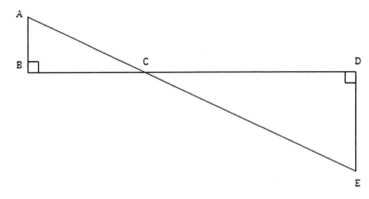

14. In the figure above, segment BC is 4 units long, segment CD is 8 units long, and segment DE is 6 units long. What is the length of segment AC?
    A. 4 units
    B. 5 units
    C. 6 units
    D. 8 units

15. If a rectangle's length and width are doubled, by what percentage does its area increase?

A. 80%
B. 160%
C. 240%
D. 300%

16. Which of the following are complementary angles?

A. 71° and 19°
B. 90° and 90°
C. 90° and 45°
D. 15° and 30°

17. Given the double bar graph shown below, which of the following statements is true?

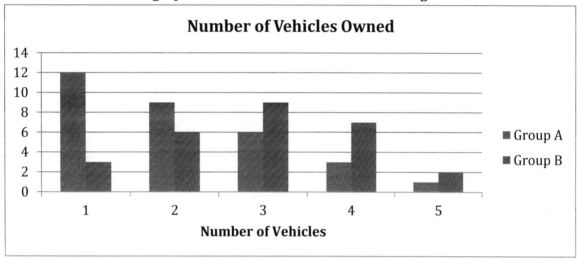

A. Group A is negatively skewed, while Group B is approximately normal.
B. Group A is positively skewed, while Group B is approximately normal.
C. Group A is approximately normal, while Group B is negatively skewed.
D. Group A is approximately normal, while Group B is positively skewed.

18. Which of the following correlation coefficients represents the weakest correlation?

A. 0.3
B. −0.1
C. 0.4
D. −0.9

19. Elizabeth rolls a standard die, labeled 1 to 6, 100 times. Which of the following experimental outcomes is *not* likely?

A. 67 rolls will show a number greater than 2.
B. 50 rolls will show an even number.
C. 75 rolls will show a number less than 4.
D. 33 rolls will show a number less than 3.

20. A bag contains 8 red marbles, 3 blue marbles, and 4 green marbles. What is the probability Carlos draws a red marble, does not replace it, and then draws another red marble?

    A. $\dfrac{4}{15}$

    B. $\dfrac{32}{105}$

    C. $\dfrac{64}{225}$

    D. $\dfrac{2}{15}$

Reading

Directions for questions 1–6

Read the statement or passage and then choose the best answer to the question. Answer the question based on what is stated or implied in the statement or passage.

1. The Amazon Rainforest is one of the most important ecosystems in the world. However, it is slowly being destroyed. Areas of the rainforest are being cleared for farms and roads, and much of the wood is also being harvested and sold. There are several compelling reasons to protect this area. First, a significant number of pharmaceuticals are made from plants that have been discovered in the rainforest, and it's quite possible there are still important plants that have not yet been discovered. Secondly, the rainforest provides a significant portion of the world's oxygen and also absorbs great amounts of carbon dioxide. Without rainforests, global warming could accelerate.

The main purpose of the passage is

    A. to present the major reasons why the Amazon Rainforest is being destroyed.
    B. to explain why the Amazon Rainforest should be protected.
    C. to argue that rainforest destruction is a major cause of global warming.
    D. to discuss how the rainforest has helped in the development of medications.

2. Howard Gardner was a psychologist best known for developing the theory of multiple intelligences. Basically, the theory states that the idea of general intelligence or overall intelligence is somewhat inaccurate. This is because people often show intelligence in different areas. He argued that there are actually different types of intelligence. One type of intelligence that Gardner identified was interpersonal intelligence. People who possess this type of intelligence relate and interact well with others. Intrapersonal intelligence, on the other hand, implies that people are in touch with their own feelings. They enjoy thinking about theories and developing their own thoughts and ideas. People who have linguistic intelligence learn best by taking notes and reading textbooks. These people usually excel in traditional academic environments, as many academic subjects stress these types of activities. The other types of intelligence are kinesthetic, musical, spatial, and logical/mathematical.

We can conclude from the passage that

    A. Gardner believed that linguistic intelligence was the most desirable type to have.
    B. most people who have a high level of intrapersonal intelligence do well in school.
    C. people who have a high level of interpersonal intelligence work well in groups.
    D. people who have mathematical intelligence would do the best on a standard IQ test.

3. The Internet has made life a whole lot easier for many people, but being online also brings with it very real risks. Hackers can steal personal and financial information. There are several precautions that computer users can take to minimize the level of risk that is involved with being online. One of the most obvious safety precautions is to purchase a good anti-virus and anti-spyware program. Passwords are also a very important part of online security, and several tips can help users create more secure passwords. First, a password should be something that can easily be remembered, but it shouldn't be something others can guess easily. Your first or last name, phone number, or the name of your street are all bad choices, as people could learn this information quite easily. Longer passwords are more secure, and those that use a mixture of upper- and lowercase letters and a combination of letters and numbers are more secure than those that don't. Finally, passwords should be changed often. This can make remembering them more difficult, but the extra effort is worth the added security.

The main purpose of this passage is to

    A. discuss the major risks associated with Internet use.
    B. talk about the importance of anti-virus programs.
    C. outline important considerations for passwords.
    D. discuss why certain types of passwords shouldn't be used.

4. When people are conducting research, particularly historical research, they usually rely on primary and secondary sources. Primary sources are the more direct type of information. A primary source is an account of an event that is produced by individuals who were actually present. Some examples of primary sources include a person's diary entry about an event, an interview with an eyewitness, a newspaper article, or a transcribed conversation. Secondary sources are pieces of information that are constructed through the use of other, primary sources. Often, the person who creates the secondary source was not actually present at the event. Secondary sources could include books, research papers, and magazine articles.

From the passage it can be assumed that

    A. primary sources are easier to find than secondary sources.
    B. primary sources provide more accurate information than secondary sources.
    C. secondary sources give more accurate information than primary sources.
    D. secondary sources are always used when books or articles are being written.

5. Many people fail to realize just how crucial getting a good night's sleep actually is. It is usually suggested that adults should get about seven hours of sleep every night, and younger children should get even more. Sleep has several benefits. First, it is believed to improve memory. This is one reason why it is always preferable to sleep the night before a test rather than stay up for the entire night to review the information. On a related note, sleep also improves concentration and mental alertness. Those who get sufficient sleep are able to concentrate on work tasks better and also react faster when they are driving a car, for example. Finally, people who get enough sleep have better immunity against illness. The reason for this is not fully understood, but researchers believe that an increase in the production of growth hormone and melatonin plays a role.

The main purpose of this passage is

    A. to talk about the benefits of sleep.
    B. to discuss how much sleep people should get.
    C. to identify which hormones can boost immunity.
    D. to present strategies for improving memory and concentration.

6. Feudalism was a type of social system that existed in parts of Europe during the Middle Ages. Essentially, there were several different classes within a feudal society. The king controlled all of the land in his jurisdiction. He divided this land among a few barons. The barons then divided up the land they were given and distributed it to knights. It was then split up again and distributed to serfs, who were the lowest members of feudal society. They were permitted to farm small sections of land, but they had to give a portion of their food to the knights in exchange for this privilege. They also had to give free labor to the knights who allowed them to use their land. Serfs had very few rights; they weren't even allowed to leave their land without permission from the knight who controlled the land. The system of feudalism ended when money began to be used as currency instead of land.

It can be concluded that

    A. serfs were in a better position when the economy changed to a money-based one.

    B. there were more knights in a typical feudal society than barons.

    C. the knights did not have to do anything for the barons in exchange for land.

    D. most feudal societies in Europe were ruled by more than one king.

Questions 7–13 are based upon the following passage:

In the United States, where we have more land than people, it is not at all difficult for persons in good health to make money. In this comparatively new field there are so many avenues of success open, so many vocations which are not crowded, that any person of either sex who is willing, at least for the time being, to engage in any respectable occupation that offers, may find lucrative employment.

Those who really desire to attain an independence, have only to set their minds upon it, and adopt the proper means, as they do in regard to any other object which they wish to accomplish, and the thing is easily done. But however easy it may be found to make money, I have no doubt many of my hearers will agree it is the most difficult thing in the world to keep it. The road to wealth is, as Dr. Franklin truly says, "as plain as the road to the mill." It consists simply in expending less than we earn; that seems to be a very simple problem. Mr. Micawber, one of those happy creations of the genial Dickens, puts the case in a strong light when he says that to have annual income of twenty pounds per annum, and spend twenty pounds and sixpence, is to be the most miserable of men; whereas, to have an income of only twenty pounds, and spend but nineteen pounds and sixpence is to be the happiest of mortals.

Many of my readers may say, "we understand this: this is economy, and we know economy is wealth; we know we can't eat our cake and keep it also." Yet I beg to say that perhaps more cases of failure arise from mistakes on this point than almost any other. The fact is, many people think they understand economy when they really do not.

7. Which of the following statements best expresses the main idea of the passage?

    A. Getting a job is easier now than it ever has been before.

    B. Earning money is much less difficult than managing it properly.

    C. Dr. Franklin advocated getting a job in a mill.

    D. Spending money is the greatest temptation in the world.

8. What would this author's attitude likely be to a person unable to find employment?

   A. descriptive
   B. conciliatory
   C. ingenuous
   D. incredulous

9. According to the author, what is more difficult than making money?

   A. managing money
   B. traveling to a mill
   C. reading Dickens
   D. understanding the economy

10. Who is the most likely audience for this passage?

   A. economists
   B. general readers
   C. teachers
   D. philanthropists

11. What is the best definition of *economy* as it is used in this passage?

   A. exchange of money, goods, and services
   B. delegation of household affairs
   C. efficient money management
   D. less expensive

12. Which word best describes the author's attitude towards those who believe they understand money?

   A. supportive
   B. incriminating
   C. excessive
   D. patronizing

13. This passage is most likely taken from a(n) ____.

   A. self-help manual
   B. autobiography
   C. epistle
   D. novel

Questions 14–20 are based upon the following passage:

We all know the drill: the consequences of urban sprawl, Americans' long work hours, and devotion to television and the Internet are doing nothing good for American communities.

A new study by sociologists at Duke University and the University of Arizona adds more grist to this mill, noting that Americans in 2004 had smaller networks of people with whom they talk about matters important to them than they did in 1985. (*Social Isolation in America: Changes in Core Discussion Networks Over Two Decades*, American Sociological Review, June 2006.) In 1985, Americans had three confidants, in 2004, we averaged two. The number of Americans who had no one with whom to talk about important matters almost doubled in 2004 to over 25%. Increasingly,

142

most confidants are family: in 2004, 80% of people talked only to family about important matters and about 9% of people depended totally on their spouse.

This decrease in confidants is part (a result) of the same trend that's leaving fewer people knowing their neighbors or participating in social clubs or public affairs than in the past (phenomena noted in the book <u>Better Together: Restoring the American Community</u> by Robert Putnam and Lewis Feldstein). We know a lot of people, but not necessarily very well.

Left to our own devices and cultural trends then, we seem to be moving in an unpleasant direction. Communities are formed ad hoc, around specific shared individual interests. This wouldn't be bad, of course, except that those communities seem to exist only within the constraints of those shared interests, and don't develop into close and meaningful relationships. The transient and specific nature of many of our relationships today can keep us socially busy without building the lasting relationships and communities that we want.

So what do we do about it if we want to change things? Harvard University's School of Government put together 150 ways to increase what they call "social capital" (the value of our social networks). Among their suggestions are: support local merchants, audition for community theater or volunteer to usher, participate in political campaigns, start or join a carpool, eat breakfast at a local gathering spot on Saturdays, and stop and make sure the person on the side of the highway is OK.

14. According to the author, which of the following was true in 2004:
- A. The average American had three confidants and 9% of people depended totally on their spouse for discussion of important matters.
- B. The average American had two confidants, and 80% of people discussed important matters only with their spouses.
- C. The average American had two confidants, and 9% of people discussed important matters only with family members.
- D. The average American had two confidants, and 80% of people discussed important matters only with family members.

15. The author argues that the transient nature of many of today's relationships is problematic because:
- A. we don't share specific interests
- B. we don't know many people
- C. it prevents us building lasting relationships and communities
- D. we have too much social capital

16. Which of the following are some of the causes to which the author attributes problems in American communities:
- A. too much homework and devotion to television
- B. urban sprawl and long work hours
- C. long work hours and too much homework
- D. urban sprawl and decline of sports team membership

17. Which of the following is not something the author states was suggested by Harvard University as a way to increase social capital:

   A. eat breakfast at a local gathering spot
   B. join a bowling team
   C. support local merchants
   D. join a carpool

18. In what year was the Duke University study cited by the author published?

   A. 2006
   B. 2000
   C. 1985
   D. 2004

19. How many ways did Harvard University's School of Government suggest to increase social capital?

   A. 25
   B. 80
   C. 100
   D. 150

20. According to the author, "social capital" means which of the following:

   A. the value of our social networks
   B. the number of confidants with whom we share information
   C. the value we place on friendships outside family members
   D. the number of activities in which we engage

Questions 21–24 are based on the following passage.

In the American Southwest of the late 1800s, the introduction of barbed wire fencing led to fierce disputes between ranchers and farmers, both eager to protect their rights and their livelihood. The farmers were the clear winners of the two groups, and the barbed wire fences stayed and proliferated. Barbed wire proved to be ideal for use in western conditions; it was cheaper and easier to use than the alternatives of wood fences, stone walls or hedges. Within a few decades all the previously open range land became fenced-in private property. This change was so dramatic to the western culture that some consider the introduction of barbed wire fencing to be the event that ended the Old West period of our history.

21. According to the author, which group supported the use of barbed wire fences?

   A. the ranchers
   B. the farmers
   C. both the ranchers and the farmers
   D. neither the ranchers nor the farmers

22. According to the author, what do some believe the introduction of barbed wire ended?

   A. the disputes between the farmers and the ranchers
   B. the controversy over whether wood fences or stone walls were better
   C. the Old West period of our history
   D. the livelihood of the farmers

23. Which of the following did the author <u>not</u> imply would have been found in the Old West prior to the introduction of barbed wire fencing?

    A. no fencing in some places
    B. wood fences
    C. hedges
    D. brick walls

24. According to the author, when did the introduction of barbed wire fencing occur?

    A. the late 16th century
    B. the late 17th century
    C. the late 18th century
    D. the late 19th century

Writing

Johnna's American history teacher has assigned a research essay on a figure from the American Revolution. Johnna decided to write about Paul Revere and would like your help revising and improving the essay. After you read her essay, answer questions 1–10.

(1) In the early 1760s, Paul Revere, ran a busy metalworking shop. (2) People from all over Boston came to buy the silver and gold cups, medals, and cutlery he made. (3) Everything changed in 1765. (4) Many colonists ran low on money and stopped shopping at Paul's shop.

(5) Things got worse when the british passed the Stamp Act. (6) The Stamp Act created a tax to help the British earn money. (7) Colonists like Paul Revere hated the Stamp Act because it would make things more expensive.

(8) Under the Stamp Act, colonists needed to pay for everything that was printed, such as newspapers, magazines, and business contracts. (9) After a colonist paid the tax, the tax collector put a stamp on the paper to show that the tax had been paid. (10) The Stamp Act made it very expensive for Paul to run his business. (11) For example, if he wanted a new apprentice for his silver shop, he needed to buy a Stamp for the signed contract.

(12) Paul wasn't just angry about buying stamps. (13) He also felt that the British shouldn't be allowed to tax the colonies. (14) There was no American colonists in the British parliament, which passed the tax. (15) Paul and the other colonists didn't want taxation without representation. (16) They wanted to be able to choose their own taxes.

(17) The colonists refused to buy stamps. (18) They were determined to get the Stamp Act repealed.

(19) Paul joined a group called the Sons of Liberty. (20) They wore silver medals on their coats that said "Sons of Liberty." (21) Paul may have helped make the medals in his silver shop.

(22) The Sons of Liberty staged demonstrations at the Liberty Tree, a huge elm tree, that stood in Boston. (23) Paul drew cartoons and wrote poems about liberty. (24) He published them in the local newspaper, *The Boston Gazette*.

(25) After a year of hard work fighting the Stamp Act Paul and the Sons of Liberty received the happy news. (26) The Stamp Act had been repealed!

(27) People celebrated all over Boston; they lit bonfires, set off fireworks, and decorated houses and ships with flags and streamers. (28) Paul attended the biggest celebration, which took place at the Liberty Tree. (29) The people hung 280 lanterns on the tree's branches lighting up the night sky.

(30) Some members of the Sons of Liberty constructed a paper obelisk. (31) An obelisk is the same shape as the Washington Monument. (32) They decorated the obelisk with pictures and verses about the struggle to repeal the Stamp Act and hung it from the Liberty Tree.

(33) Paul may have helped construct the obelisk, even if he wasn't involved in the direct construction, he probably knew about and supported it. (34) After the celebration, he made a copper engraving showing the pictures and verses on the obelisk's four sides. (35) His engraving records the celebration under the Liberty Tree. (36) Even though Paul Revere may be better known for his silver work and famous ride, his engravings, like the engraving of the obelisk, help us see the American Revolution through his eyes.

1. What change should be made to sentence 1?

A. Change *1760s* to *1760's*
B. Delete the comma after *1760s*
C. Delete the comma after *Revere*
D. Add a comma after *busy*

2. What change should be made to sentence 5?

A. Change *got* to *get*
B. Change *worse* to *worst*
C. Change *british* to *British*
D. Change *Stamp Act* to *stamp act*

3. What change should be made to sentence 11?

A. Delete the comma after *example*
B. Delete the comma after *shop*
C. Change *Stamp* to *stamp*
D. Change *signed contract* to *Signed Contract*

4. What change should be made to sentence 14?

A. Change *was* to *were*
B. Change *parliament* to *parlaiment*
C. Delete the comma after *parliament*
D. Change *which* to *that*

5. What is the most effective way to combine sentences 17 and 18?

A. The colonists refused to buy stamps and they were determined to get the Stamp Act repealed.
B. The colonists refused to buy stamps, and they were determined to get the Stamp Act repealed.
C. The colonists refused to buy stamps, and were determined to get the Stamp Act repealed.
D. The colonists refused to buy stamps, were determined to get the Stamp Act repealed.

6. What change should be made to sentence 22?

A. Change *demonstrations* to *demonstration*
B. Insert *and* after the comma
C. Delete the comma after *elm tree*
D. Change *in* to *at*

7. What change, if any, should be made to sentence 25?
- A. Add a comma after *work*
- B. Add a comma after *Act*
- C. Change *received* to *recieved*
- D. No change

8. What change should be made to sentence 29?
- A. Change *280* to *two-hundred-eighty*
- B. Change *tree's* to *trees*
- C. Add a comma after *branches*
- D. Change *night* to *nightly*

9. What is the most effective way to combine sentences 30 and 31?
- A. Some members of the Sons of Liberty constructed a paper obelisk, which is the same shape as the Washington Monument.
- B. Some members of the Sons of Liberty constructed a paper obelisk which is the same shape as the Washington Monument.
- C. Some members of the Sons of Liberty constructed a paper obelisk, that is the same shape as the Washington Monument.
- D. Some members of the Sons of Liberty constructed a paper obelisk; which is the same shape as the Washington Monument.

10. What change should be made to sentence 33?
- A. Delete *may*
- B. Change the comma after *obelisk* to a semicolon
- C. Delete the comma after *construction*
- D. Change *knew* to *knows*

For questions 11–15, select the best option for replacing the underlined portion of the sentence. The first option listed is always the same as the current version of the sentence.

11. Children who aren't nurtured during infancy are more likely to develop attachment disorders, <u>which can cause persisting and severely problems</u> later in life.
- A. which can cause persisting and severely problems
- B. that can cause persisting and severe problem
- C. they can cause persistent and severe problem
- D. which can cause persistent and severe problems

12. While speed is a measure of how fast an object is moving, velocity measures how fast an object is moving <u>and also indicates in what direction</u> it is traveling.
- A. and also indicates in what direction
- B. and only indicates in which direction
- C. and also indicate in which directions
- D. and only indicated in what direction

13. Many companies are now using social networking sites like Facebook and MySpace <u>to market there service and product.</u>
- A. to market there service and product
- B. to market their services and products
- C. and market their service and products
- D. which market their services and products

14. An autoclave is a tool used mainly in hospitals <u>to sterilizing surgical tools and hypodermic needles</u>.
- A. to sterilizing surgical tools and hypodermic needles
- B. for sterilize surgical tools and hypodermic needles
- C. to sterilize surgical tools and hypodermic needles
- D. for sterilizing the surgical tool and hypodermic needle

15. <u>The bizarre creatures known by electric eels</u> are capable of emitting an incredible 600 volts of electricity.
- A. The bizarre creatures known by electric eels
- B. A bizarre creature known as electric eels
- C. The bizarre creatures known to electric eels
- D. The bizarre creatures known as electric eels

16. Bats and dolphins use a process known as echolocation, which means they emit and receive frequencies that can help them navigate through the dark night and murky waters, and also allows them to locate food sources like insects or fish.

Rewrite, beginning with

<u>Locating food sources like insects or fish ...</u>

The next words will be
- A. during which they emit and receive frequencies
- B. is done through a process known as echolocation
- C. helps them navigate through the dark night
- D. is done by bats and dolphins

17. Carbon dating is an accepted method used by archaeologists to figure out the age of artifacts, even though it may not be entirely accurate if samples are contaminated or if the objects to be dated are not extremely old.

Rewrite, beginning with

<u>Even though carbon dating is not always entirely accurate, ...</u>

The next words will be
- A. it is an accepted method
- B. objects to be dated
- C. to figure out the age
- D. samples are contaminated

18. Chemical changes are sometimes difficult to distinguish from physical changes, but some examples of physical changes, such as melting water, chopped wood, and ripped paper, are very easy to recognize.

Rewrite, beginning with

<u>Melting water, chopped wood, and ripped paper</u> ...

The next words will be

- A. are sometimes difficult to distinguish
- B. are very easy to recognize
- C. are chemical changes
- D. are some examples of physical changes

19. The theory of repressed memory was developed by Sigmund Freud, and it stated that all people store memories that cannot be accessed during daily life, but can be accessed through hypnotherapy and hypnosis.

Rewrite, beginning with

<u>Developed by Sigmund Freud,</u> ...

The next words will be

- A. it stated that all people
- B. that cannot be accessed
- C. hypnotherapy and hypnosis
- D. the theory of repressed memory

20. Romantic poetry is an important genre, and the works are easily distinguished from other types of poetry by several characteristics, including their focus on nature and the importance that is ascribed to everyday occurrences.

Rewrite, beginning with

<u>A focus on nature and the importance that is ascribed to everyday occurrences</u> ...

The next words will be

- A. are easily distinguished
- B. from other types of poetry
- C. are several characteristics
- D. is an important genre

Essay

Some states have legalized the sale and use of marijuana, bringing attention to the possibility of national legalization and regulation of the drug. Please write a multiple-paragraph persuasive essay (approximately 350–500 words) discussing what you believe the federal government's position should be on this issue.

Answers and Explanations for Test #1

Math

1. D: First, test each expression to see which satisfies the condition $x > y$. This condition is met for all the answer choices except B and C, so these need not be considered further. Next, test the remaining choices to see which satisfy the inequality $x + y > 0$. It can be seen that this inequality holds for choice A, but not for choice D, since $x + y = 3 + (-3) = 3 - 3 = 0$. In this case the sum $x + y$ is not greater than 0.

2. A: This equation represents a linear relationship that has a slope of 3.60 and passes through the origin. The table indicates that for each hour of rental, the cost increases by \$3.60. This corresponds to the slope of the equation. Of course, if the bicycle is not rented at all (0 hours) there will be no charge (\$0). If plotted on the Cartesian plane, the line would have a y-intercept of 0. Relationship A is the only one that satisfies these criteria.

3. C: Rafael's profit on each computer is given by the difference between the price he pays and the price he charges his customer, or \$800 – \$450. If he sells n computers in a month, his total profit will be n times this difference, or $n(800 - 450)$. However, it is necessary to subtract his fixed costs of \$3000 from this to compute his final profit per month.

4. B: Subtracting 7 from both sides of the equation yields $-\frac{1}{3}x = -3$. In order to get the term 'x' by itself, multiply both sides by –3, which leads to $x = 9$. Now we substitute this value into the given equation: $\frac{1}{3}(9) + 3$. This gives us $3 + 3$, which is 6.

5. B: Every possible combination of scores is a multiple of 7, since the two terms of the ratio have a sum of seven.

6. B: There are 12 inches in a foot and 3 feet in a yard. Four and a half yards is equal to 162 inches. To determine the number of 3-inch segments, divide 162 by 3.

7. A: Compute the product using the FOIL method, in which the *First* term, then the *Outer* terms, the *Inner* terms, and finally the *Last* terms are figured in sequence of multiplication. As a result, $(a + b)(a - b) = a^2 + ba - ab - b^2$. Since ab is equal to ba, the middle terms cancel each other which leaves $a^2 - b^2$.

8. A: $2^4 = 2 \cdot 2 \cdot 2 \cdot 2 = 16$. Therefore, $4^x = 16$, so $x = 2$.

9. A: $(2x^2 + 3x + 2) - (x^2 + 2x - 3) = (2x^2 + 3x + 2) + (-1)(x^2 + 2x - 3)$. First, distribute the -1 to remove the parentheses: $2x^2 + 3x + 2 - x^2 - 2x + 3$. Next, combine like terms: $(2x^2 - x^2) + (3x - 2x) + (2 + 3) = x^2 + x + 5$.

10. C: The nth root of x is equivalent to x to the power of $\frac{1}{n}$, i.e. $\sqrt[n]{x} = x^{\frac{1}{n}}$. This means in particular that $\sqrt[3]{x} = x^{\frac{1}{3}}$, and so $\left(\sqrt[3]{(x^4)}\right)^5 = \left((x^4)^{\frac{1}{3}}\right)^5$. Raising a power to another power is equivalent to multiplying the exponents together, so this equals $x^{4 \cdot \frac{1}{3} \cdot 5} = x^{\frac{20}{3}}$.

152

11. C: The perimeter (P) of the quadrilateral is simply the sum of its sides, or

$$P = m + (m + 2) + (m + 3) + 2m$$

Combine like terms by adding the variables (m terms) together and then adding the constants resulting in: $P = 5m + 5$

12. A: This is a typical plot of an inverse variation, in which the product of the dependent and independent variables, x and y, is always equal to the same value. In this case the product is always equal to 1, so the plot occupies the first and third quadrants of the coordinate plane. As x increases and approaches infinity, y decreases and approaches zero, maintaining the constant product. In contrast, answer B is a linear plot corresponding to an equation of the form $y = x$. C is a quadratic plot corresponding to $y = x^2$. D is an exponential plot corresponding to $y = 2^x$.

13. D: The slopes of perpendicular lines are reciprocals of opposite sign. For example, in the figure below, line A has a slope of $-\frac{1}{2}$, while line B has a slope of 2.

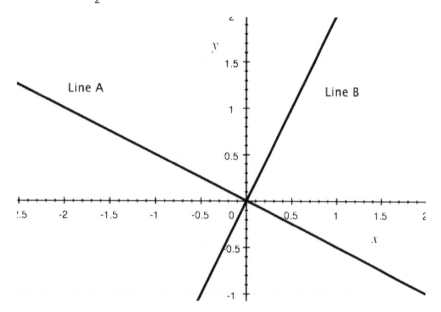

14. B: The two right triangles are similar because they share a pair of vertical angles. Vertical angles are always congruent (angle ACB and angle ECD). Obviously both right angles (angle B and angle D) are congruent. Thus, angles A and E are congruent because of the triangular sum theorem.

With similar triangles, corresponding sides will be proportional. Segment BC is ½ the length of segment CD, therefore AC will be ½ the length of CE. The length of CE can be computed from the Pythagorean theorem, since it is the hypotenuse of a right triangle for which the lengths of the other two sides are known: $CE = \sqrt{6^2 + 8^2} = \sqrt{100} = 10$.

The length of segment AC will be ½ of this value, or 5 units.

15. D: Let x stand for the length and let y stand for the width of the rectangle. Then the area is expressed as the product xy. But if the length and width are doubled to $2x$ and $2y$ respectively, the area becomes $(2x)(2y) = 4xy$, which is 4 times as large as the original rectangle. "Four times as large" is equivalent to a 300 percent increase.

16. A: Complementary angles are two angles that equal 90° when added together. Of the given answer choices, only 71° and 19° add up to 90°.

17. B: Data is said to be positively skewed when there are a higher number of lower values, indicating data that is skewed right. An approximately normal distribution shows an increase in frequency, followed by a decrease in frequency, of approximately the same rate.

18. B: Weak correlation coefficients are those with absolute values close to 0. Since −0.1 has an absolute value of 0.1 and 0.1 is closer to 0 than any of the absolute values of the other correlation coefficients, it is the weakest.

19. C: The theoretical probability of rolling a number less than 4 is the same as the theoretical probability of rolling an even number; the probability is $\frac{1}{2}$. The expected value is equal to the product of the number of rolls of 100 and the probability of $\frac{1}{2}$. Thus, it is likely that 50 of the rolls will show a number less than 4, not 75 of the rolls.

20. A: The events are dependent, since the first marble was not replaced. The sample space of the second draw will decrease by 1 because there will be one less marble to choose. The number of possible red marbles for the second draw will also decrease by 1. Thus, the probability may be written as $P(A \text{ and } B) = \frac{8}{15} \cdot \frac{7}{14}$. The probability Carlos draws a red marble, does not replace it, and draws another red marble is $\frac{4}{15}$.

Reading

1. B: Answer choices A and C are mentioned only briefly. D is discussed, but it falls under the more general purpose of the passage, which is discussing why the Amazon Rainforest is a valuable area that should be protected.

2. C: Answer choice A is not a logical conclusion because there is no indication that Gardner ranked the intelligences in any way. Answer choice B cannot be concluded from the passage, as there is no mention of the value placed on intrapersonal intelligences in a traditional academic environment. IQ tests (answer choice D) are not mentioned at all, so we cannot conclude anything about them based on this passage. Answer choice C is the correct choice. Those with interpersonal intelligence interact well with others, so it is reasonable to assume they would perform well in a group setting.

3. C: Answer choices A and B are touched upon only very briefly. Answer choice D is discussed, but it is encompassed by the broader purpose of the passage, which is to outline the most important considerations related to passwords.

4. B: Answer choice B is the most logical conclusion. The passage states that, "Primary sources are the more direct type of information. A primary source is an account of an event that is produced by individuals who were actually present." Therefore, it is reasonable to assume that an account prepared by someone who was present would be more accurate than one prepared by somebody decades later who had to rely on the accounts of others. A is not mentioned or implied, C is counter to the point of the passage, and D is simply a false statement.

5. A: Answer choices B and C are mentioned only briefly, and D is not really discussed in the passage. The passage focuses mainly on discussing some of the major benefits of sleep, so that is the main purpose of the passage.

6. B: Answer choice B is the logical conclusion. The passage states that "The king controlled all of the land in his jurisdiction. He divided this among a few barons. The barons then divided up the land they were given and distributed it to knights." If the barons divided up their lands, it would stand to reason that each baron would distribute his land to several knights. Therefore, there would have to be more knights than barons. Choice A could be a point made later in the passage, but is not found within the given section. Both choices C and D directly contradict the passage.

7. B: The author asserts both that earning money is increasingly easy and that managing money is difficult. Answer choices A, C, and D are not really discussed in the passage. Although the author does indicate that good jobs are prevalent, it is not mentioned in a way that compares the relative ease of acquiring employment to any prior time period.

8. D: The author seems to believe that there are plenty of lucrative jobs for everyone. Incredulous means hard to believe and as such is the best choice. Answers A, B, and C do not suit the message of the passage.

9. A: The author insists that many people who have no trouble earning money waste it through lavish spending. Answer choices B, C, and D are phrases or ideas mentioned in the passage but not in comparison to the difficulty of making money.

10. B: This passage is clearly intended for a non-expert adult readership, especially since the author calls out the audience as readers. As the tone of this article is persuasive and does not delve deeply into economics, it is not intended for economists or teachers (A or C). Philanthropists (D) would likely not be reading such an article as they are looking to give of their excess finances generously.

11. C: Here, the author is speaking of money management on a personal or household level. Answer choices A and D are other definitions of "economy," but they do not match the usage in the passage. Answer choice B is connected to the meaning implied in the passage, but is more of a source of economy rather than the definition.

12. D: The author suggests that many people who believe they understand economy in fact do not. Answer choices A and C do not fit the tone or message implied by the passage. Answer choice B is too strong for the author's attitude.

13. A: It seems clear that the author is about to describe the correct means of personal economy. Speaking with a tone of condescension, the author is trying to build credibility and authority before offering the solution to those who could not find it on their own. Answer choices B, C, and D would have very different styles and tones.

14. D: The author listed these facts in the second paragraph. Answer choices A, B, and C mix up the cited facts.

15. C: The passage is focused on the impact of the cultural shift on relationships and communities. Answer choices A and D are counter to some of the points mentioned by the author. Answer choice B is relevant but not the root cause argued by the author.

16. B: These are listed in the first paragraph. Answer choices A, C, and D are incorrect because the author never mentions homework or sports team membership.

17. B: Joining a bowling team was not listed. All the other options were listed in the fourth paragraph.

18. A: The in-line citation is in the second paragraph. B is not found in the article at all. C and D are other dates found in the article, but not the year the study was published.

19. D: The figure was stated in the fourth paragraph. None of the other answer choices are mentioned.

20. A: The definition of the term immediately follows the use in a parenthetical insertion in the fifth paragraph. Answer choices B, C, and D are ideas found in the article, but not the definition of "social capital."

21. B: The farmers are stated to be the winners of the dispute and subsequently the use of barbed wire increased significantly. The ranchers were not in favor of the barbed wire since they lost the dispute. Choices C and D are incorrect because if both or neither supported the use of barbed wire, there would have been no dispute.

22. C: This opinion is stated in the last sentence of the passage. Barbed wire led to disputes between farmers and ranchers, rather than ending them (answer choice A). Answer choice B was not disputed in the article. Answer choice D does not follow from the message of the passage.

23. D: Brick walls were not part of the list of predecessors to barbed wire found in the third sentence of the passage. All the other choices (A, B, and C) were in that list.

24. D: The count of centuries starts at 1, indicating years 0-99 being the first century, thus the 1800s would be the 19th century. As such, each of the other choices (A, B, and C) would indicate a different century.

Writing

1. C: A comma should not be used to separate the sentence's subject (Paul Revere) and verb (ran). Choice A is incorrect because an apostrophe would make *1760s* possessive, which it is not. Choice B is incorrect because the comma is used to separate a non-essential clause from the rest of the sentence. Choice D is incorrect because the words *busy* and *metalworking* are not a series of adjectives. Instead, *busy* is an adjective modifying the noun *metalworking shop*.

2. C: *British* is a proper noun and should always be capitalized. Choice A is incorrect because the passage is written in past tense; therefore, *got* should remain in past tense. Choice B is incorrect because it is referring to something becoming worse, rather than something that is the superlative *worst*. Choice D is incorrect because *Stamp Act* is both a proper noun and the proper name of the act.

3. C: This is the correct answer because *stamp* in this sentence is not a proper noun and does not need to be capitalized. In this context, *stamp* only needs to be capitalized when it is used in the name *Stamp Act*. Choice A is incorrect because the comma sets off a nonessential phrase at the beginning of the sentence. Choice B is incorrect because the comma sets off the initial dependent clause from the independent clause in the second half of the sentence. Choice D is incorrect because *signed contract* is not a proper noun or formal name.

4. A: In this sentence, *were* is referring to the plural *colonists*. As a singular verb form, *was* is incorrect in this case. Choice B is incorrect because *parliament* is the correct spelling. Choice C is incorrect because the comma is required to set off the nonessential phrase that follows. Choice D is incorrect because *that* is used to set off a dependent phrase and should not be preceded by a comma.

5. B: A comma and conjunction are correctly used to separate two independent clauses in choice B. Although choice A has the conjunction *and*, it is missing the required comma. Choice C is incorrect because no comma is required to separate an independent clause from a dependent clause. Choice D is incorrect because the comma creates a run-on sentence.

6. C: A comma should not be used to separate independent clauses from essential phrases that begin with *that*. Choice A is incorrect because the Sons of Liberty staged multiple demonstrations. The reader can determine this because there is no article before the word *demonstrations*. Choice B is incorrect because a comma is not needed to separate an independent clause from a dependent clause when the clauses are connected by a conjunction. Choice D is incorrect because the tree was *in* the city of Boston, not *at* a specific location.

7. B: A comma is needed to separate the dependent clause beginning with the word *after* from the independent clause beginning with *Paul*. Choice A is incorrect because the comma would divide a clause. Choice C is incorrect because *received* is the correct spelling. Choice D is incorrect because a comma is required after the word *Act*.

8. C: The phrase *lighting up the sky* is nonessential and should be separated from the rest of the sentence by a comma. While the number *280* could be written out, choice A is incorrect because it should be written as *two hundred and eighty*. Choice B is incorrect because *tree's* is possessive and requires the apostrophe. Choice D is incorrect because *nightly* is an adverb, which should modify a verb. However, the word is modifying a noun and must be written as an adjective.

9. A: A comma should be used to separate the independent clause beginning with *some members* from the nonessential phrase beginning with *which is*. Choice B is incorrect because it is missing the comma. Choice C is incorrect because it incorrectly uses *that* instead of *which*. Choice D is incorrect because it uses a semicolon instead of a comma.

10. B: A semicolon should be used to separate two independent clauses. Choice A is incorrect because *may* provides important meaning to the sentence. Choice C is incorrect because the comma correctly separates the two clauses. Choice D is incorrect because the passage is talking about a figure from history and should use the past tense.

11. D: Answer choice A is incorrect because *severely* is an adverb and not an adjective. B and C are incorrect because *problem* instead of the grammatically correct *problems* is used. D uses the correct, plural form *problems* and uses adjectives to describe the problems.

12. A: The sentence implies that *velocity* is used to indicate more than one value, which eliminates B and D. The phrase refers to velocity, which is singular, but the construction of choice C refers to a plural noun. Choice A agrees with the singular noun, and the *and* indicates that velocity is used to indicate more than one value.

13. B: Answer choice B uses the grammatically correct *their* instead of *there*. The *to* indicates the companies are using these sites for something, and *services* and *products* agree with each other because they are both plural.

14. C: Answer choice C states that an autoclave is a tool used *to sterilize*. A and B, which begin with *to sterilizing* and *for sterilize*, are not grammatically correct. D indicates that the machine is used to sterilize a single tool and needle, which does not make sense in the context of the sentence.

15. D: Answer choices A and C are incorrect because they imply that the bizarre creatures are something other than electric eels. The *a* in choice B does not agree with the plural *electric eels*.

Choice D is best because it is grammatically correct and identifies electric eels as the bizarre creatures being discussed in the sentence.

16. B: The original sentence indicates that bats and dolphins are able to do many things, including locating food sources like insects or fish through a process known as echolocation. Answer choice B best expresses the fact that locating food is accomplished through echolocation. Answer choice C cannot logically follow the phrase. Answer choices A and D do not tell how bats and dolphins locate food.

17. A: The new sentence begins with the phrase "even though," indicating that a contrast is being constructed. "Even though carbon dating is not always entirely accurate, it is still an accepted method" provides this contrast, while the other choices do not.

18. D: Melting water, chopped wood, and ripped paper are identified in the original sentence as examples of physical changes that are easy to distinguish from chemical changes. Therefore, answer choices A and C are entirely incorrect. Answer choice B indicates that these objects are easy to recognize, but the sentence should convey that they are examples of physical changes that are easy to recognize, making this choice somewhat inaccurate. Choice D is best because it identifies the previously mentioned objects as examples of physical changes.

19. D: The only phrase that describes something developed by Sigmund Freud is D. Answer choice A does not identify what the *it* is referring to, and B cannot logically follow the given phrase. Answer choice C describes ways to access repressed memories, but these were not developed by Freud.

20. C: A focus on nature and ascribing importance to everyday occurrences are identified in the original sentence as important characteristics of Romantic poetry. Answer choice C clearly identifies them as characteristics, and is the only choice that can logically follow the given phrase.

TSI Practice Test #2

Math

1. A combination lock uses a 3-digit code. Each digit can be any one of the ten available integers 0–9. How many different combinations are possible?

    A. 1000
    B. 30
    C. 81
    D. 100

2. The cost, in dollars, of shipping x computers to California for sale is $3000 + 100x$. The amount received when selling these computers is $400x$ dollars. What is the least number of computers that must be shipped and sold so that the amount received is at least equal to the shipping cost?

    A. 10
    B. 15
    C. 20
    D. 25

3. If $\frac{3}{s} = 7$ and $\frac{4}{t} = 12$, then $s - t =$

    A. $-\frac{1}{7}$
    B. $\frac{2}{12}$
    C. $\frac{2}{7}$
    D. $\frac{2}{21}$

4. If the average of 7 and x is equal to the average of 9, 4, and x, what is the value of x?

    A. 4
    B. 5
    C. 6
    D. 7

5. How many integers are solutions of the inequality $|x| < 4$?

    A. An infinite number
    B. 0
    C. 3
    D. 7

6. For what real number x is it true that $3(2x - 10) = x$?

    A. −6
    B. −5
    C. 5
    D. 6

159

7. Expand the following expression: $(y + 1)(y + 2)(y + 3)$

    A. $y^3 + 3y + 2$
    B. $3y^2 + 6y + 3$
    C. $y^3 + 6y^2 + 11y + 6$
    D. $8y^3 + 6y + 8$

8. Which of the following is *not* a factor of $x^3 - 3x^2 - 4x + 12$ **?**

    A. $x - 2$
    B. $x + 2$
    C. $x - 3$
    D. $x + 3$

9. Simplify $\frac{x^6}{y^4} \cdot x^2 y^3$.

    A. $x^4 y$
    B. $\dfrac{x^4}{y}$
    C. $x^8 y$
    D. $\dfrac{x^8}{y}$

10. Expand the following expression: $(x + 2)(x - 3)$

    A. $x^2 - 1$
    B. $x^2 - 6$
    C. $x^2 - x - 6$
    D. $x^2 - 5x - 1$

11. In the following figure, angle $\angle b = 120°$**. What is the measurement of angle** a**?**

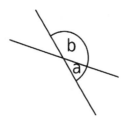

    A. $40°$
    B. $60°$
    C. $90°$
    D. $100°$

12. Which of the following figures has non-trivial rotational symmetry?

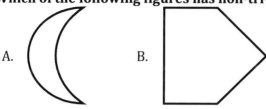

A.

B.

C.

D.

13. AC and BD are straight lines intersecting at point E. Angle BEC is 45°. What is the measure for angle AEB?

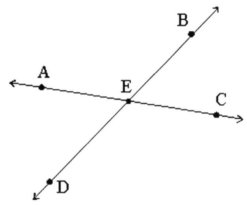

A. Angle AEB is 90°
B. Angle AEB is 115°
C. Angle AEB is 135°
D. Angle AEB is 180°

14. If the ratio of the measures of the three angles in a triangle are 2 : 6 : 10, what is the actual measure of the smallest angle?

A. 20 degrees
B. 40 degrees
C. 60 degrees
D. 80 degrees

15. In the figure below, what is the area of triangle ACD, given that AD and BC are parallel and that AB is perpendicular to both?

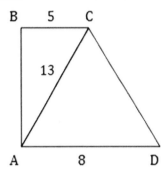

A. 13
B. 30
C. 48
D. 60

16. If the area of a rectangular game board is 336 square inches and its perimeter is 76 inches, what is the length of each of the shorter sides?

A. 10 inches
B. 14 inches
C. 19 inches
D. 24 inches

17. Given the histograms shown below, which of the following statements is true?

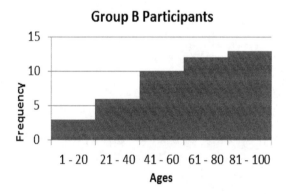

A. Group A is negatively skewed and has a mean that is less than the mean of Group B.
B. Group A is positively skewed and has a mean that is more than the mean of Group B.
C. Group B is negatively skewed and has a mean that is more than the mean of Group A.
D. Group B is positively skewed and has a mean that is less than the mean of Group A.

18. Which of the following best represents the line of best fit for the data shown in the scatter plot?

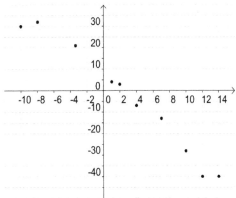

A. $y = -3.2x + 5.1$
B. $y = -2.4x + 10.3$
C. $y = -4.7x - 5.3$
D. $y = -8.2x + 3.4$

19. Using a regular deck of cards, what is the probability that Ana draws a jack, replaces the card, and then draws an ace card?

A. $\dfrac{1}{52}$
B. $\dfrac{3}{208}$
C. $\dfrac{1}{169}$
D. $\dfrac{17}{52}$

20. What is the expected value of drawing a ball from a bag when the balls are labeled 1–5?

A. 1.5
B. 2
C. 2.5
D. 3

Reading

Directions for questions 1–6

Read the statement or passage and then choose the best answer to the question. Answer the question based on what is stated or implied in the statement or passage.

1. A bird's feathers are extremely important, and when they clean and smooth them, it is known as preening. Birds in the wild preen their feathers on a regular basis. This is true of most captive birds as well, but not all. For example, some birds do not preen their feathers at all. This problem is most common in birds that are taken from their mothers at a very young age. Presumably, the absence of preening is due to the fact that they were never shown how to do it properly. A more common problem among captive birds is excessive preening. Some birds may pull out large numbers of their feathers or bite them down to the skin. It should be noted that wild birds never exhibit this kind of behavior. There are several suggestions about how the problem of excessive preening can be solved. Giving birds baths or placing them in an area that has more activity to prevent boredom are suggestions. However, these measures are often not sufficient to solve the problem.

The purpose of the passage is

    A. to give an overview of abnormal preening in birds.
    B. to compare captive birds to wild birds.
    C. to discuss why preening is important.
    D. to explain how excessive preening problems can be solved.

2. Hibernation in animals is an extremely fascinating phenomenon, one that biologists are not yet close to understanding fully. However, it is quite easy to understand why animals hibernate during the cold winter months. Usually, it is because their food is scarce during this time. Animals that are herbivores will find the winters extremely tough, because all of the vegetation will have died off by the time winter arrives. Hibernation is essentially a way of dealing with this food shortage. Animals like birds rely on seeds and small insects for sustenance. Obviously, these will also be quite scarce in the winter when the ground becomes covered and frozen. Many birds address their upcoming food shortage in a different way: they migrate to warmer areas where their sources of food will be plentiful.

The main reason animals hibernate is

    A. to travel to a warmer area where food will be more plentiful.
    B. to cut down on their food consumption during the winter months.
    C. to avoid the harsh weather that occurs during the winter months.
    D. to avoid food shortages that occur during the winter months.

3. At one time, the use of leeches to treat medical problems was quite common. If a person suffered from a snake bite or a bee sting, leeches were believed to be capable of removing the poison from the body if they were placed on top of the wound. They have also been used for bloodletting and to stop hemorrhages, although neither of these leech treatments would be considered acceptable by present-day physicians. Today, leeches are still used on a limited basis. Most often, leeches are used to drain blood from clogged veins. This results in little pain for the patient and also ensures the patient's blood will not clot while it is being drained.

The main purpose of the passage is

    A. to discuss the benefits of using leeches to treat blocked veins.
    B. to give an overview of how leeches have been used throughout history.
    C. to compare which uses of leeches are effective and which are not.
    D. to explain how leeches can be used to remove poison from the body.

4. When online file-sharing programs emerged, the music industry changed forever. Perhaps the first widely-used music file-sharing program was Napster. It allowed users to sign up to use the service at no charge. Then they could download music files from other users all over the world by simply typing in what song or album they wanted. Obviously, this was bad news for music artists and record labels because they weren't making any profits from downloaded music. Eventually, Napster was shut down. While it later reinvented itself as a paying service, other free music-sharing sites cropped up almost immediately. Even though several sites and individual users have been charged, there are still countless individuals who log onto these sites to obtain free music.

The main problem associated with peer file-sharing sites is

    A. it is hard to locate users to criminally charge them.
    B. there are too many of them currently in existence.
    C. they prevent artists and labels from earning money.
    D. they allow users to sign up for the service free of charge.

5. The so-called anti-aging industry is worth a staggering amount of money in North America. Women are sold all sorts of creams and ointments, and are promised that these will make them look younger over time. Unfortunately, these claims are entirely false. Lotions cannot penetrate to the inner layers of the skin where wrinkles typically form. Therefore, no over-the-counter creams are effective at erasing lines and wrinkles.

According to the author, the anti-aging industry

    A. targets its products at men and women equally.
    B. sells products that are highly effective.
    C. is still a relatively small industry.
    D. sells goods that do not do what they promise.

6. There is a clear formula that many students are taught when it comes to writing essays. The first is to develop an introduction, which outlines what will be discussed in the work. It also includes the thesis statement. Next come the supporting paragraphs. Each paragraph contains a topic sentence, supporting evidence, and finally a type of mini-conclusion that restates the point of the paragraph. Finally, the conclusion sums up the purpose of the paper and emphasizes that the thesis statement was proven.

After the topic sentence,

    A. a thesis statement is included.
    B. supporting evidence is presented.
    C. the conclusion is stated.
    D. the author outlines what will be discussed.

Questions 7–13 are based on the following passage:

For those of you not in the know in the world of invented languages, Esperanto was created in the late 1800s by a Mr. Ludwik Zamenhof of Poland. Zamenhof bemoaned the tension created by the literal inability of we humans to understand each other. In Esperanto he sought to provide a sort of neutral universal second language that privileged no one linguistically, confining us all only by our ability to be articulate, rather than by our familiarity with whatever language happens to be spoken at a given time.

While not the worldwide form of communication Zamenhof and other Esperantists have hoped for, Esperanto has grown impressively since its inception. Estimates of numbers of speakers range from 100,000 to 2 million, in 115 different countries; native speakers are estimated to number more than 1000. Many books have been translated and written in Esperanto, and two movies have been made in Esperanto—including *Incubus* starring William Shatner.

Reasons to Learn Esperanto:

It's Easy. A common argument for learning Esperanto is the ease of learning it: it's phonetic, grammatically regular, and a relatively small amount of words can be combined to create additional words—so you need to know less vocabulary to sound smart than you would in other languages. In addition to being able to be learned many times more quickly than anything else, studies show that learning Esperanto increases people's ability to learn a next language.

You Can Stay in People's Houses for Free. Some of these Esperanto speakers really put their money where their mouths are when it comes to supporting international understanding. There's a list Esperantists can put themselves on called the *Pasporta Serva*; speak Esperanto and, bang, you can stay with any of those fellow speakers for free. The list currently has around 1350 hosts in more than 85 countries. Does any other language come with that kind of perk?

I am Esperanto. A final reason to pin a green 5-pointed star (symbol of Esperanto) to your shirt and try and learn this crazy human-made language is to support the ideals that motivated Zamenhof to create the thing in the first place. He wanted to help usher in peace among cultures by giving people a place to be on equal footing, at least linguistically. In this time of tensions and divisions between pretty much every group you can find, that seems like a goal worth sharing. So, go ahead and call yourself Esperanto—it means, in Esperanto, "one who hopes."

7. According to the author, estimates of Esperanto speakers range from:
   A. 115 to 1000
   B. 100,000 to 2 million
   C. around 1350
   D. 85 to 1350

8. Which of the following is <u>not</u> a reason given by the author for learning Esperanto?
   A. Esperanto speakers can stay in some other speakers' homes for free
   B. It is phonetic
   C. It increases speakers' ability to learn a next language.
   D. It is spoken by most Europeans

9. According to the author, why did Zamenhof create Esperanto?
   A. To give people a place to be on equal footing and thereby help create peace among cultures
   B. To assist people in staying with other speakers around the world
   C. To combine what he thought were the best elements of Spanish and English in one language
   D. To eliminate political differences

10. According to the author, in how many countries is Esperanto spoken, and how many countries are represented on the *Pasporta Serva*?
   A. 115/ more than 1000
   B. 1350/more than 85
   C. 115/ more than 85
   D. 1350/ more than 1000

11. The author writes that "he sought to provide a sort of neutral universal second language that privileged no one linguistically..." Which of the following words is most synonymous with the word "privileged" as used in that sentence?
   A. benefited
   B. hindered
   C. advantage
   D. fortunate

12. What are Esperanto speakers called?
   A. Esperantos
   B. Esperantis
   C. Esperantists
   D. Esperantons

13. According to the author, what have studies shown about Esperanto?
   A. That it is spoken in 115 countries
   B. That learning it increases people's ability to learn a next language
   C. That it has grown impressively since its inception
   D. That it increases global understanding and communication

Questions 14–18 are based on the following passage:

It could be argued that all American war movies take as their governing paradigm that of the Western, and that we, as viewers, don't think critically enough about this fact. The virtuous hero in the white hat, the evil villain in the black hat, the community threatened by violence; these are the obvious elements of the paradigm. In addition, the hero is highly skilled at warfare, though reluctant to use it, the community is made up of morally upstanding citizens, and there is no place for violence in the community: the hero himself must leave the community he has saved once the battle is complete. This way of seeing the world has soaked into our storytelling of battle and conflict. It's hard to find a U.S.-made war movie that, for example, presents the enemy as complex and potentially fighting a legitimate cause, or that presents the hero (usually the U.S.) as anything other than supremely morally worthy. It is important to step back and think about the assumptions and frameworks that shape the stories we're exposed to; if we're careless and unquestioning, we absorb biases and worldviews with which we may not agree.

14. The primary purpose of this passage is to:

A. analyze an interesting feature of American cinema.
B. refute the Western paradigm.
C. suggest a way that war movies could be made better.
D. suggest that viewers think critically about underlying assumptions in the movies we watch.

15. The author claims that it is hard to find a U.S. made movie that "presents the hero (usually the U.S.) as anything other than supremely morally worthy." The author implies that she:

A. believes the hero should always appear to be morally worthy.
B. believes the hero should never appear to be morally worthy.
C. believes the hero should be more nuanced and less unconditionally good.
D. believes the hero is an uninteresting character.

16. Which of the following is <u>not</u> an example given by the author of an element of the Western paradigm:

A. Hero highly skilled at warfare
B. Evil villain in black hat
C. Everyone riding horses
D. Community made up of upstanding citizens

17. Which of the following is part of the worldview with which we may not agree but that the author implies we might absorb from these movies if we're careless and unquestioning:

A. Enemies of the U.S. do not ever fight for legitimate causes.
B. The community is morally bankrupt.
C. The U.S. is complex.
D. The U.S. is not skilled at warfare.

18. The author writes that "the virtuous hero in the white hat, the evil villain in the black hat, the community threatened by violence; these are the obvious elements of the paradigm." Which of the following words is most synonymous with the word "paradigm" as used in that sentence?

    A. story
    B. moral
    C. pattern
    D. example

Questions 19–21 are based on the following passage:

Black History Month is unnecessary. In a place and time in which we overwhelmingly elected an African American president, we can and should move to a post-racial approach to education. As *Detroit Free Press* columnist Rochelle Riley wrote in a February 1 column calling for an end to Black History Month, "I propose that, for the first time in American history, this country has reached a point where we can stop celebrating separately, stop learning separately, stop being American separately."

In addition to being unnecessary, the idea that African American history should be focused on in a given month suggests that it belongs in that month alone. It is important to instead incorporate African American history into what is taught every day as American history. It needs to be recreated as part of mainstream thought and not as an optional, often irrelevant, side note. We should focus efforts on pushing schools to diversify and broaden their curricula.

There are a number of other reasons to abolish it: first, it has become a shallow, commercial ritual that does not even succeed in its (limited and misguided) goal of focusing for one month on a sophisticated, intelligent appraisal of the contributions and experiences of African Americans throughout history. Second, there is a paternalistic flavor to the mandated bestowing of a month in which to study African American history that is overcome if we instead assert the need for a comprehensive curriculum. Third, the idea of Black History Month suggests that the knowledge imparted in that month is for African Americans only, rather than for all people.

19. The author's primary purpose is to:

    A. argue that Black History Month should not be so commercial.
    B. argue that Black History Month should be abolished.
    C. argue that Black History Month should be maintained.
    D. suggest that African American history should be taught in two months rather than just one.

20. It can be inferred that the term "post-racial" in the second sentence is an approach that:

    A. is not based on or organized around concepts of race.
    B. treats race as one factor, but not the most important, in determining an individual's experience.
    C. considers race after considering all other elements of a person's identity.
    D. prohibits discussion of race.

21. Which of the following does the author *not* give as a reason for abolishing Black History Month?

    A. It has become a shallow ritual.
    B. There is a paternalistic feel to being granted one month of focus.
    C. It suggests that the month's education is only for African Americans.
    D. No one learns anything during the month.

Questions 22–24 are based on the following passage:

> On April 30, 1803, the United States bought the Louisiana Territory from the French. Astounded and excited by the offer of a sale and all that it would mean, it took less than a month to hear the offer and determine to buy it for $15 million. Right away the United States had more than twice the amount of land as before, giving the country more of a chance to become powerful. They had to move in military and governmental power in this region, but even as this was happening, they had very little knowledge about the area. They did not even really know where the land boundaries were, nor did they have any idea how many people lived there. They needed to explore.

22. Based on the facts in the passage, what prediction could you make about the time immediately following the Louisiana Purchase?

    A. Explorers were already on the way to the region.
    B. The government wanted to become powerful.
    C. People in government would make sure explorers went to the region.
    D. Explorers would want to be paid for their work.

23. Why did the United States decide to buy the Louisiana Territory?

    A. They wanted to be more powerful.
    B. They wanted to find out the land boundaries.
    C. They wanted to know how many people lived there.
    D. They were astounded.

24. The author writes that the United States were "astounded and excited by the offer of a sale and all that it would mean…" Which of the following words is most synonymous with the word "astounded" as used in that sentence?

    A. eager
    B. confused
    C. greedy
    D. shocked

Writing

Landon's German teacher has assigned a research project on the culture and history of Germany. Landon has made a poster and written detailed captions for each set of pictures on the poster. He would like your help revising and improving the captions. After you read Landon's captions, answer questions 1–10.

Berlin

(1) For almost 30 years, the Berlin Wall divided Berlin in two. (2) On November 9, 1989, citizens from both sides of the city joined together to break down the wall and reunite the city. (3) Today, most of the wall has fallen, but a line of bricks snakes across the city, marking its old path.

(4) Although bombing during World War II destroyed most of Berlins buildings, the city has been rebuilt as a cultural center. (5) It has art, history, and science museums, as well as famous historical monuments.

(6) The majestic Brandenburg Gate was built in 1791 as a symbols of peace. (7) For many years, it was part of the Berlin Wall and reminded people of the divisions between east and west. (8) Today, the Brandenburg Gate symbolizes reunification and freedom. (9) Near the Brandenburg Gate is the German parliament building, called the Reichstag. (10) It was built in 1894 and was at the center of many important events in German politics. (11) Today, visitors can take an elevator up to the sparkling glass dome at the top of the Reichstag for a view of the city.

Ich bin ein Berliner

(12) On June 26, 1963, President John F. Kennedy visited West Berlin. (13) His visit took place a few years after the Berlin Wall was built and tensions between the United States and Communist East Germany were running high. (14) He gave an inspiring speech about freedom and democracy to the people of democratic West Berlin that ended with words of unity: "Ich bin ein Berliner." (15) He meant to say, "I am a citizen of Berlin," but his words really meant, "I am a doughnut." (16) A Berliner is a jelly doughnut popular in Germany. (17) The Germans in the audience appreciated President Kennedy's support, and cheered his message of freedom enthusiastically.

Cuisine

(18) German cuisine is known for its hearty, meat and potato dishes. (19) Families often enjoy a rich Sunday dinner of roast meat, potatoes, and cabbage. (20) A typical Sunday dinner might feature juicy Rinderrouladen, creamy Kartoffelpuree, and sweet Apfelkuchen. (21) In English, that would be stuffed beef rolls, mashed potatoes, and apple cake.

(22) Germans eat their heaviest meal of the day at lunchtime. (23) School cafeterias usually serve hearty stews and side dishes. (24) For dinner, families often eat thin slices of whole wheat bread with sausage, sliced meat, and cheese.

(25) Many Germans enjoy late afternoon Kaffee. (26) They visit a neighborhood café and relax with a cup of coffee and slice of creamy, rich cake. (27) Bakeries dot the

streets of German towns and cities, selling from small sandwiches to rich pastries. (28) The Amerikaner cookie, a bakery favorite, is a cakey sugar cookie topped with a vanilla and chocolate glaze. (29) The Americaner got its name because it looks like New York City's famous black and white cookies.

1. What could be deleted from sentence 2 without changing the meaning?

A. 1989
B. from both sides of the city
C. together
D. break down

2. What change should be made to sentence 4?

A. Change *Although* to *However*
B. Add a comma after *World War II*
C. Change *Berlins* to *Berlin's*
D. Change *has* to *had*

3. What change should be made to sentence 6?

A. Change *Gate* to *gate*
B. Change *was* to *were*
C. Insert a comma after *1791*
D. Change *symbols* to *symbol*

4. What change should be made to sentence 13?

A. Change *years* to *year's*
B. Add a comma after *built*
C. Add a comma after *States*
D. Change *were* to *was*

5. What change should be made to sentence 17?

A. Insert commas after *Germans* and *audience*
B. Change *appreciated* to *apreciated*
C. Delete the comma after *support*
D. Change *enthusiastically* to *enthusiaticaly*

6. What change should be made to sentence 18?

A. Change *German* to *Germany*
B. Change *is known* to *knew*
C. Change *its* to *it's*
D. Delete the comma after *hearty*

7. What is the most effective way to combine sentences 18 and 19?

A. German cuisine is known for its hearty meat and potato dishes but families often enjoy a rich Sunday dinner of roast meat, potatoes, and cabbage.
B. German cuisine is known for its hearty meat and potato dishes, but families often enjoy a rich Sunday dinner of roast meat, potatoes, and cabbage.
C. German cuisine is known for its hearty meat and potato dishes and families often enjoy a rich Sunday dinner of roast meat, potatoes and cabbage.
D. German cuisine is known for its hearty meat and potato dishes, and families often enjoy a rich Sunday dinner of roast meat, potatoes, and cabbage.

8. What is the most concise way to combine sentences 20 and 21 without confusing the reader?

    A. A typical Sunday dinner might feature juicy Rinderrouladen, which are stuffed beef rolls, creamy Kartoffelpuree, which are mashed potatoes, and sweet Apfelkuchen, which is apple cake.

    B. A typical Sunday dinner might feature juicy Rinderrouladen (stuffed beef rolls), creamy Kartoffelpuree (mashed potatoes), and sweet Apfelkuchen (apple cake).

    C. A typical Sunday dinner might feature juicy Rinderrouladen, creamy Kartoffelpuree, and sweet Apfelkuchen, and these are stuffed beef rolls, mashed potatoes, and apple cake.

    D. A typical Sunday dinner might feature juicy Rinderrouladen, creamy Kartoffelpuree, and sweet Apfelkuchen.

9. What change should be made to sentence 27?

    A. Insert *that* after *Bakeries*

    B. Insert *big* after *of*

    C. Insert *everything* after *selling*

    D. Insert *and* after *rich*

10. What change, if any, should be made to sentence 29?

    A. Change *Americaner* to *Amerikaner*

    B. Change *name* to *names*

    C. Change *City's* to *Cities*

    D. No change

For questions 11–15, select the best option for replacing the underlined portion of the sentence. The first option listed is always the same as the current version of the sentence.

11. <u>A key factor taken into account during city planning is</u> where major services and amenities will be located.

    A. A key factor taken into account during city planning is

    B. Key factors taken into account during city planning is

    C. A key factor taking into account during city planning is

    D. Key factors, taken into accounting during city planning are

12. <u>Jupiter with its numerous moons, and Great Red Spot,</u> has been studied extensively by astronomers.

    A. Jupiter with its numerous moons, and Great Red Spot,

    B. Jupiter with, its numerous moons and Great Red Spot,

    C. Jupiter, with its numerous moons and Great Red Spot,

    D. Jupiter with, its numerous moons, and Great Red Spot,

13. Many gardeners are now making their own backyard compost, <u>which is not only cheap, but also helps to cut down on landfill waste</u>.

    A. which is not only cheap, but also helps to cut down on landfill waste

    B. which is not only cheaper, but also cuts down on landfill's waste

    C. which is, not only cheap, but also, helps to cut down on landfill waste

    D. which is not only done cheaply, but is also cutting down on landfills wastes

14. The growth of the security industry can be large attributable to the fact that people are less trusting of others than they once were.

    A. The growth of the security industry can be large attributable
    B. The growing of the securities industry can be largely attributable
    C. The growth on the security industry can be large attributed
    D. The growth of the security industry can be largely attributed

15. Claude Monet was a famous painter who's well-known painting includes *San Giorgio Maggiore at Dusk* and *The Water Lily Pond*.

    A. who's well-known painting includes
    B. whose well-known painting including
    C. whose well-known paintings include
    D. who well-known paintings include

16. The Sugar Act was implemented in 1764 by England, and it required individuals residing in the colonies of the United States to pay a tax on sugar, as well as on dyes and other goods.

Rewrite, beginning with

Implemented in 1764 by England ...

The next words will be

    A. the Sugar Act
    B. it required individuals
    C. in the colonies
    D. on sugar

17. Oil spill, as the phrase suggests, refers to the accidental introduction of oil into environments, and even though it can refer to land spills, the phrase is usually understood to refer to spills in water.

Rewrite, beginning with

Even though the phrase "oil spill" is usually understood to refer to spills in water ...

The next words will be

    A. as the name suggests
    B. it can refer to land spills
    C. and the introduction of oil
    D. known as oil spills

18. Radar was first used in 1904, and at that time all it was capable of was determining whether objects were present, but now it can determine the size and shape of an object, among other things, as well.

Rewrite, beginning with

Although once only capable of determining the presence of objects, ...

The next words will be

    A. radar was first used
    B. among other things
    C. radar can now determine
    D. the size and shape of an object

19. Placebos are often used in drug studies, and the effectiveness of a drug can be determined by measuring whether people with illnesses or diseases show significantly more improvement when they are given a real drug rather than a placebo.

Rewrite, beginning with

By measuring whether people with illnesses show significantly more improvement when given a real drug, ...

The next words will be

    A. the effectiveness of a drug
    B. placebos can be used in drug studies
    C. it is rather than a placebo
    D. is often used in drug studies

20. Employees value salary and good benefits in a job, but many also consider having an enjoyable job important, so it's difficult to say what the majority of people value most in a career.

Rewrite, beginning with

While many people consider having an enjoyable job important, ...

The next words will be

    A. it's what the majority of people
    B. it's difficult to say
    C. salary and good benefits
    D. other employees value

Essay

Preemptive war has long been discussed as an option to prevent certain countries that are viewed as dangerous or unstable from acquiring nuclear weapons. Please write a multiple-paragraph persuasive essay (approximately 350–500 words) discussing whether you support or oppose the idea of a preemptive war for this purpose.

Answers and Explanations for Test #2

Math

1. A: In this probability problem, there are three independent events (the codes for each digit), each with ten possible outcomes (the numerals 0–9). Since the events are independent, the total number of possible outcomes equals the product of the possible outcomes for each of the three events, that is:

$$P = P_1 \cdot P_2 \cdot P_3 = 10 \cdot 10 \cdot 10 = 1000$$

This makes sense when you also relate the problem to a sequence, beginning with the combinations 0-0-0, 0-0-1, 0-0-2.... In ascending order, the last 3-digit combination would be 9-9-9. Although it may seem that there would be 999 possible combinations, you must include the initial combination, 0-0-0.

2. A: Setting the cost of shipping equal to the amount received gives us the equation $3{,}000 + 100x = 400x$. Subtract $100x$ from both sides to get $3{,}000 = 300x$, then divide both sides by 300 to see that $x = 10$.

3. D: Multiply both sides of the first equation by s to get $3 = 7s$, then divide both sides by 7 to find that $s = \frac{3}{7}$. Multiply both sides of the second equation by t to get $4 = 12t$, then divide both sides by 12 to find that $t = \frac{4}{12}$, which reduces to $\frac{1}{3}$. To find the difference, we must convert to a common denominator. In this case, the common denominator is 21. Multiplying by appropriate fractional equivalents of 1, we find that $\frac{3}{7}\left(\frac{3}{3}\right) = \frac{9}{21}$ and $\frac{1}{3}\left(\frac{7}{7}\right) = \frac{7}{21}$. Therefore, $s - t = \frac{9}{21} - \frac{7}{21} = \frac{2}{21}$.

4. B: The average of 7 and x is $7 + x$ divided by 2. The average of 9, 4, and x is $9 + 4 + x$ divided by 3. Thus, $\frac{7+x}{2} = \frac{13+x}{3}$. Cross-multiply: $3(7 + x) = 2(13 + x)$. This gives us $21 + 3x = 26 + 2x$. Solving for x yields $x = 26 - 21 = 5$.

5. D: There are 7 integers whose absolute value is less than 4: –3, –2, –1, 0, 1, 2, 3.

6. D: To solve $3(2x - 10) = x$, first expand the left side by multiplying through by 3: $6x - 30 = x$. Therefore, $5x = 30$, and $x = 6$.

7. C: This equation is asking you to multiply three algebraic expressions. When multiplying more than two expressions, multiply any two expressions (using the FOIL method), and then multiply the result by the third expression. Start by multiplying the first two:

$$(y + 1)(y + 2) = (y \cdot y) + (y \cdot 2) + (1 \cdot y) + (1 \cdot 2)$$

$$= y^2 + 2y + y + 2$$

$$= y^2 + 3y + 2$$

Then multiply the result by the third expression:

$$(y^2 + 3y + 2)(y + 3) = (y^2 + 3y + 2)(y) + (y^2 + 3y + 2)(3)$$

$$= (y^3 + 3y^2 + 2y) + (3y^2 + 9y + 6)$$

$$= y^3 + 3y^2 + 3y^2 + 9y + 2y + 6$$

$$= y^3 + 6y^2 + 11y + 6$$

8. D: Note that the first two terms and the last two terms of $x^3 - 3x^2 - 4x + 12$ are each divisible by $x - 3$. Thus:

$$x^3 - 3x^2 - 4x + 12 = x^2(x - 3) - 4(x - 3) = (x^2 - 4)(x - 3)$$

The term $x^2 - 4$ is a difference of squares, and since $x^2 - a^2 = (x + a)(x - a)$, we know $x^2 - 4 = (x + 2)(x - 2)$. The full factorization of $x^3 - 3x^2 - 4x + 12$ is therefore $(x + 2)(x - 2)(x - 3)$. Thus, all of the answer choices except $x + 3$ are factors.

Alternatively, instead of factoring the polynomial, we could have divided the polynomial $x^3 - 3x^2 - 4x + 12$ by the expression contained in each answer choice. Of those listed, only the expression x + 3 yields a nonzero remainder when divided into $x^3 - 3x^2 - 4x + 12$, so it is not a factor.

9. D:

$$\frac{x^6}{y^4} \cdot x^2 y^3 = x^6 y^{-4} \cdot x^2 y^3$$

$$= (x^6 x^2)(y^{-4} y^3)$$

$$= x^{6+2} y^{-4+3}$$

$$= x^8 y^{-1}$$

$$= \frac{x^8}{y}$$

10. C: A method commonly taught to multiply binomials is the "FOIL" method, an acronym for First, Outer, Inner, Last: multiply the first terms of each factor, then the outer terms, and so forth. Applied to $(x + 2)(x - 3)$, this yields:

$$(x)(x) + (x)(-3) + (2)(x) + (2)(-3) = x^2 - 3x + 2x - 6 = x^2 - x - 6$$

11. B: These are supplementary angles. That means that the two angles will add up to a total of 180°, which is the angle of a straight line. To solve, subtract as follows:

$$b = 180° - 120°$$

$$b = 60°$$

12. C: Rotational symmetry is defined as a figure that looks exactly the same after being rotated any amount. Answer choice C is the only example given that would stay the same if rotated. Trivial rotational symmetry involves not rotating the figure at all.

13. C: A straight line is 180°. Subtract to solve: 180° – 45° = 135°.

14. A: The sum of the measures of the three angles of any triangle is 180. The equation of the angles of this triangle can be written as $2x + 6x + 10x = 180$, or $18x = 180$. Therefore, $x = 10$. We multiply 2 by 10 to find that the measure of the smallest angle is 20°.

15. C: Since we are told that angle ABC is a right angle, we can use the Pythagorean Theorem to find AB:

$$AB^2 + BC^2 = AC^2$$

$$AB^2 + 5^2 = 13^2$$

$$AB^2 + 25 = 169$$

$$AB^2 = 144$$

$$AB = 12$$

Next, notice that AB is the same as the height of triangle ACD, perpendicular to base AD. Using the formula for the area of a triangle, $A = \frac{1}{2}bh$, we can calculate the area of triangle ACD:

$$A = \frac{1}{2}(8)(12) = 48$$

16. B: Using the formula for the perimeter of a rectangle, we know that $P = 2l + 2w$. Substituting the value given, we get $76 = 2l + 2w$ or $38 = l + w$. We can now solve for l: $38 - w = l$.

Using the formula for the area of a rectangle, we know that $A = l \cdot w$. Substituting the value given, we get $336 = l \cdot w$.

If we substitute the $38 - w$ we found in the first step for l, we get $(38 - w)w = 336$. Thus:

$$38w - w^2 = 336$$

$$0 = w^2 - 38w + 336$$

$$0 = (w - 14)(w - 24)$$

$$w = 14 \; or \; 24$$

The shorter of these two possibilities is 14. Answer choice A is incorrect because it is the difference of the two sides, 24 – 14. Answer choice C is incorrect because it is obtained by dividing the perimeter by 4. Answer choice D is incorrect because it is the length of the longer sides.

17. C: Group B is negatively skewed since there are more high scores. With more high scores, the mean for Group B will be higher.

18. A: The correlation is negative with a slope of approximately –3 and a y-intercept of approximately 5. Choices B and C can be eliminated, since a y-intercept of 10.3 is too high and a y-intercept of –5.3 is too low. Choice D may also be eliminated since the slope of –8.2 is too steep for the slope shown on the graph.

19. C: The probability of independent events, A and B, may be found using the formula, $P(A \text{ and } B) = P(A) \cdot P(B)$. Thus, the probability she draws a jack, replaces it, and then draws an ace card may be represented as $P(A \text{ and } B) = \frac{4}{52} \cdot \frac{4}{52}$, which simplifies to $P(A \text{ and } B) = \frac{1}{169}$.

20. D: The expected value is equal to the sum of the products of each ball value and its probability. Thus, the expected value is $\left(1 \cdot \frac{1}{5}\right) + \left(2 \cdot \frac{1}{5}\right) + \left(3 \cdot \frac{1}{5}\right) + \left(4 \cdot \frac{1}{5}\right) + \left(5 \cdot \frac{1}{5}\right)$, which equals $\frac{15}{5} = 3$.

Reading

1. A: Answer choice B is not correct, because wild birds are not discussed at length. Answer choice C is not really discussed, and D is touched upon only briefly. The passage focuses on lack of preening and excessive preening, which are both examples of abnormal preening behavior. The main purpose of the passage is to discuss abnormal preening in birds.

2. D: The passage states that "Animals that are herbivores will find the winters extremely tough, because all of the vegetation will have died off by the time winter arrives. Hibernation is essentially a way of dealing with this food shortage." Therefore, D is the correct answer. Answer choice A is the purpose of migration, and answer choices B and C are not mentioned.

3. B: Answer choices A, C, and D are all mentioned in the passage, but they are part of the overall purpose, which is to give an overview of how leeches have been used throughout history.

4. C: The passage states that "Obviously, this was bad news for music artists and record labels because they weren't making any profits from downloaded music." Therefore, answer choice C is the correct choice. None of the other choices are identified as problems associated with file-sharing sites.

5. D: The passage states, "Women are sold all sorts of creams and ointments, and are promised that these will make them look younger over time. Unfortunately, these claims are entirely false. Lotions cannot penetrate to the inner layers of the skin where wrinkles typically form." Therefore, these goods do not deliver what they promise. Answer choice A is not mentioned. Answer choices B and C are negated by the passage.

6. B: The topic sentence is placed at the beginning of each supporting paragraph. Supporting evidence is presented after the topic sentence in each supporting paragraph. The passage states, "Next come the supporting paragraphs. Each paragraph contains a topic sentence, supporting evidence, and finally a type of mini-conclusion that restates the point of the paragraph."

7. B: This is stated in the second paragraph. All the other answer choices are simply other numbers found in the article.

8. D: This is the only answer choice that is not given as a reason for learning Esperanto. The other choices are all listed in the third and fourth paragraphs.

9. A: Answer choice B is incorrect because, although it is a benefit the author claims comes from learning Esperanto, the author does not state that it is the reason the language was initially developed. Answer choices C and D are incorrect as they were never brought up in the text at all.

10. C: This information is given in the second and fourth paragraphs, respectively.

11. A: In the sentence quoted, the author uses *privileged* to mean benefited or favored. Answer choice B is not a meaning of the word privileged in any situation. Answer choice C does not fit grammatically in this form. Answer choice D is the meaning of the word privileged but is not appropriate in this context.

12. C: This word is used to refer to speakers of Esperanto in the second and fourth paragraphs.

13. B: The only answer option about which the author claimed a study had shown something is that Esperanto increased one's ability to learn a next language (Paragraph 3).

14. D: The point of the passage is to suggest that viewers should think more critically about assumptions and frameworks (such as the Western paradigm) that underlie the stories in movies they watch. Answer choice A describes the passage but does not explain its purpose. Answer choice B is incorrect because while the passage warns about the dangers of the Western paradigm, it does not necessarily refute it. Answer choice C is incorrect because the passage does not give suggestions for how to make war movies better, but merely to point out possible dangers.

15. C: The author recommends that viewers think more critically about frameworks that underlie stories in movies; she argues that, if not, viewers may absorb biases with which they do not agree. An example the author gives of that bias is that it is hard to find a movie in which the hero is not supremely morally worthy. The author's identification of this as a bias implies that she thinks it is not the right choice. Her comment about the difficulty of finding a portrayal of an enemy that allows the enemy to be complex suggests that the author believes that more nuance and less absolutes would be an improvement in the U.S. storytelling of war.

16. C: The author said nothing about horseback riding. The other answer choices are all mentioned in the passage.

17. A: The author suggests that these movies rarely show enemies of the U.S. to be complex or fighting for a legitimate cause. Answer choices B, C, and D are not at all implied by the article.

18. C: Based on the context clues of the sentence the reader can infer that these are elements of a *paradigm* or *pattern*. The passage is about stories (answer choice A), but the point of this statement is about a specific pattern that these stories follow. *Moral* (B) and *example* (D) do not fit the meaning.

19. B: The entire passage makes the argument that Black History Month should be abolished, offering various reasons why this is the best course of action. There is no reference to Black History Month being commercial (answer choice A). Choices C and D are directly in contradiction to the message of the passage.

20. A: The context of the sentence suggests that post-racial refers to an approach in which race is not a useful or positive organizing principle.

21. D: The author of the passage never suggests that people do not learn about African American history during Black History Month. Every other choice is part of the argument made.

22. C: People in government knew that the purchase would make the country more powerful, but the last sentence specifically states that they needed to explore. Answer choice C is the best prediction of what would occur next. Answer choices A and D infer too much, since you cannot assume any of these based on this passage given. Answer choice B is simply a statement that does not predict anything for the future.

23. A: While all of the answer choices are in the passage, only answer choice A answers the question of why this purchase was made. The desire to become more powerful is listed in the passage as one of the reasons that the United States decided to buy the land.

24. D: The reader can use the word *excited* to help infer that the best synonym for *astounded* is *shocked*. While they were eager (answer choice A), this goes more with *excited* than *astounded*. There is no evidence for *confused* (B) or *greedy* (C).

Writing

1. C: The word *together* reinforces the word *join* but is not required, so *joined together* is slightly redundant. Choice A is incorrect because the year is required to help the reader know when these events are taking place. Choice B is incorrect because the phrase *from both sides of the city* tells the reader that citizens from both East Berlin and West Berlin participated. Choice D is incorrect because *break down* makes it clear that the wall was torn down.

2. C: *Berlin* is a possessive that modifies *buildings* (the buildings are in Berlin). Choice A is incorrect because the word *however* is a conjunctive that should stand on its own and be followed by a comma. The word *although* correctly sets up the dependent clause that begins the sentence. Choice B is incorrect because *during World War II* is part of the subject and should not be separated by a comma from the verb *destroyed*. Choice D is incorrect because the verb should be the present tense *has*. Present tense is required because the city is still rebuilt.

3. D: The article *a* indicates that *symbol* should be singular rather than plural. Choice A is incorrect because *gate* is part of the proper noun *Brandenburg Gate*. Choice B is incorrect because the subject of the sentence is singular, which means the verb must be singular. Choice C is incorrect because a comma is not required after the year as it is essential to the sentence.

4. B: The conjunction *and* is separating two independent clauses. When this happens, a comma is required before the conjunction. Choice A is incorrect because the sentence is talking about *years*, which is plural rather than possessive. Choice C is incorrect because a comma is not needed before the *and* in a two-item series. Choice D is incorrect because the subject *tensions* is plural, which means the verb *were* needs to remain in the plural form.

5. C: The conjunction *and* connects an independent clause and a dependent clause. When these two types of clauses are connected, a comma should not be used. Choice A is not correct because the prepositional phrase *in the audience* is essential and should not be separated by commas. Choices B and D are incorrect because both words are spelled correctly in the original passage.

6. D: A comma should not separate an adjective from the noun it modifies. Choice A is incorrect because the word *German* is an adjective that is correctly modifying *cuisine*, while *Germany* is a noun. Choice B is incorrect because the sentence is constructed as a passive sentence and needs the passive verb form *is known*. Choice C is incorrect because *it's* means *it is* and is not a possessive.

7. D: A comma and the conjunction *and* are required to combine the sentences. *And* is a better choice than *but* because the second sentence is a continuation of the first rather than a contradiction. Choices A and B are incorrect because the conjunction *but* doesn't fit the meaning of the sentences. Choice A is also missing the required comma. Choice C uses the correct conjunction but is missing the comma.

8. B: This answer choice is correct because it uses parentheses to define the German words. This version is both the least wordy choice and also one that defines the unknown words. Choices A and

C also define the unknown words, but they are longer and wordier than choice B. Choice D is the most concise, but it does not define the German words, which might confuse a reader who does not understand German.

9. C: The word *everything* is the object of the clause and the sentence would be incomplete without it. Choice A is incorrect because the word *that* would turn the first part of the sentence into a complex subject rather than a subject and verb. Choice B is incorrect because *big* changes the meaning of the sentence. While the towns may be big, it is not required to fix the sentence. Choice D is incorrect because *rich* is an adjective that modifies the noun *pastries*; these words should not be separated by *and*.

10. A: *Amerikaner* should be spelled with a k," as can be seen in the previous sentence. Choice B is incorrect because *name* is referring to a singular subject. Choice C is incorrect because the word *City's* should be singular possessive, not plural. Choice D is incorrect because it misspells *Amerikaner* as *Americaner*.

11. A: Answer choice B is incorrect because the plural *key factors* and the singular *is* do not agree. The *taking* in choice C makes it incorrect. Choice D has a misplaced comma. Choice A makes sense and the singular *a key factor* and *is* agree with each other.

12. C: Choice C is the only choice that has correctly placed commas. The *numerous moons* and the *Great Red Spot* both refer to the planet Jupiter, which is maintained in answer choice C.

13. A: Answer choice B is incorrect because of the possessive "landfill's" without an article as well as the comparative word "cheaper" without anything with which to compare. Choice C has two unnecessary commas. Answer choice D is too wordy, and *landfills wastes* sounds quite awkward. Answer choice A is succinct, the comma is in the correct place, and it expresses the information is a clear way that is not awkward.

14. D: Answer choices A and C are incorrect because *large* is used in front of *attributable* and *attributed*. Both of these phrases are grammatically incorrect as *large* is an adjective rather than an adverb. Choice B describes *the growing of the securities industry*, which is quite awkward. D is the best choice because it refers to *the growth of the security industry* and uses the phrase *largely attributed*, which is grammatically correct.

15. C: The correct way to refer to a person, in this case Monet, is through the use of the pronoun *whose*, which eliminates A and D. Two paintings are identified, so the plural form must be used, eliminating choice B. Choice C uses *whose* and *paintings*, indicating there is more than one and making it the correct choice.

16. A: The Sugar Act is identified in the first sentence as something that was implemented in 1764 by England. Therefore, answer choice A is the best choice. Answer choice B does not indicate what was implemented. Answer choice C indicates where but not what was implemented, and choice D does not tell the reader what was implemented.

17. B: The phrase "even though" indicates a contrast. Answer choice A is more of an agreement than a contrast. Answer choice C is somewhat redundant, and choice D cannot logically follow the given phrase. Answer choice B provides a contrast because the given phrase talks about spills in water, while choice B talks about spills on land. It is also a logical choice because "it" in choice B refers to "the phrase" that is mentioned in the given wording.

18. C: Answer choice C is the only choice that provides a distinction between then and now. The given phrase says that radar was *once* used to determine the presence of objects, and C indicates that radar can *now* determine other things as well.

19. A: The word "by" indicates a cause/effect relationship. By measuring whether people respond significantly more favorably when given a real drug, something is being accomplished. Answer choices C and D do not imply this relationship. Answer choice B does not make logical sense in the context of the sentence, as placebos do not do the measuring. Answer choice A states "the effectiveness of a drug," which is a good choice because it could logically be followed with a phrase like "can be determined."

20. D: The word "while" is used to establish a contrast, making D the obvious choice. The given phrase speaks about *some people*, while D identifies *other employees*, which creates an effective contrast.

TSI Practice Test #3

Math

1. If $2x + 3y = 13$ and $4x - y = 5$, then $3x + 2y =$

   A. 3

   B. 6

   C. 12

   D. 24

2. If a movie reached the 90-minute mark 12 minutes ago, what minute mark had it reached m minutes ago?

   A. $m - 102$

   B. $m - 78$

   C. $102 - m$

   D. $78 - m$

3. If $x > 2500$, then the value of $\frac{x}{1-2x}$ is closest to

   A. $-\frac{50}{99}$

   B. $-\frac{1}{2}$

   C. $\frac{50}{99}$

   D. $\frac{1}{2}$

4. If $520 \div x = 40n$, then which of the following is equal to nx?

   A. 13

   B. 26

   C. 40

   D. $13x$

5. If $a - 16 = 8b + 6$, what does $a + 3$ equal?

   A. $b + 3$

   B. $8b + 19$

   C. $8b + 22$

   D. $8b + 25$

6. Janice weighs x pounds. Elaina weighs 23 pounds more than Janice. June weighs 14 pounds more than Janice. In terms of x, what is the sum of their weights minus 25 pounds?

   A. $3x + 37$

   B. $3x + 12$

   C. $x + 12$

   D. $3x - 25$

185

7. If $x > 2$, **then** $\left(\frac{x^2-5x+6}{x+1}\right) \cdot \left(\frac{x+1}{x-2}\right) =$

   A. $x + 1$

   B. $x - 3$

   C. $\frac{x^2+2x+1}{x-2}$

   D. $\frac{x^2-2x-3}{x+1}$

8. What is $\frac{x^3+2x}{x+3}$ **when** $x = -1$?

   A. $-\frac{3}{2}$

   B. $-\frac{2}{3}$

   C. $\frac{1}{2}$

   D. $\frac{3}{4}$

9. $(x + 6)(x - 6) =$

   A. $x^2 - 12x - 36$

   B. $x^2 + 12x - 36$

   C. $x^2 + 12x + 36$

   D. $x^2 - 36$

10. If $x + 2y = 3$ **and** $-x - 3y = 4$, **then** $x =$

   A. 1

   B. 5

   C. 7

   D. 17

Use the figure below to answer questions 11-13.

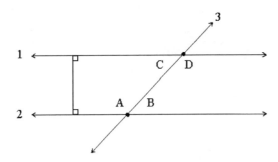

11. Which of the following statements is true about the figure above?

   A. Lines 1 and 2 are parallel.

   B. Lines 1 and 3 are parallel.

   C. Lines 1 and 2 intersect.

   D. Line 1 bisects line 3.

12. In the figure, which of the following is a pair of alternate interior angles?

    A. angle A and angle B
    B. angle A and angle C
    C. angle B and angle D
    D. angle A and angle D

13. In the figure, which of the following is obtuse?

    A. line 1
    B. line 3
    C. angle A
    D. angle B

14. Which of the following letters has a vertical line of symmetry?

    A. V
    B. K
    C. B
    D. L

15. In the following figure, if $\frac{b}{a+b+c} = \frac{3}{5}$, then $b =$

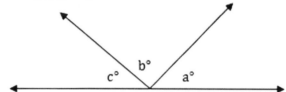

    A. 60
    B. 72
    C. 108
    D. 120

16. If the radius of circle O is one-quarter the diameter of circle P, what is the ratio of the circumference of circle O to the circumference of circle P?

    A. $\frac{1}{4}$
    B. $\frac{1}{2}$
    C. 2
    D. 4

17. Suppose two variables show a correlation of 0.9. Which of the following statements *best* describes the relationship?

    A. The variables show a strong correlation.
    B. The variables show some correlation, which is neither weak nor strong.
    C. The variables show a weak correlation.
    D. The variables show a perfect correlation.

18. Edward draws a card from a deck of cards, does not replace it, and then draws another card. What is the probability that he draws a heart and then a spade?

    A. $\dfrac{1}{16}$

    B. $\dfrac{1}{2}$

    C. $\dfrac{1}{17}$

    D. $\dfrac{13}{204}$

19. Suppose Ashley will receive a $6,000 scholarship if she chooses University A, a $4,500 scholarship if she chooses University B, and a $5,500 scholarship if she chooses University C. The probabilities that she will attend each university are equal. Which of the following best represents the expected value for the scholarship amount she will receive?

    A. $4,833

    B. $5,155

    C. $5,333

    D. $5,525

20. Nia spends $5 on a raffle ticket. If she is the winner, she will win $500. A total of 250 raffle tickets were sold. What is the expected value?

    A. −$2

    B. −$3

    C. −$5

    D. −$7

Reading

Directions for questions 1–6

Read the statement or passage and then choose the best answer to the question. Answer the question based on what is stated or implied in the statement or passage.

1. The importance of a comfortable workspace cannot be overstated. Developing a comfortable work environment is relatively simple for employers. Ergonomic chairs, large computer screens, personal desk space, and some level of privacy are all essential. This involves some expense, but not a great deal. Not surprisingly, employees are happier in this type of environment, but it is the employers who really benefit. Reduced sick time, higher levels of employee satisfaction, higher productivity, and more creativity have all been observed.

The main idea expressed in this passage is

    A. a comfortable workspace is not as important as people say.
    B. developing a comfortable workspace is easy.
    C. establishing a comfortable workspace is not expensive.
    D. employers benefit greatly when they provide comfortable workspaces.

2. Planning weddings is tough. One important part of the planning process is choosing bridesmaid dresses. Although there used to be a lot of rules when it came to picking out a color, many of them are not observed any more. However, one that is still observed is that the bridesmaids should not wear the same color as the bride. The most popular colors for bridesmaid dresses in recent years have been white and black.

It can be concluded that

    A. picking dresses is the hardest part of planning a wedding.
    B. many brides are choosing to wear colors other than white.
    C. most bridesmaids are allowed to choose their own dress.
    D. bridesmaids were not traditionally allowed to wear black.

3. Those so-called green fuels may not be as environmentally friendly as once thought. For example, producing natural gas is a much more labor-intensive process than producing an equal amount of conventional gasoline. Also, producing natural gas involves burning fossil fuels. Transporting natural gas also involves burning fossil fuels.

A weakness of green fuels is that

    A. they are not as abundant as conventional fuel.
    B. they require a lot more work to produce.
    C. burning them releases fossil fuels.
    D. they must be transported greater distances.

4. The media has done a lot to promote racism in North America. For example, it was found that the majority of crimes discussed on the nightly news featured African American suspects. However, when the total number of crimes committed in North America was examined, it was found that white people were also suspects 50% of the time.

If the above information were true, it could be concluded that

    A. there are more white criminals than African American criminals.
    B. most people believe that African Americans commit more crimes.
    C. many crimes committed by white people are not discussed on the news.
    D. the total number of crimes committed has decreased in the last several years.

5. Many people feel that the use of stem cells in research is unethical. However, they fail to realize that such research could lead to cures for some of the world's most troubling diseases. Diseases like Parkinson's and MS could possibly be cured through the use of stem cells, and those with spinal cord injuries could possibly walk again. Therefore, it is entirely ethical to engage in stem cell research aimed at easing the suffering of those who have life-altering conditions.

The main purpose of the passage is

    A. to discuss why people believe stem cell research is unethical.
    B. to discuss the possible benefits of stem cell research.
    C. to identify diseases that have been cured through stem cell research.
    D. to argue that not conducting stem cell research is unethical.

6. Many people do not know the difference between precision and accuracy. While accuracy means that something is correct, precision simply means that you are able to duplicate results and that they are consistent. For example, if a glass of liquid was 100 degrees, an accurate measurement would be one that was close to this temperature. However, if you measured the temperature five times, and came up with a measurement of exactly 50 degrees each time, your measurement would be extremely precise, but not accurate.

The term *accurate results* refers to

    A. results that are correct.
    B. results that are consistent.
    C. results that can be duplicated.
    D. results that are measurable.

Questions 7–11 are based on the following passage:

Who Was This Man?

"You have a visitor, you see," said Monsieur Defarge.

"What did you say?"

"Here is a visitor."

The shoemaker looked up as before, but without removing a hand from his work.

"Come!" said Defarge. "Here is monsieur, who knows a well-made shoe when he sees one. Show him that shoe you are working at. Take it, monsieur."

Mr. Lorry took it in his hand.

"Tell monsieur what kind of shoe it is, and the maker's name."

There was a longer pause than usual, before the shoemaker replied: "I forget what it was you asked me. What did you say?"

"I said, couldn't you describe the kind of shoe, for monsieur's information?"

"It is a lady's shoe. It is a young lady's walking-shoe. It is in the present mode. I never saw the mode. I have had a pattern in my hand."

He glanced at the shoe with some little passing touch of pride.

"And the maker's name?" said Defarge.

Now that he had no work to hold, he laid the knuckles of the right hand in the hollow of the left, and then the knuckles of the left hand in the hollow of the right, and then passed a hand across his bearded chin, and so on in regular changes, without a moment's intermission. The task of recalling him from the vagrancy into which he always sank when he had spoken, was like recalling some very weak person from a swoon, or endeavouring, in the hope of some disclosure, to stay the spirit of a fast-dying man.

"Did you ask me for my name?"

"Assuredly I did."

"One Hundred and Five, North Tower."

"Is that all?"

"One Hundred and Five, North Tower."

With a weary sound that was not a sigh, nor a groan, he bent to work again, until the silence was again broken.

"You are not a shoemaker by trade?" said Mr. Lorry, looking steadfastly at him.

His haggard eyes turned to Defarge as if he would have transferred the question to him: but as no help came from that quarter, they turned back on the questioner when they had sought the ground.

"I am not a shoemaker by trade? No, I was not a shoemaker by trade. I-I learnt it here. I taught myself. I asked leave to..."

He lapsed away, even for minutes, ringing those measured changes on his hands the whole time. His eyes came slowly back, at last, to the face from which they had wandered; when they rested on it, he started, and resumed, in the manner of a sleeper that moment awake, reverting to a subject of last night.

"I asked leave to teach myself, and I got it with much difficulty after a long while, and I have made shoes ever since."

—Excerpted from *A Tale of Two Cities* by Charles Dickens

7. Monsieur Defarge and Mr. Lorry are visiting

    A. an art gallery in Paris.
    B. a man who has been ill.
    C. a member of the British government.
    D. a doctor making hospital calls.

8. Based on the name he gives, the reader can infer that the man

    A. has spent time in a prison tower.
    B. has been traveling throughout Europe.
    C. has been homeless a long time.
    D. first left home as a young man.

9. Which of the following is NOT a sign of the man's mental condition?

    A. his inability to complete a thought
    B. his identifying himself by a location instead of a name
    C. the repetitive motion of his hands
    D. his cheerful laughter

10. The man had asked to learn the trade of

    A. woodcarving.
    B. glassblowing.
    C. shoemaking.
    D. dressmaking.

11. What can the reader infer about the identity of Monsieur Defarge?

    A. He is the unkind jailer at the prison.
    B. He is a friend keeping the man safe.
    C. He is the man's loving son or grandson.
    D. He is a cruel doctor in a hospital.

Questions 12–15 are based on the following passages:

Passage 1:

Fairy tales, fictional stories that involve magical occurrences and imaginary creatures like trolls, elves, giants, and talking animals, are found in similar forms throughout the world. This occurs when a story with an origin in a particular location spreads geographically to, over time, far-flung lands. All variations of the same story must logically come from a single source. As language, ideas, and goods travel from place to place through the movement of peoples, stories that catch human imagination travel as well through human retelling.

Passage 2:

Fairy tales capture basic, fundamental human desires and fears. They represent the most essential form of fictionalized human experience: the bad characters are pure evil, the good characters are pure good, the romance of royalty (and of commoners becoming royalty) is celebrated, etc. Given the nature of the fairy tale genre, it is not surprising that many different cultures come up with similar versions of the same essential story.

12. On what point would the authors of both passages agree?

A. Fairy tales share a common origin.
B. The same fairy tale may develop independently in a number of different cultures.
C. There are often common elements in fairy tales from different cultures.
D. Fairy tales capture basic human fears.

13. What does the "nature of the fairy tale genre" refer to in Passage 2?

A. The representation of basic human experience
B. Good characters being pure good and bad characters being pure evil
C. Different cultures coming up with similar versions of the same story
D. Commoners becoming royalty

14. Which of the following is not an example of something the author of Passage 1 claims travels from place to place through human movement?

A. Fairy tales
B. Language
C. Ideas
D. Foods

15. Which of the following is not an example of something that the author of Passage 1 states might be found in a fairy tale?

A. Trolls
B. Witches
C. Talking animals
D. Giants

Questions 16–21 are based on the following passage:

Peanut allergy is the most prevalent food allergy in the United States, affecting around one and a half million people, and it is potentially on the rise in children in the United States. While thought to be the most common cause of food-related death, deaths from food allergies are very rare. The allergy typically begins at a very young age and remains present for life for most people. Approximately one-fifth to one-quarter of children with a peanut allergy, however, outgrow it. Treatment involves careful avoidance of peanuts or any food that may contain peanut pieces or oils. For some sufferers, exposure to even the smallest amount of peanut product can trigger a serious reaction.

Symptoms of peanut allergy can include skin reactions, itching around the mouth, digestive problems, shortness of breath, and a runny or stuffy nose. The most severe peanut allergies can result in anaphylaxis, which requires immediate treatment with epinephrine. Up to one-third of people with peanut allergies have severe reactions. Without treatment, anaphylactic shock can result in death due to obstruction of the airway, or heart failure. Signs of anaphylaxis include constriction of airways and difficulty breathing, shock, a rapid pulse, and dizziness or lightheadedness.

As of yet, there is no treatment to prevent or cure allergic reactions to peanuts. In May of 2008, however, Duke University Medical Center food allergy experts announced that they expect to offer a treatment for peanut allergies within five years.

Scientists do not know for sure why peanut proteins induce allergic reactions, nor do they know why some people develop peanut allergies while others do not. There is a strong genetic component to allergies: if one of a child's parents has an allergy, the child has an almost 50% chance of developing an allergy. If both parents have an allergy, the odds increase to about 70%.

Someone suffering from a peanut allergy needs to be cautious about the foods he or she eats and the products he or she puts on his or her skin. Common foods that should be checked for peanut content are ground nuts, cereals, granola, grain breads, energy bars, and salad dressings. Store prepared cookies, pastries, and frozen desserts like ice cream can also contain peanuts. Additionally, many cuisines use peanuts in cooking—watch for peanut content in African, Chinese, Indonesian, Mexican, Thai, and Vietnamese dishes.

Parents of children with peanut allergies should notify key people (child care providers, school personnel, etc.) that their child has a peanut allergy, explain peanut allergy symptoms to them, make sure that the child's epinephrine auto injector is always available, write an action plan of care for when their child has an allergic reaction to peanuts, have their child wear a medical alert bracelet or necklace, and discourage their child from sharing foods.

16. According to the passage, approximately what percentage of people with peanut allergies have severe reactions?

- A. Up to 11%
- B. Up to 22%
- C. Up to 33%
- D. Up to 44%

17. By what date do Duke University allergy experts expect to offer a treatment for peanut allergies?

- A. 2008
- B. 2009
- C. 2010
- D. 2013

18. Which of the following is not a type of cuisine the passage suggests often contains peanuts?

- A. African
- B. Italian
- C. Vietnamese
- D. Mexican

19. Which allergy does the article state is thought to be the most common cause of food-related death?

- A. Peanut
- B. Tree nut
- C. Bee sting
- D. Poison oak

20. It can be inferred from the passage that children with peanut allergies should be discouraged from sharing food because:

    A. Peanut allergies can be contagious.

    B. People suffering from peanut allergies are more susceptible to bad hygiene.

    C. Many foods contain peanut content and it is important to be very careful when you don't know what you're eating.

    D. Scientists don't know why some people develop peanut allergies.

21. Which of the following does the passage not state is a sign of anaphylaxis?

    A. running or stuffy nose

    B. shock

    C. a rapid pulse

    D. constriction of airways

Questions 22–24 refer to the following passage:

"His pride," said Miss Lucas, "does not offend me so much as pride often does, because there is an excuse for it. One cannot wonder that so very fine a young man, with family, fortune, everything in his favour, should think highly of himself. If I may so express it, he has a *right* to be proud."

"That is very true," replied Elizabeth, "and I could easily forgive his pride, if he had not mortified mine."

"Pride," observed Mary, who piqued herself upon the solidity of her reflections, "is a very common failing I believe. By all that I have ever read, I am convinced that it is very common indeed, that human nature is particularly prone to it, and that there are very few of us who do not cherish a feeling of self-complacency on the score of some quality or other, real or imaginary. Vanity and pride are different things, though the words are often used synonymously. A person may be proud without being vain. Pride relates more to our opinion of ourselves, vanity to what we would have others think of us."

22. Why doesn't the gentleman's pride offend Miss Lucas?

    A. She admires his vanity.

    B. He is handsome and rich.

    C. It is human nature to be proud.

    D. He is poor and homeless.

23. Which sentence best states the theme of this passage?

    A. Pride and vanity are offensive.

    B. Fame and fortune can make a person proud.

    C. Every person is proud in one way or another.

    D. Pride can bring you fortune.

24. According to the passage, what is the difference between pride and vanity?

    A. Pride relates to a person's abilities; vanity relates to a person's looks.

    B. Men are proud; women are vain.

    C. Pride and vanity are synonymous.

    D. Pride is what you think of yourself; vanity is what you want others to think of you.

Writing

Margot's high school may be adopting a dress code. Margot is against this idea and has written an article for her school newspaper arguing against the dress code. Margot wrote the article and would like your help revising and improving the essay. After you read the article, answer questions 1–10.

(1) Mrs. Conwer, the Jackson High principal, announced last week that Jackson High is considering a student dress code. (2) She is saying that some of the outfits students are wearing to school is being distracting and inappropriate. (3) For example, she says that some of the boys like to wear their pants too low and that some of the girls like to wear very short skirts. (4) I don't agree that there is a problem. (5) Furthermore, I think there are several reasons why it is important that Jackson High does not have a dress code.

(6) When people are in high school, they are teenagers. (7) Being a teenager means that your at a time in life when you are exploring new things and learning about yourself. (8) Many teens also like to express themselves. (9) For example, some people I know keep a blog where they write about things that are important to them. (10) Other people play in a band and can express themselves through music. (11) A lot of teens express themselves through fashion. (12) Since many teens start earning their own money, they can buy their own clothes and choose the fashions that they want. (13) If Jackson High adopts a dress code the students won't be able to express themselves. (14) Self expression is important and are often taught at Jackson High. (15) Ms. Riley, my dance teacher, tells me to express myself through dance. (16) Mr. Hunter, my English teacher, tells me to express myself through writing. (17) Taking away expression through fashion is hypocritical because it goes against what is taught in many classes.

(18) A dress code at Jackson High will never please everyone. (19) Who gets to decide what is appropriate and what is not? (20) What happens if the students disagree with the code? (21) In school, we learn about respecting different opinions and making compromises. (22) However, if Mrs. Conwer or just a couple of teacher's choose the dress code, they will be ignoring the students. (23) Jackson High should stop ignoring the lessons that we learn in our classes every day.

(24) How can Jackson High make sure that students dress appropriately if it doesn't have a dress code? (25) That's what some teachers have said to me. (26) I think the answer is obvious. (27) Teach us, the students, how people are supposed to dress in the real world when they have jobs. (28) Explain why certain choices might be inappropriate. (29) Than let us make our own decisions. (30) That's what we learn in all our classes, and that's how it should be for the dress code.

1. What is the most effective way to rewrite sentence 2?

A. Some of the outfits students wear to school, she is saying, are distracting and not appropriate.

B. The outfits are distracting and inappropriate, she says, that students wear to school.

C. She says that some of the outfits that students wear to school are distracting and inappropriate.

D. She says that it is distracting and inappropriate that students wear outfits to school.

2. What change, if any, should be made to sentence 7?
- A. Change *your* to *you're*
- B. Insert a comma before *and*
- C. Change *about* to *on*
- D. No change

3. What is the most effective way to combine sentences 11 and 12?
- A. A lot of teens express themselves through fashion, and since many teens start earning their own money, they can buy their own clothes and choose the fashions that they want.
- B. A lot of teens express themselves through fashion and since many teens start earning their own money, they can buy their own clothes and choose the fashions that they want.
- C. A lot of teens express themselves through fashion, but since many teens start earning their own money, they can buy their own clothes and choose the fashions that they want.
- D. A lot of teens express themselves through fashion but since many teens start earning their own money, they can buy their own clothes and choose the fashions that they want.

4. What change should be made to sentence 13?
- A. Change *if* to *because*
- B. Add a comma after *code*
- C. Change *students* to *students'*
- D. Change *themselves* to *theirselves*

5. What change should be made in sentence 14?
- A. Change *expression* to *expresion*
- B. Insert a comma before *and*
- C. Delete *are*
- D. Insert *the* after *at*

6. What transition should be added to the beginning of sentence 18?
- A. However
- B. Furthermore
- C. First of all
- D. Therefore

7. What change should be made to sentence 22?
- A. Change *however* to *nevertheless*
- B. Change *a couple* to *several*
- C. Change *teacher's* to *teachers*
- D. Delete the comma after *code*

8. What change should be made in sentence 27?
- A. Delete the comma after *us*
- B. Change *suppossed* to *supposed*
- C. Change *real world* to *real-world*
- D. Change *jobs* to *job's*

9. What change, if any, should be made to sentence 28?

    A. Change *explain* to *explaining*
    B. Insert *not* after *might*
    C. Change *inappropriate* to *inapropriate*
    D. No change

10. What change should be made in sentence 29?

    A. Change *than* to *then*
    B. Insert *you* before *let*
    C. Insert *to* after *us*
    D. Change *decisions* to *descisions*

For questions 11–15, select the best option for replacing the underlined portion of the sentence. The first option listed is always the same as the current version of the sentence.

11. If he stops to consider the ramifications of this decision, <u>it is probable that he will rethink his original decision a while longer</u>.

    A. it is probable that he will rethink his original decision a while longer.
    B. he will rethink his original decision over again.
    C. he will probably rethink his original decision.
    D. he will most likely rethink his original decision for a bit.

12. When you get <u>older," she said "you will no doubt</u> understand what I mean."

    A. older," she said "you will no doubt
    B. older" she said "you will no doubt
    C. older," she said, "you will no doubt
    D. older," she said "you will not

13. <u>Dr. Anderson strolled past the nurses examining a bottle of pills.</u>

    A. Dr. Anderson strolled past the nurses examining a bottle of pills.
    B. Dr. Anderson strolled past the nurses to examining a bottle of pills.
    C. Examining a bottle of pills Dr. Anderson strolled past the nurses.
    D. Examining a bottle of pills, Dr. Anderson strolled past the nurses.

14. Karl and Henry <u>raced to the reservoir, climbed the ladder, and then they dove into</u> the cool water.

    A. raced to the reservoir, climbed the ladder, and then they dove into
    B. first raced to the reservoir, climbed the ladder, and then they dove into
    C. raced to the reservoir, they climbed the ladder, and then they dove into
    D. raced to the reservoir, climbed the ladder, and dove into

15. Did either <u>Tracy or Vanessa realize that her decision would be</u> so momentous?

    A. Tracy or Vanessa realize that her decision would be
    B. Tracy or Vanessa realize that each of their decision was
    C. Tracy or Vanessa realize that her or her decision would be
    D. Tracy or Vanessa realize that their decision would be

16. The Burmese python is a large species of snake that is native to parts of southern Asia, although the snake has recently begun infesting the Florida Everglades and causing environmental concerns by devouring endangered species.

Rewrite the sentence, beginning with the phrase,

<u>The Burmese python has recently caused environmental concerns in the Florida Everglades</u>...

The words that follow will be:

    A. because it is devouring endangered species in Florida
    B. where it has made a home for itself away from its origins in southern Asia
    C. by leaving its native home of southern Asia with an infestation of its natural prey
    D. and is altering the delicate balance of species in that area

17. In the wild, the Burmese python typically grows to around twelve feet in length, but in captivity the snakes can often grow much longer than that, to upwards of fifteen or twenty feet in length.

Rewrite the sentence, beginning with the phrase,

<u>Burmese pythons in captivity can grow to be as long as fifteen or twenty feet</u>...

The words that follow will be:

    A. as a result of the controlled environment that allows them to eat more
    B. while it is typically shorter in the wild
    C. but in the wild are shorter and may only be twelve feet long
    D. which is much longer than a python in the wild grows to be

18. Florida biologists and environmentalists blame the exotic animals industry for the snake's introduction into the Everglades, because many snake owners are unable or unwilling to continue taking care of the creatures once they grow too large and become too expensive, abandoning them.

Rewrite the sentence, beginning with the phrase,

<u>The Burmese python can grow large and become too expensive for snake owners to maintain</u>...

The words that follow will be:

    A. and Florida biologists and environmentalists blame the exotic animals industry
    B. so the python has been introduced into the Everglades
    C. leaving the exotic animals industry at risk in the United States
    D. resulting in abandoned snakes that have infested the Everglades

19. Lawmakers called for action against owning Burmese pythons after a pet python got out of its cage in a Florida home and killed a young child while she was sleeping, a situation that left responsible snake owners objecting and claiming that this was an isolated event.

Rewrite the sentence, beginning with the phrase,

<u>Responsible Burmese python owners have claimed that the death of a young child in Florida after a python attack was an isolated event</u>...

The words that follow will be:

    A. but lawmakers have called for action against owning the pythons
    B. because the python accidentally got out of its cage and attacked the child
    C. that does not reflect accurately on conscientious snake owners
    D. resulting in angry lawmakers who called for a prohibition of Burmese pythons

20. Biologists were initially concerned that the Burmese python could spread throughout much of the United States, due to its ability to adapt to its environment, but recent evidence suggests that the snake is content to remain within the Everglades.

Rewrite the sentence, beginning with the phrase,

<u>**Recent evidence suggests that the Burmese python is content to remain within the Everglades**</u>...

The words that follow will be:

    A. due to its ability to adapt to its environment
    B. and comes as a surprise to biologists who believed the snake would spread outside Florida
    C. despite concerns that the snake could spread throughout much of the United States
    D. because it is unable to adapt to cooler environments outside of south Florida

Essay

NSA wiretapping and spying policies have been a topic of interest lately, with much discussion taking place over the need for security as it relates to the right to individual privacy. Please write a multiple-paragraph persuasive essay (approximately 350–500 words) discussing whether you support or oppose government collection of private data for the purpose of national security.

Answers and Explanations for Test #3

Math

1. C: Solving for y in the second equation gives $y = 4x - 5$. If we plug this into the first equation, we get $2x + 3(4x - 5) = 13$, which expands to $2x + 12x - 15 = 13$. Solving for this equation gives us $14x = 28$, or $x = 2$. Then, plug the value of x into either equation to solve for y: $y = 3$. Therefore, $3x + 2y = 3(2) + 2(3) = 12$.

2. C: The movie is now at the $90 + 12 = 102$-minute mark. Therefore, m minutes ago, it had reached the $102 - m$ mark. Answer choice A is incorrect because it reverses the constant and variable. Answer choice B is incorrect because it subtracts 12 from 90 instead of adding and reverses constant and variable. Answer choice D is incorrect because it subtracts 12 from 90 instead of adding.

3. B: For all large values of x, the value of $\frac{x}{1-2x}$ will be very close to the value of $\frac{x}{-2x} = -\frac{1}{2}$. Answer choice A is less than $-1/2$, so it is not the closest. Answer choices C and D are incorrect because they are positive rather than negative.

4. A: If $520 \div x = 40n$, then

$$40nx = 520$$

$$nx = 13$$

5. D: Isolate a: $a = 8b + 6 + 16$. Thus, $a = 8b + 22$. Next add 3 to both side of the equation:

$$a + 3 = 8b + 22 + 3 = 8b + 25$$

6. B: Translate this word problem into a mathematical equation. Let Janice's weight = x. Let Elaina's weight = x + 23. Let June's weight = x + 14. Add their weights together and subtract 25 pounds:

$$= x + x + 23 + x + 14 - 25$$

$$= 3x + 37 - 25$$

$$= 3x + 12$$

7. B: $\left(\frac{x^2-5x+6}{x+1}\right) \cdot \left(\frac{x+1}{x-2}\right) = \frac{(x^2-5x+6)\cdot(x+1)}{(x+1)\cdot(x-2)}$. Before carrying out the multiplication of the polynomials, notice that there is a factor of $x + 1$ in both the numerator and denominator, so the expression reduces to $\frac{x^2-5x+6}{x-2}$. We can simplify further by factoring the numerator. One way to factor a quadratic expression with a leading coefficient of 1 is to look for two numbers that add to the coefficient of x (in this case -5) and multiply to the constant term (in this case 6). Two such numbers are -2 and -3: $(-2) + (-3) = -5$ and $(-2) \cdot (-3) = 6$. So $x^2 - 5x + 6 = (x - 2)(x - 3)$. That means $\frac{x^2-5x+6}{x-2} = \frac{(x-2)(x-3)}{x-2}$. The $x - 2$ in the numerator and denominator can cancel, so we are left with just $x - 3$. (Note that if $x = -1$ or $x = 2$, the obtained simplified expression would not be true: either value of x would result in a denominator of zero in the original expression, so the whole expression would be undefined. Therefore, it is necessary to state that these values of x are excluded from the domain. For a domain of $x > 2$, both $x = -1$ and $x = 2$ would be excluded.)

8. A: To evaluate $\frac{x^3+2x}{x+3}$ at $= -1$, substitute in -1 for x in the expression: $\frac{(-1)^3+2(-1)}{(-1)+3} = \frac{(-1)+(-2)}{2} = \frac{-3}{2} = -\frac{3}{2}$.

9. D: Use the rule that $(a + b)(a - b) = a^2 - b^2$ or multiply the bionomials using the FOIL method: multiply together the First term of each factor, then the Outer, then the Inner, then the Last, and add the products together.

$$(x + 6)(x - 6) = x \cdot x + x \cdot (-6) + 6 \cdot x + 6 \cdot (-6) = x^2 - 6x + 6x - 36 = x^2 - 36.$$

10. D: There are several ways to solve a system of equations like this. Likely the simplest is by elimination. We add the two equations together to cancel out the x-values: $(x + 2y = 3) + (-x - 3y = 4) \Rightarrow x + 2y - x - 3y = 3 + 4 \Rightarrow -y = 7 \Rightarrow y = -7$. Now, putting that value for y back into one of the original equations, we get $x + 2(-7) = 3 \Rightarrow x - 14 = 3 \Rightarrow x = 17$.

11. A: Lines 1 and 2 are parallel because they are both perpendicular to the same line. If the parallel lines continued on into infinity, they would never cross, as lines 1 and 3 do (answer choice B). To *intersect* (answer choice C) means that the lines cross. *Bisect* (answer choice D) means that a line cuts another line or figure in two equal halves.

12. D: The degree measurement for alternate interior angles is exactly the same. In the figure, there are two pairs of alternate interior angles: B and C; A and D.

13. C: An obtuse angle is one that is more than 90° (a right angle) and less than 180°. Answer choices A and B are not angles. Answer choice D (angle B) is an acute angle since it is smaller than a 90° angle.

14. A: If you draw a vertical line down the center of the letter V, the two sides will be symmetrical. None of the other letters in the answer choices are symmetrical when thus divided.

15. C: The angles a, b, and c form a straight line, so $a + b + c = 180$. Substituting 180 for $a + b + c$ in the proportion, we have:

$$\frac{b}{180} = \frac{3}{5}$$

By cross-multiplying, we can solve for b: $5b = 3(180)$ or $b = 108$. Answer choice A is incorrect because it is found by dividing 180 by 3. Answer choice B is incorrect because it is found by subtracting $180 - b$. Answer choice D is incorrect because it is found by subtracting $180 - (180/3)$.

16. B: The radius of circle O is one-fourth the diameter of circle P. The diameter is twice the radius, or $d = 2r$. This means that the radius of circle O is half of the radius of circle P, or $r_O = \frac{1}{4}(2r_P) = \frac{1}{2}r_P$. The circumference of circle $P = 2\pi r_P$. The circumference of circle $O = 2\pi r_O = 2\pi(\frac{1}{2}r_P) = \pi r_P$. Since circle P's circumference is twice that of circle O, the ratio of circle O's circumference to circle P's is $\frac{\pi r_P}{2\pi r_P} = \frac{1}{2}$. Answer choice A is incorrect because it doesn't convert the diameter to the radius. Answer choice C is incorrect because it finds the ratio of circle P's circumference to circle O's, rather than vice versa. Answer choice D is incorrect because it doesn't convert the diameter to the radius and it finds the ratio of circle P's circumference to circle O's rather than vice versa.

17. A: A correlation of 0.9 is a strong correlation because it is close to 1. Recall that the closer a correlation coefficient is to −1 or 1, the stronger the correlation. A correlation of −1 or 1 is perfect.

18. D: Since he does not replace the first card, the events are dependent. The sample space will decrease by 1 for the second draw because there will be one less card to choose from. Thus, the probability may be written as $P(A \text{ and } B) = \frac{13}{52} \cdot \frac{13}{51}$, or $P(A \text{ and } B) = \frac{169}{2652}$, which simplifies to $\frac{13}{204}$.

19. C: The expected value is equal to the sum of the products of the scholarship amounts and probability she will attend each college, or $\frac{1}{3}$. Thus, the expected value is $\left(6000 \cdot \frac{1}{3}\right) + \left(4500 \cdot \frac{1}{3}\right) + \left(5500 \cdot \frac{1}{3}\right)$, which equals approximately 5,333. So, she can expect to receive $5,333.

20. B: The expected value is equal to the sum of the product of the amount of the net profit, or $495, and the probability of winning and the product of the amount of the loss, or –$5, and the probability of losing. The expected value is $\left(495 \cdot \frac{1}{250}\right) + \left((-5) \cdot \frac{249}{250}\right)$, which equals $\frac{495}{250} - \frac{1245}{250} = \frac{-750}{250} = -3$. Thus, Nia's expected value is –$3.

Reading

1. D: The main idea discussed in the passage is that employers benefit the most from establishing a comfortable workspace. The author points out that it is not extremely expensive, then identifies all of the benefits for employers: better productivity, less absenteeism, etc. Answer choice A directly opposes the opening sentence. Answer choices B and C are mentioned but are not the main idea.

2. B: It can be concluded that many brides are choosing to wear colors other than white based on two statements in the passage. First, we know that bridesmaids should not wear the same color as the bride. Secondly, it is stated that white is a popular color for bridesmaid dresses. Therefore, since the color of the bridesmaid dress is not the same as the bride's dress, it can be concluded that the bride's dress is not white. While picking dresses is an "important part" of wedding planning, the passage does not state that it is the hardest part (choice A). There is nothing in the passage about bridesmaids choosing their own dresses (choice C) or avoiding black in past times (choice D).

3. B: Many green fuels require more work to produce than conventional fuels. The passage states, "producing natural gas is a much more labor-intensive process than producing an equal amount of conventional gasoline. Also, producing natural gas also involves burning fossil fuels." There is no evidence to support answer choices A and D. Answer choice C looks promising, but the passage does not mention that *burning* the green fuels produces fossil fuels, but rather that producing and transporting them uses fossil fuels.

4. C: This conclusion can be made based on two statements. First, the passage states that "the majority of crimes discussed on the nightly news featured African American suspects." Second, "it was found that white people were also suspects 50% of the time." Therefore, if half of all suspects are white, but the majority of suspects on the news are African American, it is reasonable to conclude that the news chooses not to report crimes that involve white suspects. Answer choice A is incorrect because 50% is not a majority. The passage does not make any comment on what people believe (choice B) or the total number of crimes (choice D).

5. B: The main purpose of the passage is to discuss the possible benefits of stem cell research. The author states that many people feel it is unethical (choice A), but most of the passage is devoted to discussing the possible benefits of stem cell research. Cures for diseases and being able to repair spinal cord injuries are the possible benefits identified. The passage does not claim that any diseases have already been cured through stem cell research (choice C) or that it is unethical *not* to conduct stem cell research (choice D).

6. A: Accuracy is the same as correctness. The passage states "accuracy means that something is correct" and "if a glass of liquid was 100 degrees, an accurate measurement would be one that was close to this temperature." Consistency (choice B) refers to precision rather than accuracy, as does a result that can be duplicated (choice C). Both accurate and precise results are measurable (choice D).

7. B: The passage refers to the nameless shoemaker's haggard eyes, his inability to focus on a question, his repetitive motions, and his inability to give his name. There is no indication of any art or gallery. The setting is Paris; the passage does not indicate that. Thus, choice A is incorrect. The man being described is not identified as British or as a member of government, so choice C is incorrect. The man is making shoes, not hospital calls; therefore, choice D is incorrect.

8. A: The man gives his name as One Hundred and Five, North Tower, an address, not a personal name. The reference to a tower suggests a prison. Option B is an incorrect choice; the man has not apparently been out of the North Tower in many years. Nor is option C correct because the man is not precisely homeless. Nothing in the passage tells the reader when the man left home, so option D can be eliminated.

9. D: The man does not laugh in this passage. Choice A is clearly stated in the passage. He has lapses in conversation with Mr. Lorry. It is also clear in the passage that the man has no remembrance of a given personal name, so choice B can be eliminated. The repeated motion of his hands when they do not hold the shoe is a telling sign of derangement, so choice C is incorrect.

10. C: The man is working on a lady's walking-shoe when his visitors arrive and states that he had learned the trade, which was not his original manner of work, at his own request since arriving at the prison. He even expresses some pride in the quality of his work, which is based on a pattern because he has never seen the current mode of shoe. There is no indication that he is engaged in woodcarving (answer choice A), glassblowing (choice B), or dressmaking (choice D). All of the other choices are clearly false.

11. B: Defarge is somehow the man's keeper and is concerned with his well-being. We see from the passage that Defarge introduces the visitor, and that the man defers to Defarge as if wishing he would answer a question. Choice A suggests unkindness, which is clearly not the case—Defarge is neutral at best. That option can be eliminated. There is no evidence that he is a family member, as he does not know the man's name, so choice C can be eliminated as well. There is also no suggestion of cruelty nor of a profession nor of a definite setting, leaving choice D untenable.

12. C: Since both authors are explaining in the passages how the same story may come to be in different cultures, it is clear they both accept that there are often common elements in fairy tales from different cultures. The author of Passage 1 believes that all versions of a fairy tale share a common origin (choice A) but the author of Passage 2 does not agree, and instead states that the same fairy tale can develop independently in different cultures (choice B). The author of Passage 2 mentions human fears (choice D) but they are not discussed in Passage 1.

13. A: The author of Passage 2 claims that the essence and nature of fairy tales is their representation of basic human experience. It is this assertion that leads the author to believe that the same story could develop independently in different places. The good/bad characters are mentioned in this passage but do not capture the essence of fairy tales (choice B). Different cultures creating the same story (choice C) follows from the nature of the fairy tale rather than defining it. Commoners becoming royalty (choice D) is another aspect mentioned in the passage but not the core nature of fairy tales.

14. D: The author does not mention the movement of food in the passage. The other answer choices are all listed in this passage.

15. B: The author never mentions witches in the passage. The others are listed in the first sentence.

16. C: The second paragraph of the passage notes that "up to one-third of people with peanut allergies have severe reactions." Since one-third is approximately 33%, (C) is the correct choice.

17. D: The second paragraph of the passage notes that in 2008, Duke experts stated that they expect to offer treatment in five years. Five years from 2008 is 2013.

18. B: The last sentence in paragraph five lists the cuisines which are more likely to contain or use peanuts. Italian is not listed.

19. A: The second sentence of the first paragraph states that peanut allergy is the most common cause of food-related death. Tree nuts (choice B) are not mentioned and the other two answer choices are not foods.

20. C: The passage implies that it is not always easy to know which foods have traces of peanuts in them and that it's important to make sure you know what you're eating. This is hard or impossible if you share someone else's food. The passage does not indicate that a peanut allergy could be contagious (choice A) or mention hygiene (choice B). While the passage does say that scientists do not know why some people have allergic reactions (choice D), this is not mentioned in relation to sharing food.

21. A: Paragraph two gives examples of symptoms of peanut allergies and, more specifically, examples of symptoms of anaphylaxis. A running or stuffy nose is given as a symptom of the former, but not of the latter.

22. B: In the first paragraph, Miss Lucas states that "so very fine a young man, with family, fortune, everything in his favour, should think highly of himself. If I may so express it, he has a *right* to be proud." Basically, she feels he deserves to be proud because he is physically attractive, comes from a good family, has money, and is successful. The best choice is (B). The passage does not clearly state that Miss Lucas admires his vanity (choice A), though it is possible. Mary suggests in the third paragraph that pride is part of human nature (choice C), but this is not linked to Miss Lucas's opinion. Choice D contradicts the given information since the gentleman is stated to be rich.

23. C: A theme is a message or lesson conveyed by a written text. The message is usually about life, society, or human nature. This particular excerpt is exploring pride as it relates to human nature. Mary's observations on pride are the best summary of the theme of this passage. "By all that I have ever read, I am convinced that it is very common indeed, that human nature is particularly prone to it." The best answer choice is (C). Choice A is contradicted in the first sentence. Choice B is discussed but is not the main theme. Choice D is not mentioned in the passage.

24. D: Paragraph 3 gives the answer to this question. According to Mary, pride is an opinion of yourself, and vanity is what we want others to think of us.

Writing

1. C: This version begins with a subject and verb and is followed by a clause. It is also clear and concise. Choice A is incorrect because the words are out of order and don't logically follow the previous sentence. Sentence 2 should begin with 'She says' because it is the school principal's opinion being expressed. This choice is also incorrect because it uses the words *not appropriate* instead of *inappropriate*. Choice B is incorrect because the clause "that students wear to school" should come after the word *outfits*. Choice D is incorrect because the word order changes the meaning of the sentence by stating that all outfits are distracting and inappropriate.

2. A: This answer choice is correct because *your* is the possessive of *you* while *you're* is a conjunction that stands for *you are*. Because it makes sense to substitute *you are* for *you're*, choice A is correct. Choice B is incorrect because a comma is only required before *and* if it is concluding a series of three or more items. Choice C is incorrect because it is correct to write *learn about* but incorrect to write *learn on*. Choice D is incorrect because *your* should be written as the conjunction *you're*.

3. A: Answer choice A uses correct punctuation and a logical conjunction. Because the conjunction *and* connects two independent clauses (meaning that they can stand on their own as sentences), there must be a comma before the conjunction. Therefore, choices B and D are incorrect because they are missing this comma. While choice C does have a comma before the conjunction, it uses the conjunction *but* rather than *and*. *But* implies that the two clauses contradict each other. *And* is a better choice because the two clauses are connected and support each other.

4. B: The phrase *If Jackson high adopts a dress code* is a dependent clause that is followed by an independent clause. Because there is no conjunction, these two clauses must be separated by a comma. Choice A is incorrect because the word *because* would only be used if the dress code had already been adopted. Choice C is incorrect because *students'* would require the word to be a possessive, even though the sentence does not show the students possessing anything. Choice D is incorrect because *theirselves* is not a real word.

5. C: The plural verb *are* does not match the singular subject, *self expression*. Choice A is incorrect because *expression* is already written with the correct spelling. Choice B is incorrect because the conjunction *and* is connecting an independent clause with a dependent clause. When *and* is used in this way, there should not be a comma before the conjunction. Choice D is incorrect because an article is not needed before the name of the school, which is a proper noun.

6. B: The word *furthermore* shows that the sentence will present additional support for the writer's argument. Choice A is incorrect because *however* indicates that the following sentence will contradict what came before. Choice C is incorrect because the sentence is not presenting the first point in the writer's argument. Choice D is incorrect because the sentence is not presenting a conclusion, but an additional point.

7. C: because *teacher's* is not being used as a possessive. Instead, it is being used as a plural noun and therefore should not have an apostrophe. Choice A is incorrect because *however* is a better transition to sentence 22 due to the sentence showing a contrast with a previous point. Choice B is incorrect because the word *of* should not follow *several*. Choice D is incorrect because the comma correctly separates a dependent clause from an independent clause.

8. B: The correct spelling of the word only has a single *s*. Choice A is incorrect because the comma is required to set off the nonessential clause *the students*. Choice C is incorrect because *real* is an adjective modifying *world*, and it is incorrect to put a hyphen in between an adjective and a noun unless using the combination of adjective and noun as an adjective. Choice D is incorrect because *jobs* is a plural noun, not a possessive.

9. D: As written, the sentence does not have any errors. Choice A is incorrect because sentences should not begin with a declarative verb. Choice B is incorrect because *not* changes the meaning of the sentence to the opposite of the writer's point. Choice C is incorrect because *inappropriate* is spelled correctly.

10. A: *Than* is a comparison word while *then* indicates a conclusion. Choice B is incorrect because *you* indicates that the writer is addressing a specific person, which is not the case. Choice C is incorrect because the infinitive form is not needed here. Choice D is incorrect because *decisions* is already written with the correct spelling.

11. C: The original sentence (choice A) is redundant and wordy. Choice B changes the meaning by declaring that he *will* rethink his decision, rather than that he will likely rethink it. Choice D is redundant with the phrase *for a bit.*

12. C: The syntax of the original sentence is fine, but a comma after *said* and before the open-quotation mark is required. Choice C is the only one that includes this comma.

13. D: Choice A is incorrect because the sentence needs a comma after *nurses*. Choice B incorrectly adds the word *to*, which does not match the verb form. Choice C also omits a necessary comma after *pills*. Only choice D is grammatically correct.

14. D: The verb structure should be consistent in a sentence with parallel structures.

15. A: The singular pronoun *her* is appropriate since the antecedents are joined by *or*. Also, the subjunctive verb form is required to indicate something indefinite.

16. A: Answer choice A best completes the statement in the rewritten sentence by making the immediate connection between the environmental concerns and the reason for them. Answer choice B could work within the context of the sentence, but it does not create a sufficient link between the environmental concerns and their causes. Answer choice C provides information that is not contained within the original sentence, and answer choice D also adds information by noting that the "delicate balance" is altered. While this might be inferred from the original sentence, it cannot be added to the rewritten sentence.

17. C: Answer choice C accurately adds the statement of contrast about the python being shorter in the wild. Answer choice A adds information to the original sentence. Answer choice B is technically correct but does not contain as much information as answer choice C and is thus not the best choice. Answer choice D is also technically correct but is unnecessarily wordy and does not provide the substance of the information that answer choice C contains.

18. D: Answer choice D creates the necessary link between the snake owners and the infestation of pythons in the Everglades. Answer choice A contains accurate information, but the sentence does not flow smoothly from one idea to the next. Answer choice B is true but is vague and fails to create a sufficient link between ideas. Answer choice C contains details that make no sense within the context of the sentence.

19. A: Answer choice A provides the sense of contrast that is contained within the original sentence by showing the differences between the responsible snake owners and the lawmakers. Answer choice B offers information that is contained within the original sentence but fails to provide a clear link between ideas. Answer choice C essentially repeats the information that is in the rewritten statement and is thus repetitive. Answer choice D, though correct, does not make a great deal of sense following up the information in the rewritten statement.

20. C: Answer choice C effectively restates the sentence by capturing the entire mood of the original. Answer choice A adds correct information, but it is incomplete with respect to the original idea. Answer choice B may be inferred to a degree, but there is not enough information in the original sentence to claim that the biologists were *surprised* about the results—only that they were *concerned* about the potential. Answer choice D adds information that is not within the original sentence.

TSI Practice Test #4

Math

1. A regular toilet uses 3.2 gallons of water per flush. A low flow toilet uses 1.6 gallons of water per flush. What is the difference between the number of gallons used by the regular toilet and the low flow toilet after 375 flushes?

    A. 100 gallons
    B. 525 gallons
    C. 600 gallons
    D. 1,200 gallons

2. Solve for n in the following equation: $4n - p = 3r$

    A. $\frac{3r}{4} - p$
    B. $p + 3r$
    C. $\frac{3r}{4} + p$
    D. $\frac{3r}{4} + \frac{p}{4}$

3. What is $|x| + |x - 2|$ when $x = 1$?

    A. 0
    B. 1
    C. 2
    D. 3

4. Which of the following inequalities is correct?

    A. $\frac{1}{3} < \frac{2}{7} < \frac{5}{12}$
    B. $\frac{2}{7} < \frac{1}{3} < \frac{5}{12}$
    C. $\frac{5}{12} < \frac{2}{7} < \frac{1}{3}$
    D. $\frac{5}{12} < \frac{1}{3} < \frac{2}{7}$

5. If $6q + 3 = 8q - 7$, what is q?

    A. $-\frac{5}{7}$
    B. $\frac{5}{7}$
    C. 5
    D. -7

6. A communications company charges \$5.00 for the first ten minutes of a call and \$1.20 for each minute thereafter. Which of the following equations correctly relates the price in dollars, d, to the number of minutes, m (when $m \geq 10$)?

    A. $d = 5 + 1.2m$
    B. $d = 5 + 1.2(m - 10)$
    C. $d = 5m + 1.2(m + 10)$
    D. $d = (m + 10)(5 + 1.2)$

210

7. $\dfrac{x^2}{y^2} + \dfrac{x}{y^3} =$

   A. $\dfrac{x^3 + x}{y^3}$

   B. $\dfrac{x^2 + xy}{y^3}$

   C. $\dfrac{x^2 y + xy}{y^3}$

   D. $\dfrac{x^2 y + x}{y^3}$

8. How many solutions are there to the equation $\left| x^2 - 2 \right| = x$?

   A. 0
   B. 1
   C. 2
   D. 4

9. Which of the following represents the factors of the expression, $x^2 - 3x - 40$?

   A. $(x - 8)(x + 5)$
   B. $(x - 7)(x + 4)$
   C. $(x + 10)(x - 4)$
   D. $(x + 6)(x - 9)$

10. Given the equation, $2^x = 64$, what is the value of x?

   A. 4
   B. 5
   C. 6
   D. 7

11. In the figure below, angles b and d are equal. What is the degree measure of angle d?

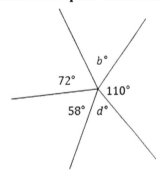

   A. 120°
   B. 80°
   C. 60°
   D. 30°

12. What is the area of the parallelogram in the figure pictured below?

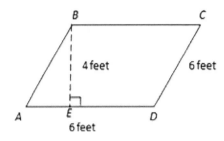

A. 10 square feet
B. 16 square feet
C. 24 square feet
D. 36 square feet

13. Find the value of x in the figure pictured below:

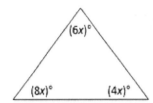

A. 10
B. 16
C. 18
D. 60

14. A rectangle is twice as long as it is wide. If its area is 200 cm², what is its width?
A. 10 cm
B. 20 cm
C. $10\sqrt{2}$ cm
D. $20\sqrt{2}$ cm

15. A building has a number of floors of equal height, as well as a thirty-foot spire above them all. If the height of each floor in feet is h, and there are n floors in the building, which of the following represents the building's total height in feet?
A. $n + h + 30$
B. $nh + 30$
C. $30n + h$
D. $30h + n$

16. Which of the following figures show parallelogram *WXYZ* being carried onto its image *W'X'Y'Z'* by a reflection across the *x*-axis?

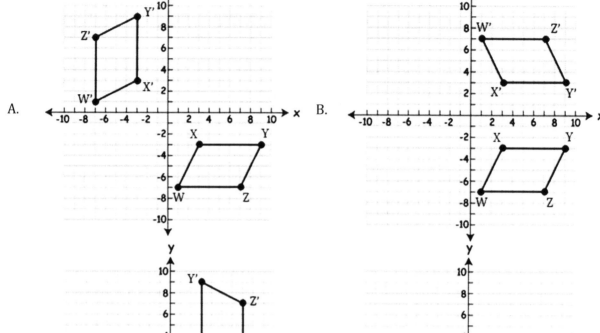

A.

B.

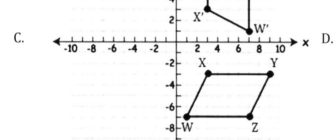

C.

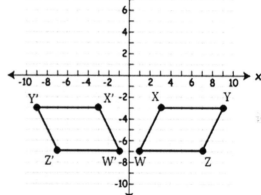

D.

17. Which of the following measures is unaffected by a skewed distribution?

    A. mean
    B. median
    C. standard deviation
    D. range

18. Which of the following correlation coefficients represents a weak correlation?

    A. −0.9
    B. 0.2
    C. −0.7
    D. 0.8

19. Elisha spins a spinner with 8 equally spaced sections labeled 1–8. What is the probability that the spinner lands on either a number greater than 5 or on 2?

A. $\frac{3}{64}$

B. $\frac{1}{2}$

C. $\frac{1}{8}$

D. $\frac{3}{8}$

20. A bag contains 2 red marbles, 3 blue marbles, and 5 green marbles. What is the probability Gitta draws a red marble, does not replace it, and then draws another red marble?

A. $\frac{1}{25}$

B. $\frac{1}{45}$

C. $\frac{2}{45}$

D. $\frac{14}{45}$

Reading

Directions for questions 1–6

Read the statement or passage and then choose the best answer to the question. Answer the question based on what is stated or implied in the statement or passage.

1. Literacy rates are lower today than they were fifteen years ago. Then, most people learned to read through the use of phonics. Today, whole language programs are favored by many educators.

If these statements are true, it can be concluded that

    A. whole language is more effective at teaching people to read than phonics.
    B. phonics is more effective at teaching people to read than whole language.
    C. literacy rates will probably continue to decline over the next 15 years.
    D. the definition of what it means to be literate is much stricter now.

2. George Washington was a remarkable man. He was born in 1732. Shortly before becoming the President of the United States in 1789, Washington was an important leader in the American Revolutionary War from 1775 to 1783. After retiring, he returned to Mount Vernon in 1797. A short time later, John Adams made him commander-in-chief of the United States Army again. This was done in anticipation that the country might go to war with France.

Which of the following happened soonest after Washington served as a leader in the American Revolutionary War?

    A. Washington returned to Mount Vernon.
    B. Washington was made commander-in-chief of the U.S. Army.
    C. Washington became the President of the United States.
    D. Washington decided to go into retirement.

3. During the 1970s, a new type of pet became popular in North America. Although they were actually just brine shrimp, they were marketed as "Sea Monkeys." They don't actually look like monkeys at all, but were branded as such due to their long tails. When sea monkeys first began to be sold in the United States, they were sold under the brand name "Instant Life." Later, when they became known as sea monkeys, the cartoon drawings that were featured in comic books showed creatures that resembled humans more than shrimp. The creative marketing of these creatures can only be described as genius, and at the height of their popularity in the 1970s, they could be found in as many as one in five homes.

Based on the information in the passage, it can be inferred that

    A. Sea monkeys were more popular when they were marketed as "instant life."
    B. Sea monkeys wouldn't have been as popular if they had been marketed as "brine shrimp."
    C. Most people thought they were actually purchasing monkeys that lived in the sea.
    D. There are more homes today that have sea monkeys than there were in the 1970s.

4. Before the battle between CDs and MP3s, there was a rivalry during the 1960s between the four-track and the eight-track tape. Four-track tapes were invented in the early 1960s by Earl Muntz, an entrepreneur from California. Later, Bill Lear designed the eight-track tape. This latter invention was similar in size to the four-track tape, but it could store and play twice as many songs. Lear had close ties with the motor company Ford, and he convinced them to include eight-track players in their vehicles, which definitely helped the eight-track tape to achieve a high level of popularity. Soon after, they were introduced into homes, and the four-track tape all but disappeared.

The main difference between the four-track and eight-track tape was

    A. The four-track tape was much larger than the eight-track tape.
    B. The eight-track tape cost a lot more to produce than the four-track tape.
    C. The eight-track tape could hold more songs than the four-track tape.
    D. The four-track tape was usually included in Ford vehicles.

5. It is natural for humans to have fears, but when those fears are completely irrational and begin to interfere with everyday activities they are known as phobias. Agoraphobia is a serious phobia, and it can be devastating for those who suffer from it. Contrary to popular belief, agoraphobia is not simply a fear of open spaces. Rather, the agoraphobic fears being in a place that he feels is unsafe. Depending on the severity of the problem, the agoraphobic might fear going to the mall, walking down the street, or even walking to the mailbox. Often, the agoraphobic will view his home as the safest possible place to be, and he may even be reluctant to leave his house. Treatments for this condition include medication and behavioral therapy.

An agoraphobic would feel safest

    A. In their yard.
    B. In their house.
    C. In a mall.
    D. On the sidewalk.

6. The butterfly effect is a somewhat poorly understood mathematical concept, primarily because it is interpreted and presented incorrectly by the popular media. It refers to systems, and how initial conditions can influence the ultimate outcome of an event. The best way to understand the concept is through an example. You have two rubber balls. There are two inches between them, and you release them. Where will they end up? Well, that depends. If they're in a sloped, sealed container, they will end up two inches away from each other at the end of the slope. If it's the top of a mountain, however, they may end up miles away from each other. They could bounce off rocks; one could get stuck in a snow bank while the other continues down the slope; one could enter a river and get swept away. The fact that even a tiny initial difference can have a significant overall impact is known as the butterfly effect.

The purpose of this passage is

    A. To discuss what could happen to two rubber balls released on top of a mountain.
    B. To show why you can predict what will happen to two objects in a sloped, sealed container.
    C. To discuss the primary reason why the butterfly effect is a poorly understood concept.
    D. To give an example of how small changes at the beginning of an event can have large effects.

Questions 7–15 are based on the following passage:

    Daylight Saving Time (DST) is the practice of changing clocks so that afternoons have more daylight and mornings have less. Clocks are adjusted forward one hour in the spring and one hour backward in the fall. The main purpose of the change is to make better use of daylight.

DST began with the goal of conservation. Benjamin Franklin suggested it as a method of saving on candles. It was used during both World Wars to save energy for military needs. Although DST's potential to save energy was a primary reason behind its implementation, research into its effects on energy conservation are contradictory and unclear.

Beneficiaries of DST include all activities that can benefit from more sunlight after working hours, such as shopping and sports. A 1984 issue of *Fortune* magazine estimated that a seven-week extension of DST would yield an additional $30 million for 7-Eleven stores. Public safety may be increased by the use of DST: some research suggests that traffic fatalities may be reduced when there is additional afternoon sunlight.

On the other hand, DST complicates timekeeping and some computer systems. Tools with built-in time-keeping functions such as medical devices can be affected negatively. Agricultural and evening entertainment interests have historically opposed DST.

DST can affect health, both positively and negatively. It provides more afternoon sunlight in which to get exercise. It also impacts sunlight exposure; this is good for getting vitamin D, but bad in that it can increase skin cancer risk. DST may also disrupt sleep.

Today, daylight saving time has been adopted by more than one billion people in about 70 countries. DST is generally not observed in countries near the equator because sunrise times do not vary much there. Asia and Africa do not generally observe it. Some countries, such as Brazil, observe it only in some regions.

DST can lead to peculiar situations. One of these occurred in November, 2007 when a woman in North Carolina gave birth to one twin at 1:32 a.m. and, 34 minutes later, to the second twin. Because of DST and the time change at 2:00 a.m., the second twin was officially born at 1:06, 26 minutes earlier than her brother.

7. According to the passage, what is the main purpose of DST?

A. To increase public safety
B. To benefit retail businesses
C. To make better use of daylight
D. To promote good health

8. Which of the following is not mentioned in the passage as a negative effect of DST?

A. Energy conservation
B. Complications with time keeping
C. Complications with computer systems
D. Increased skin cancer risk

9. The article states that DST involves:

A. Adjusting clocks forward one hour in the spring and the fall.
B. Adjusting clocks backward one hour in the spring and the fall.
C. Adjusting clocks forward in the fall and backward in the spring.
D. Adjusting clocks forward in the spring and backward in the fall.

10. Which interests have historically opposed DST, according to the passage?

A. retail businesses and sports
B. evening entertainment and agriculture
C. 7-Eleven and health
D. medical devices and computing

11. According to the article, increased sunlight exposure:

A. is only good for health.
B. is only bad for health.
C. has no effect on health.
D. can be both good and bad for health.

12. In what area does the article state DST is observed only in some regions?

A. The equator
B. Asia
C. Africa
D. Brazil

13. What is an example given in the passage of a peculiar situation that DST has caused?

A. sleep disruption
B. driving confusion
C. twin birth order complications
D. countries with DST only in certain regions

14. According to the passage, a 1984 magazine article estimated that a seven-week extension of DST would provide 7-Eleven stores with an extra $30 million. Approximately how much extra money is that per week of the extension?

A. 42,000
B. 420,000
C. 4,200,000
D. 42,000,000

15. For what purpose did Benjamin Franklin first suggest DST?

A. to save money for military needs
B. to save candles
C. to reduce traffic fatalities
D. to promote reading

Questions 16–21 refer to the following passage:

Tips for Eating Calcium-Rich Foods

- Include milk as a beverage at meals. Choose fat-free or low-fat milk.
- If you usually drink whole milk, switch gradually to fat-free milk to lower saturated fat and calories. Try reduced fat (2%), then low-fat (1%), and finally fat-free (skim).
- If you drink cappuccinos or lattes—ask for them with fat-free (skim) milk.
- Add fat-free or low-fat milk instead of water to oatmeal and hot cereals
- Use fat-free or low-fat milk when making condensed cream soups (such as cream of tomato).
- Have fat-free or low-fat yogurt as a snack.
- Make a dip for fruits or vegetables from yogurt.
- Make fruit-yogurt smoothies in the blender.
- For dessert, make chocolate or butterscotch pudding with fat-free or low-fat milk.
- Top cut-up fruit with flavored yogurt for a quick dessert.
- Top casseroles, soups, stews, or vegetables with shredded low-fat cheese.
- Top a baked potato with fat-free or low-fat yogurt.

For those who choose not to consume milk products

- If you avoid milk because of lactose intolerance, the most reliable way to get the health benefits of milk is to choose lactose-free alternatives within the milk group, such as cheese, yogurt, or lactose-free milk, or to consume the enzyme lactase before consuming milk products.
- Calcium choices for those who do not consume milk products include:
  o Calcium fortified juices, cereals, breads, soy beverages, or rice beverages
  o Canned fish (sardines, salmon with bones) soybeans and other soy products, some other dried beans, and some leafy greens.

16. According to the passage, how can you lower saturated fat and calories in your diet?
  A. Add fat-free milk to oatmeal instead of water.
  B. Switch to fat-free milk.
  C. Drink calcium-fortified juice.
  D. Make yogurt dip.

17. What device does the author use to organize the passage?
  A. headings
  B. captions
  C. diagrams
  D. labels

18. How much fat does reduced fat milk contain?
  A. 0 percent
  B. 1 percent
  C. 2 percent
  D. 3 percent

19. Which of the following is true about calcium-rich foods?

    I. Canned salmon with bones contains calcium.

    II. Cheese is a lactose-free food.

    III. Condensed soup made with water is a calcium-rich food.

    A. I only

    B. I and II only

    C. II and III only

    D. III only

20. What information should the author include to help clarify information in the passage?

    A. The fat content of yogurt.

    B. How much calcium is in fortified juice.

    C. Which leafy greens contain calcium.

    D. The definition of lactose intolerance.

21. The style of this passage is most like that found in a(n)

    A. tourist guidebook.

    B. health textbook.

    C. encyclopedia.

    D. friendly letter.

Questions 22–24 pertain to the following passage:

Leaving

Even though Martin and Beth's steps were muffled by the falling snow, Beth could still hear the faint crunch of leaves underneath. The hushed woods had often made Beth feel safe and at peace, but these days they just made her feel lonely.

"I'm glad we decided to hike the trail, Martin. It's so quiet and pretty."

"Sure."

Beth couldn't understand how it happened, but over the past few months this silence had grown between them, weighing down their relationship. Of course, there was that thing with Mary, but Beth had forgiven Martin. They moved on. It was in the past.

"Do you want to see a movie tonight?" asked Beth. "There's a new one showing at the downtown theater."

"Whatever you want."

She wanted her husband back. She wanted the laughter and games. She wanted the late-night talks over coffee. She wanted to forget Mary and Martin together. She wanted to feel some sort of <u>rapport</u> again.

"Is everything alright, Martin?"

"I'm fine. Just tired."

"We didn't have to come; we could have stayed at home."

"It's fine."

Beth closed her eyes, tilted her head back, and breathed in the crisp air. "Fine" once meant "very good," or "precious." Now, it is a meaningless word, an excuse not to tell other people what's on your mind. "Fine" had hung in the air between them for months now, a softly falling word that hid them from each other. Beth wasn't even sure she knew Martin anymore, but she was confident that it was only a matter of time before everything was not "fine," only a matter of time before he told her...

"I have to leave."

"Huh? What?"

"I got a page. My patient is going into cardiac arrest."

"I wish you didn't have to leave."

"I'm sorry, but I have to go."

"I know."

22. It is reasonable to infer that Martin and Beth's relationship is strained because:
A. Martin recently lost his job.
B. Martin was unfaithful to Beth.
C. Martin works too much.
D. Martin does not want to go to the movies.

23. Based on the passage, it is reasonable to infer that Martin is a:
A. mechanic.
B. medical doctor.
C. dentist.
D. film director.

24. The best definition of the underlined word *rapport* is:
A. a close relationship.
B. a sense of well-being.
C. a common goal.
D. loneliness.

Writing

Jordan's English class is reading a book set in the 1920s. In order to better understand that decade, his English teacher has assigned a research essay on one aspect of that time period. Jordan has written an essay on early pilots but needs help revising and improving the essay. After you read the essay, answer questions 1–10.

(1) After Orville and Wilbur Wright have flown their first airplane in 1903, the age of flying slowly began. (2) Many new pilots learned how to fly in World War I, which the United States joined in 1917. (3) During the war, the American public loved hearing stories about the daring pilots and their air fights. (4) But after the war ended, many Americans thought that men and women belonged on the ground and not in the air.

(5) In the years after the war and through the Roaring Twenties, Americas pilots found themselves without jobs. (6) Some of them gave up flying altogether. (7) Pilot Eddie Rickenbacker, who used to be called America's Ace of Aces, became a car salesman. (8) But other pilots found new and creative things to do with their airplanes.

(9) Pilot Casey Jones used his airplane to help get news across the country. (10) When a big news story broke, Jones flew news photos to newspapers in different cities. (11) Another pilot, Roscoe Turner traveled around the country with a lion cub in his plane. (12) The cub was the mascot of an oil company, and Turner convinced the company that flying the cub around would be a good advertisement. (13) The Humane Society wasn't very happy about this idea, and they convinced Turner to make sure the lion cub always wore a parachute.

(14) Other pilots took people for short airplane rides, often charging five dollars for a five-minute ride (by comparison, you could buy a loaf of bread for about ten cents in 1920). (15) These pilots, called barnstormers, often used dangerous tricks to get customers: two barnstormers once stood on a plane's wings and played tennis while the plane flew at 70 miles per hour! (16) Many barnstormers advertised their shows as a "flying circus."

(17) During the 1920s, the U.S. Post Office developed airmail. (18) Before airmail, the post traveled on trains and can take weeks to reach a destination. (19) Flying for the post office was dangerous work. (20) Early pilots didn't have sophistocated instruments and safety equipment on their planes. (21) Many of them had to bail out and use their parachutes when their planes iced up in the cold air or had other trouble.

(22) The most famous pilot of the 1920s, Charles A. Lindbergh, began as a postal pilot. (23) In May 1927, he participated in an air race to fly across the Atlantic Ocean. (24) The prize was $25,000, but the dangers were extensive. (25) Named Nungesser and Coli, two French pilots had recently tried to fly across the Atlantic.

(26) They disappeared.

(27) The newspapers called Charles Lindbergh "the dark horse" to win the race. (28) He had already set a record by making the fastest solo flight between St. Louis, Missouri, and, San Diego, California. (29) Lindbergh's record-setting flight took 23

hours and 15 minutes; today, a flight between St. Louis and San Diego takes about four hours.

(30) After several weather delays, Lindbergh took off in his small plane, The Spirit of St. Louis, on May 20, 1927. (31) He made it across the Atlantic Ocean and arrived in France after 33 hours and 30 minutes of non-stop flight; today, a flight from New York to Paris would take about seven hours.

(32) The flight was taxing. (33) Because Lindbergh flew alone, he had to stay awake for the entire trip. (34) He knew that he couldn't have made it across without a great plane. (35) He said, "I feel that the monoplane was as much a part of the trip as myself."

(36) Lindbergh's trip set off a golden age for aviation. (37) The same people who were nervous about airplanes at the beginning of the 1920s came out by the thousands to cheer Lindbergh. (38) The age of pilots doing odd jobs and dangerous stunt work had ended.

1. What change should be made to sentence 1?
- A. Add a comma after *Wright*
- B. Change *have flown* to *flew*
- C. Change *first* to *1st*
- D. Delete the comma after *1903*

2. What change should be made to sentence 5?
- A. Change *years* to *year's*
- B. Delete the comma after *Twenties*
- C. Change *Americas* to *America's*
- D. Change *themselves* to *theirselves*

3. What change should be made in sentence 11?
- A. Delete the comma before *Roscoe*
- B. Add a comma after *Turner*
- C. Change *with* to *as*
- D. Change *plane* to *airplane*

4. What change should be made to sentence 15?
- A. Change *barnstormers* to *barnstormer*
- B. Change the colon after *customers* to a semicolon
- C. Change *plane's* to *planes*
- D. Change *while* to *when*

5. What change should be made to sentence 18?
- A. Delete the comma after *airmail*
- B. Change *traveled* to *travelled*
- C. Change *can* to *could*
- D. Change *a* to *it's*

6. What change should be made to sentence 20?
- A. Change *pilots* to *pilot's*
- B. Change sophistocated to sophisticated
- C. Add a comma after *instruments*
- D. Change *their* to *they're*

7. What's the most effective way to rewrite sentence 25?
- A. Two French pilots, named Nungesser and Coli, had recently tried to fly across the Atlantic.
- B. Two French pilots Nungesser and Coli had recently tried to fly across the Atlantic.
- C. Recently having tried to fly across the Atlantic, two French pilots were named Nungesser and Coli.
- D. No change

8. What change should be made to sentence 28?
- A. Delete the comma after *St. Louis*
- B. Delete the comma after *Missouri*
- C. Delete the comma after *and*
- D. Delete the comma after *San Diego*

9. How could sentences 34 and 35 best be combined?
- A. He knew that he couldn't have made it across without a great plane and he said, "I feel that the monoplane was as much a part of the trip as myself."
- B. He knew that he couldn't have made it across without a great plane, he said, "I feel that the monoplane was as much a part of the trip as myself."
- C. He knew that he couldn't have made it across without a great plane and says, "I feel that the monoplane was as much a part of the trip as myself."
- D. He knew that he couldn't have made it across without a great plane and said, "I feel that the monoplane was as much a part of the trip as myself."

10. What transition could be added at the beginning of sentence 36?
- A. In conclusion
- B. Furthermore
- C. Therefore
- D. Additionally

For questions 11–15, select the best option for replacing the underlined portion of the sentence. The first option listed is always the same as the current version of the sentence.

11. Despite their lucky escape, <u>Jason and his brother could not hardly enjoy themselves</u>.
- A. Jason and his brother could not hardly enjoy themselves.
- B. Jason and his brother could not enjoy themselves.
- C. Jason and Jason's brother could not hardly enjoy themselves.
- D. Jason and his brother could not enjoy them.

12. Stew recipes call <u>for rosemary, parsley, thyme, and these sort of herbs</u>.
- A. for rosemary, parsley, thyme, and these sort of herbs.
- B. for: rosemary; parsley; thyme; and these sort of herbs.
- C. for rosemary, parsley, thyme, and these sorts of herbs.
- D. for rosemary, parsley, thyme, and this sorts of herbs.

13. Mr. King, <u>an individual of considerable influence, created a personal fortune and gave back</u> to the community.

    A. an individual of considerable influence, created a personal fortune and gave back
    B. an individual of considerable influence, he created a personal fortune and gave back
    C. an individual of considerable influence created a personal fortune and gave back
    D. an individual of considerable influence, created a personal fortune and gave it back

14. <u>She is the person whose opinion matters the most</u>.

    A. She is the person whose opinion matters the most.
    B. She is the person to whom her opinion matters the most.
    C. She is the person her opinion matters the most.
    D. She is the person for whom her opinion matters the most.

15. Minerals are nutritionally significant elements <u>that assist to make your body</u> work properly.

    A. that assist to make your body
    B. that help your body
    C. that making your body
    D. that work to make your body

16. The most prolific predator in the Florida Everglades has always been the alligator, which preys on local birds and wildlife, while the introduction of the Burmese python adds another, and often insatiable, predator to compete with the alligator.

Rewrite the sentence, beginning with the phrase,

<u>The introduction of the Burmese python to the Everglades adds another predator to compete with the alligator</u>...

The words that follow will be:

    A. which has always been the most prolific predator in the Everglades
    B. thus leaving the local birds and wildlife in serious danger of becoming endangered
    C. and the alligator was never as serious a predator as the python has become
    D. which does not have the python's reputation for being insatiable

17. Not only does the Burmese python compete with the alligator for prey, but it also competes with the alligator as prey, because pythons have been known to engorge full-grown alligators, thus placing the python at the top of the food chain and leaving them with no native predators in the Everglades.

Rewrite the sentence, beginning with the phrase,

<u>The Burmese python is now at the top of the food chain in the Everglades and has no native predator</u>...

The words that follow will be:

    A. so it competes with the alligator as prey
    B. as evidence shows that pythons are capable of engorging full-grown alligators
    C. although the python still competes with alligators for prey
    D. leaving the Everglades with a serious imbalance of predators

18. Biologists and environmentalists recognize the considerable dangers of the python's expansion in the Everglades as it consumes endangered creatures native to that area, and in one instance researchers were shocked to discover that the tracking device for a tagged rodent led them to the python that had already consumed the unlucky creature.

Rewrite the sentence, beginning with the phrase,

Researchers in the Everglades were shocked to discover that the tracking device for a tagged rodent led them to the python that had already consumed the unlucky creature...

The words that follow will be:

A. thus showing how the python is destroying endangered species within the Everglades
B. causing concerns that the python expansion might be more dangerous than biologists and environmentalists originally believed
C. which was one of the few of its species that had managed to survive the python expansion in the Everglades
D. leaving biologists and environmentalists to recognize the considerable dangers of the python's expansion in the Everglades

19. In an attempt at controlling the python, Florida dispatched hunters to destroy as many pythons as possible, but after several months of searching the hunters were only able to make a dent in the python population of thousands by killing several dozen.

Rewrite the sentence, beginning with the phrase,

The python population of thousands was reduced only by several dozen...

The words that follow will be:

A. even after many months of searching for and destroying the creatures
B. because the hunters were only given a few months for the task and needed more time to destroy as many pythons as possible
C. after the hunters sent to destroy as many pythons as possible failed to make a dent in the number
D. resulting in concerns that more hunters were needed to locate and destroy as many pythons as possible

20. Although eradication is preferred when non-native species are introduced into the United States, researchers have found that is it virtually impossible, and controlling the species becomes the only real option in avoiding the destruction of native habitats and endangered species.

Rewrite the sentence, beginning with the phrase,

Controlling an invasive species is the only real option in avoiding the destruction of native habitats and endangered species...

The words that follow will be:

A. because the total eradication of non-native species that are introduced into the United States is virtually impossible
B. because the total eradication of non-native species that are introduced into the United States is generally frowned upon
C. although researchers prefer the total eradication of non-native species and continue to make efforts to destroy the python in the Everglades
D. in spite of the many attempts at totally eradicating the non-native species that are introduced into the United States

Essay

There is an ongoing struggle between those who would like to develop the oil reserves in Alaska and the Gulf of Mexico to help the US gain energy independence and those who oppose doing so because of possible environmental consequences. Please write a multiple-paragraph persuasive essay (approximately 350–500 words) discussing whether you support or oppose developing the oil reserves.

Answers and Explanations for Test #4

Math

1. C: To solve this problem, first calculate how many gallons each toilet uses in 375 flushes:

$$3.2 \cdot 375 = 1{,}200 \text{ gallons}$$

$$1.6 \cdot 375 = 600 \text{ gallons}$$

The problem is asking for the difference, so find the difference between the regular toilet and the low-flow toilet:

$1{,}200 - 600 = 600$ gallons. Note that you could also find the difference in water use for one flush, and then multiply that amount by 375:

$$3.2 - 1.6 = 1.6$$

Then multiply 1.6 by 375 to obtain 600 gallons.

2. D: To solve for n, you have to isolate that variable by putting all of the other terms of the equation, including coefficients, integers, and variables on the other side of the equal sign.

Add p to each side of the equation:

$$4n - p = 3r$$

$$4n - p + p = 3r + p$$

$$4n = 3r + p$$

Divide each term by 4:

$$\frac{4n}{4} = \frac{3r}{4} + \frac{p}{4}$$

$$n = \frac{3r}{4} + \frac{p}{4}$$

3. C: $|x| + |x - 2| = |1| + |1 - 2| = |1| + |-1| = 1 + 1 = 2.$

4. B: One way to compare fractions is to convert them to equivalent fractions with common denominators. In this case the lowest common denominator of the three fractions is $7 \cdot 12 = 84$. Converting each of the fractions to this denominator, $\frac{1}{3} = \frac{1 \cdot 28}{3 \cdot 28} = \frac{28}{84}, \frac{2}{7} = \frac{2 \cdot 12}{7 \cdot 12} = \frac{24}{84}$, and $\frac{5}{12} = \frac{5 \cdot 7}{12 \cdot 7} = \frac{35}{84}$. Since $24 < 28 < 35$, it must be the case that $\frac{2}{7} < \frac{1}{3} < \frac{5}{12}$.

5. C: $6q + 3 = 8q - 7 \Rightarrow 6q + 3 + 7 = 8q \Rightarrow 6q + 10 = 8q \Rightarrow 10 = 8q - 6q \Rightarrow 10 = 2q \Rightarrow q = 5.$

6. B: The charge is \$1.20 for each minute *past* the first ten minutes. The number of minutes after the first ten minutes is $m - 10$, so this amount charged for the part of the phone call exceeding 10 minutes is $1.2(m - 10)$. Adding this to the \$5.00 charge for the first ten minutes gives $d = 5 + 1.2(m - 10)$.

7. D: To add the two fractions, first rewrite them with the least common denominator, which is in this case y^3. $\frac{x}{y^3}$ already has this denominator, and we can rewrite $\frac{x^2}{y^2}$ as $\frac{x^2 \cdot y}{y^2 \cdot y} = \frac{x^2 y}{y^3}$. Thus, $\frac{x^2}{y^2} + \frac{x}{y^3} = \frac{x^2 y}{y^3} + \frac{x}{y^3} = \frac{x^2 y + x}{y^3}$.

8. C: To solve an equation with an absolute value like $|x^2 - 2| = x$, we need to treat it as two separate cases. If $x^2 - 2$ is positive, then $|x^2 - 2| = x^2 - 2$. The equation then becomes $x^2 - 2 = x$, which can be rewritten as $x^2 - x - 2 = 0$. If $x^2 - 2$ is negative, then $|x^2 - 2| = -(x^2 - 2)$, and the equation becomes $-(x^2 - 2) = x$, which we can rewrite as $x^2 + x - 2 = 0$. We will need to examine both of these equations.

We can factor $x^2 - x - 2 = 0$ by finding two numbers that sum to the coefficient of x (–1) and multiply to the constant term (–2). The two qualifying numbers are 1 and –2; thus, this equation factors to $(x + 1)(x - 2) = 0$, yielding the solutions $x = -1$ and $x = 2$.

We can factor $x^2 + x - 2 = 0$ in the same way. In this case, the two qualifying numbers are -1 and 2; thus, this equation factors to $(x - 1)(x + 2) = 0$, yielding the solutions $x = 1$ and $x = -2$.

From solving these two equations, we have solutions of $x = -2, -1, 1, 2$, but this method of solving absolute value equations can yield invalid solutions. We must verify that our solutions are valid.

Notice that in the original equation, x is set equal to an absolute value. By definition, this means that x cannot be a negative number, which eliminates two of our possible solutions. We can verify the positive values by plugging them into the original equation:

$$|1^2 - 2| = |-1| = 1; \quad |2^2 - 2| = |2| = 2$$

Since $x = 1$ and $x = 2$ are both valid, we can see that there are 2 solutions to the equation.

9. A: The expression may be factored as $(x - 8)(x + 5)$. The factorization may be checked by distributing each term in the first factor over each term in the second factor. Doing so gives $x^2 + 5x - 8x - 40$, which can be rewritten as $x^2 - 3x - 40$.

10. C: The power to which 2 is raised to give 64 is 6; $2^6 = 64$ because $2 \cdot 2 \cdot 2 \cdot 2 \cdot 2 \cdot 2 = 64$. Thus, $x = 6$.

11. C: Angles around a point add up to 360 degrees. Add the degrees of the given angles: 72° + 110° + 58° = 240°. Then subtract: 360° – 240° = 120°. Remember to divide 120° in half, since the question is asking for the degree measure of one angle, angle d.

12. C: The area of a parallelogram is base times height or $A = bh$, where b is the length of a side and h is the length of an altitude to that side. In this problem, $A = 6 \cdot 4$; $A = 24$. Remember, use the length of BE, not the length of CD for the height.

13. A: The sum of the measures of the angles in a triangle equals 180°. Use the numbers given in the figure to make the following equation:

$$(6x)° + (8x)° + (4x)° = 180°$$

$$(18x)° = 180°$$

$$x = 10$$

14. A: The area A of a rectangle is equal to its length l times its width w: $A = l \cdot w$. The rectangle is twice as long as it is wide, so $l = 2w$. By replacing l with its equivalent $2w$, the area of this rectangle can be written as $A = 2w \cdot w = 2w^2$. So $2w^2 = 200$ cm^2; $w^2 = 100$ cm^2; $w = \sqrt{100 \text{ cm}^2} = 10$ cm.

15. B: If there are n floors, and each floor has a height of h feet, then to find the total height of the floors, we just multiply the number of floors by the height of each floor: nh. To find the total height of the building, we must also add the height of the spire, 30 feet. So, the building's total height in feet is $nh + 30$.

16. B: A reflection is a transformation producing a mirror image. A figure reflected over the x-axis will have its vertices in the form (x, y) transformed to $(x, -y)$. The point W at $(1,-7)$ reflects to W' at $(1,7)$, and so on. Only answer choice C shows $WXYZ$ being carried onto its image $W'X'Y'Z'$ by a reflection across the x-axis. Choice A shows a reflection across the line $y = x$. Choice C shows a 90° counterclockwise rotation about the origin. Choice D shows a reflection across the y-axis.

17. B: The median is unaffected by a skewed distribution, or data with extreme outliers. The median represents the value, at which 50% of the scores fall above and 50% of the scores fall below. The mean, standard deviation, and range are all impacted by non-normal data.

18. B: Correlation coefficients range from −1 to 1, with values close to −1 or 1 representing strong relationships. Thus, a correlation coefficient of 0.2 represents a weak correlation because it is close to 0 rather than 1.

19. B: The probability of mutually exclusive events, A or B, occurring may be written as $P(A \text{ or } B) = P(A) + P(B)$. The probability of obtaining a number greater than 5 is $\frac{3}{8}$ because 3 of the 8 sections are greater than 5 (6, 7, 8). The probability of obtaining a 2 is $\frac{1}{8}$ because this refers to 1 of the 8 sections. Thus, $P(A \text{ or } B) = \frac{3}{8} + \frac{1}{8}$ or $\frac{1}{2}$.

20. B: The events are dependent since the first marble was not replaced. The sample space of the second draw will decrease by 1 because there will be one less marble to choose from. The number of possible red marbles for the second draw will also decrease by 1. Thus, the probability may be written as $P(A \text{ and } B) = \frac{2}{10} \cdot \frac{1}{9}$. Thus, the probability she draws a red marble, does not replace it, and draws another red marble is $\frac{2}{90}$ or $\frac{1}{45}$.

Reading

1. B: It can be concluded that phonics is a more effective way to learn to read for two reasons. First, the passage states that literacy rates are lower now than they were 15 years ago, meaning that more people knew how to read 15 years ago. Then, the passage states that phonics was the main way people learned how to read then. Therefore, based on these two facts, it can be concluded that phonics is more effective. Choice A is incorrect because it states the opposite. Choice C cannot be inferred from the passage, nor can choice D.

2. C: The passage states that "Shortly before becoming the President of the United States in 1789, Washington was an important leader in the American Revolutionary War from 1775 to 1783." Retiring (choice D) and returning to Mount Vernon (choice A) came after this. Washington being made commander-in-chief for the second time is the last event in the passage.

3. B: In describing the marketing of "sea monkeys," the author describes it as creative genius, and attributes their popularity to the drawings and advertisements that appeared in comic books. It is reasonable to conclude that without the branding and (somewhat misleading) ads, they wouldn't have been as popular. Marketing them under the less exciting brand name "brine shrimp" likely wouldn't have resulted in as many sales. The passage does not mention whether "instant life" or "sea monkeys" was a more popular name (choice A). While the passage does mention "creative marketing" that showed drawings different from the actual creatures, it does not say that people thought they were buying actual monkeys (choice C). The passage states that sea monkeys were "at the height of their popularity" in the 1970s, so it is unreasonable to think that more homes have them today (choice D).

4. C: Choice A is incorrect because the passage states they were similar in size. The cost of production is not mentioned, eliminating choice B as a possibility. Choice D is incorrect because it was the eight-track tape that was included in these vehicles. Choice C is correct because the passage states the eight-track tape could store and play twice as many songs.

5. B: The passage states that, "Often, the agoraphobic will view his home as the safest possible place to be, and he may even be reluctant to leave his house," making B the correct choice. In the yard (choice A) or on the sidewalk (D) can be inferred as a possible fear (walking to the mailbox), and at the mall (choice C) is listed as a possible fear.

6. D: Choices B and C are only briefly mentioned, allowing them to be eliminated as possibilities. Although the passage does discuss what could happen to two balls released at the top of a mountain, that is not the purpose of the passage, so choice A can be eliminated. The purpose is to show how small differences (in this case two inches between two rubber balls) can have large effects. This is essentially what the butterfly effect is, and the purpose of the passage is to give an example to demonstrate this principle.

7. C: The first paragraph states that the main purpose of DST it to make better use of daylight. Public safety (choice A), benefit for retail businesses (choice B), and health (choice D) are mentioned but none of these is the main purpose.

8. A: Energy conservation is discussed as a possible benefit of DST, not a negative effect of it. The other choices are all listed as possible drawbacks.

9. D: The first paragraph states that DST involves setting clocks forward one hour in the spring and backward one hour in the fall.

10. B: The last sentence in paragraph four notes that agricultural and evening entertainment interests have historically been opposed to DST. Choices A and C list interests that benefit from DST, while choice D lists interests that can experience negative effects, but does not state that they oppose DST.

11. D: The passage gives examples of both good and bad effects extra daylight can have on health. This negates the other options.

12. D: The sixth paragraph notes that DST is observed in only some regions of Brazil. The other answer choices are all regions that generally do not observe DST.

13. C: The last paragraph of the passage notes that DST can lead to peculiar situations, and relays an anecdote about the effect of DST on the birth order of twins. The other answer choices are all possible complications but are not mentioned in the passage.

14. C: If $30,000,000 is gained over 7 weeks, each week has a gain of 1/7 of that, or approximately $4,200,000.

15. B: In the second paragraph, the author asserts that Benjamin Franklin suggested DST as a way to save candles. It was later used for military purposes (choice A) and it has been suggested that it could help reduce traffic fatalities (choice C), but neither of these was Franklin's purpose. There is no mention of reading (choice D).

16. B: Tip number 2 best answers this question. The tip recommends that those who drink whole milk gradually switch to fat-free milk. Since the question asks about ways to reduce saturated fat and calories, using skim milk in the place of water (choice A) does not address the issue being raised. The other two choices do not address lowering saturated fat and calories either.

17. A: The author uses headings to organize the passage. While the headings are bold print, such font is not used to organize the passage (i.e. notify the reader of what information is forthcoming), but rather to draw the reader's eyes to the headings. The passage does not include captions (choice B), which are used to label graphics; diagrams (choice C), which are graphics representing material; or labels (choice D), which again are used to identify graphics.

18. C: Tip number 2 bests answers this detail question. Reduced fat milk contains 2% fat.

19. B: Statement I and Statement II are both true statements about calcium-rich foods, according to the passage. Canned fish, including salmon with bones, is recommended as a calcium-rich food. Cheese is mentioned as a lactose-free alternative within the milk group. Statement III is false. According to the passage, condensed cream soups should be made with milk, not water, to be considered calcium-rich.

20. D: The best choice for this question is choice D. The other options would clarify information for minor details within the passage and would provide little new information for the reader. However, food recommendations for those who do not consume milk products are listed under a separate heading, and lactose intolerance is the only reason listed. The reader can deduce that this is a main idea in the passage and the definition of "lactose intolerance" would help explain this main idea to the reader.

21. B: The author's style is to give facts and details in a bulleted list. Of the options given, you are most likely to find this style in a health textbook. A tourist guidebook (choice A) would most likely make recommendations about where to eat, not what to eat. An encyclopedia (choice C) would list and define individual foods. A friendly letter (choice D) would have a date, salutation, and closing.

22. B: This question is concerned with the main idea of the passage. Although the passage is not explicit about why Martin and Beth's relationship is strained, by eliminating a number of answer choices, the right answer can easily be found. Choice A can be eliminated because Martin has not lost his job—he receives a page at the end of the passage concerning one of his patients. Choice B is not contradicted by the passage, but all that the reader is told is that Martin and Mary were once together. Choice C can be eliminated because the passage does not indicate how much Martin works. Choice D can be eliminated because Martin tells Beth that if she wants to go to the movies, they can go. The best choice, then, is B.

23. B: This question asks the reader to make a conclusion based on details from the passage. The reader knows that (1) Martin wears a pager for his job, (2) he has patients, and (3) one of his patients is going into cardiac arrest. Choices A and D can be eliminated because mechanics, film directors, and television producers do not see patients. Choice C seems like a possibility. After all, dentists see patients. Choice B is the best choice because if a person goes into cardiac arrest it is more likely a medical doctor rather than a dentist would be paged.

24. A: This question asks for the best definition of "rapport." A "rapport" is a relationship based on mutual understanding. With this in mind, Choice A might be a good answer, even though it is not an exact match. Choice B can be eliminated because it does not describe a relationship. Choice C can be eliminated because individuals can have a relationship based on mutual understanding without sharing a common goal. Choice D can be eliminated because loneliness has nothing to do with the definition of "rapport."

Writing

1. B: The verb should be in past tense rather than present tense. Choice A is incorrect because a comma should not separate the subject and verb of a sentence. Choice C is incorrect because it is better to write out *first* than it is to use numerical digits. Choice D is incorrect because a comma is required to separate the dependent clause at the beginning of the sentence from the independent clause at the end of the sentence.

2. C: *America's* is possessive. The sentence is referring to the pilots who lived in America. Choice A is incorrect because *years* is plural and not possessive. Choice B is incorrect because the comma correctly separates the dependent clause at the beginning of the sentence from the independent clause at the end of the sentence. Choice D is incorrect because *theirselves* is not a real word.

3. B: A comma is needed to offset the nonessential clause *Roscoe Turner*. Choice A is incorrect because *Roscoe Turner* is a nonessential clause; it is not required to understand the meaning of the sentence. The clause should be offset by commas on both sides. Choice C is incorrect because *as* would change the meaning of the sentence to imply that Roscoe Turner dressed as a lion cub. Choice D is incorrect because the words *plane* and *airplane* can be used interchangeably.

4. B: A semicolon is used to separate two related independent clauses. In contrast, a colon is used to set off lists. Choice A is incorrect because *barnstormers* is referring to multiple pilots and should remain in the plural. Choice C is incorrect because *plane's* is correctly written as a possessive. Choice D is incorrect because *while* correctly implies that the barnstormers played tennis at the same time as the plane flew.

5. C: The passage is discussing the past. Therefore, the past tense *could* is preferable over the present tense *can*. Choice A is incorrect because the comma is needed to set off the phrase at the beginning of the sentence. Choice B is incorrect because *traveled* only has a single *l*. Although both *a* and *its* could be used in this sentence, choice D is incorrect because *it's* is a conjunction for *it is* and would be incorrect if used in this part of the sentence.

6. B: *Sophisticated* is the correct spelling. Choice A is incorrect because *pilots* is not a possessive in this context. Choice C is incorrect because a comma is not needed to separate a list that only has two items. Choice D is incorrect because *their* is a possessive, which fits the sentence. *They're* refers to *they are*, which does not work in this sentence.

7. A: The word order in answer choice A best conveys the meaning of the sentence concisely. Choice B is incorrect because *Nungesser and Coli* is a nonessential phrase and needs to be separated from the rest of the sentence with commas. Choice C inverts the order of the sentence and makes it more awkward; it is better to have a simple subject and verb at the beginning of a sentence. Choice D is incorrect because the word order confuses the sentence's meaning.

8. C: A comma is rarely needed after the word *and*. A comma would only be required if a nonessential phrase followed *and*. However, the word *and* in this sentence simply separates a two-item series. The other commas are correct because commas should be used both before and after a state's name.

9. D: This answer choice uses the correct punctuation and verb tense. Choice A is incorrect because the conjunction *and* separates two independent clauses; when the conjunction is used in this way, a comma must come before it. Choice B is incorrect because there is no conjunction between the two independent clauses, making the answer choice a run-on sentence. Choice C is incorrect because the passage is written in the past tense but *says* is incorrectly written in the present tense.

10. A: is the best answer choice because *in conclusion* sums up the essay and leads into the final paragraph. Choices B and D are incorrect because the words *furthermore* and *additionally* indicate that an additional argument will be made. However, sentence 35 begins a concluding paragraph with no significant information added. Choice C is incorrect because the word *therefore* should be used as a conclusion to a specific point rather than the conclusion of an entire essay.

11. B: The combination of *hardly* and *not* constitutes a double negative, so answer choices A and C are incorrect. Answer choice D is incorrect because "them" refers to some unknown objects rather than "themselves."

12. C: The plural demonstrative adjective *these* should be used with the plural noun *sorts*. Choices A and B use the singular "sort," and choice D uses the singular "this."

13. A: This sentence contains a number of parallel structures that must be treated consistently. Choice B adds the subject *he*, which makes the second part of the sentence an independent clause, so the comma is not appropriate. Choice C fails to set off the nonessential clause "an individual of considerable influence" with commas. Choice D changes the meaning by suggesting that Mr. King gave his entire fortune to his community rather than the broader meaning suggested in the original sentence.

14. A: In this sentence, *whose* is the appropriate possessive pronoun to modify *opinion*. Choices B and D are grammatically correct but convoluted and awkward. Choice C combines two independent clauses with no punctuation, so it is incorrect.

15. B: Answer choice B is precise and clear. Answer choice A keeps the meaning, but is awkward and wordy. Answer choice C uses the wrong verb tense. Answer choice D would put the word *work* into the sentence twice. It is not completely incorrect, but it is not the best choice.

16. A: Answer choice A correctly adds the necessary information about the alligator's traditional role within the Everglades. Answer choice B reassembles the information from the original sentence but does not provide the key detail about the alligator's place in the Everglades. Answer choices C and D add information that cannot be inferred from the original sentence.

17. B: Answer choice B provides the full information that is needed to complete the original idea. Answer choice A provides only partial information and is thus insufficient. Answer choice C is repetitive and does not offer any new information to complete the original idea. Answer choice D offers inferred information that is not contained within the original sentence, so it cannot be added.

18. D: Answer choice D adds the correct information about the concern that follows the python's expansion within the Everglades, without adding inferred information. Answer choice A is correct but is not necessarily effective in explaining the reason for concern. Answer choice B adds

234

information that cannot be clearly inferred (i.e., what biologists and environmentalists originally believed about the python in the Everglades). Answer choice C adds information that has no place in the original sentence.

19. C: Answer choice C effectively links the ideas contained in the original sentence. Answer choice A is accurate but ineffective and incomplete, because it fails to explain *who* was doing the searching and destroying. Answer choices B and D add judgment statements that are not in the original sentence.

20. A: Answer choice A sufficiently links the ideas in the original sentence, connecting the reality of control with the hope for eradication. Answer choice B contradicts information that is not in the original sentence; that is to say, the original sentence states clearly that "eradication is preferred," not frowned upon. Answer choice C is partially correct but adds information about researchers continuing to search for means of eradication. Answer choice D contains correct information but does not encompass the full meaning of the original sentence and leaves out valuable information (i.e., the virtual impossibility of eradication).

TSI Practice Test #5

Math

1. Which of the following graphs represents the inequality $-2 < x \leq 4$?

A.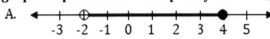

B.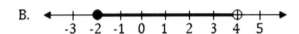

C.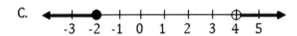

D.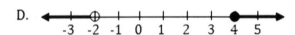

2. Which of the following is equivalent to $3 - 2x < 5$?

   A. $x < 1$
   B. $x > 1$
   C. $x < -1$
   D. $x > -1$

3. A certain exam has 30 questions. A student gets 1 point for each question he gets right and loses half a point for a question he answers incorrectly; he neither gains nor loses any points for a question left blank. If C is the number of questions a student gets right and B is the number of questions he leaves blank, which of the following represents his score on the exam?

   A. $C - \frac{1}{2}B$
   B. $C - \frac{1}{2}(30 - B)$
   C. $C - \frac{1}{2}(30 - B - C)$
   D. $(30 - C) - \frac{1}{2}(30 - B)$

4. Every person attending a certain meeting hands out a business card to every other person at the meeting. If there are a total of 30 cards handed out, how many people are at the meeting?

   A. 5
   B. 6
   C. 10
   D. 15

5. Which of the following is equal to this expression: $x(y - 2) + y(3 - x)$?

   A. $xy + y$
   B. $-2x + 3y$
   C. $2xy - 2x + 3y$
   D. $xy + 3y - x - 2$

6. At a school carnival, three students spend an average of $10. Six other students spend an average of $4. What is the average amount of money spent by all nine students?
  A. $5
  B. $6
  C. $7
  D. $8

7. The formula for finding the volume of a cone is $V = \frac{1}{3}\pi r^2 h$. Which of the following equations is correctly solved for r?
  A. $r = \frac{1}{3}\pi h$
  B. $r = \sqrt{\frac{3V}{\pi h}}$
  C. $r = \frac{3V}{\pi h}$
  D. $r = V - \frac{1}{3}\pi h$

8. Given the equation: $\frac{2}{x+4} = \frac{3}{x}$, what is the value of x?
  A. 10
  B. 12
  C. −12
  D. −14

9. What is the solution to the equation: $4\sqrt{x} + 8 = 24$?
  A. $x = 2$
  B. $x = 4$
  C. $x = 12$
  D. $x = 16$

10. Which of the following represents the solution to the following system of linear equations:

$$5x + 9y = -7$$
$$2x - 4y = 20$$

  A. $x = 3, y = 2$
  B. $x = 4, y = 3$
  C. $x = 4, y = -3$
  D. $x = 3, y = -2$

11. In the figure pictured below, *AD* = 5 and *AB* = 12. What is the length of *AC* (not shown)?

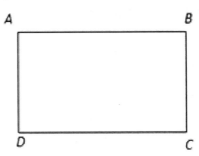

A. 10
B. 13
C. 17
D. 60

12. In the figure pictured below, find the value of *x*:

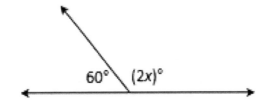

A. 30
B. 60
C. 100
D. 120

13. Which of the following is the best estimate of the circumference of the circle shown below?

A. 12
B. 24
C. 36
D. 48

14. Based on the figure below, describe how rectangle *ABCD* can be carried onto its image *A′B′C′D′*.

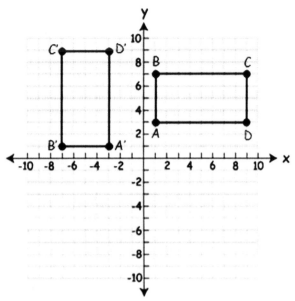

    A. Reflection across the x-axis
    B. Reflection across the y-axis
    C. Rotation 90° clockwise about the origin
    D. Rotation 90° counterclockwise about the origin

15. Examine the triangles below:

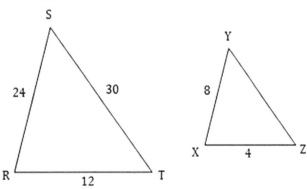

In order for Δ*RST* to be similar to Δ*XYZ*, what must be the length of $\overline{YZ}$?

    A. 10
    B. 14
    C. 15
    D. 22

16. Two hikers start at a ranger station and leave at the same time. One hiker heads due west at 3 miles/hour. The other hiker heads due north at 4 miles/hour. How far apart are the hikers after 2 hours of hiking?

    A. 5 miles
    B. 7 miles
    C. 10 miles
    D. 14 miles

17. Which frequency table is represented by the histogram shown below?

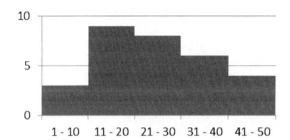

A.

Interval	Frequency
1 – 10	3
11 – 20	9
21 – 30	8
31 – 40	6
41 – 50	4

B.

Interval	Frequency
1 – 10	3
11 – 20	8
21 – 30	8
31 – 40	6
41 – 50	3

C.

Interval	Frequency
1 – 10	3
11 – 20	9
21 – 30	8
31 – 40	5
41 – 50	4

D.

Interval	Frequency
1 – 10	2
11 – 20	9
21 – 30	8
31 – 40	6
41 – 50	4

18. Abram rolls a die. What is the probability he rolls an even number or a number greater than 4?

    A. $\frac{2}{3}$
    B. $\frac{1}{6}$
    C. $\frac{3}{4}$
    D. $\frac{5}{6}$

19. What is the expected value of spinning a spinner with 10 equally spaced sections labeled 1–10?

    A. 4.5
    B. 5
    C. 5.5
    D. 6

20. Amanda rolls a die. She will lose $6 if the die lands on a 3 or 5. She will win $3 if the die lands on a 1 or 2. She will lose $9 if the die lands on a 4 or 6. What is the expected value?

    A. −$2
    B. −$4
    C. −$5
    D. −$6

Reading

Directions for questions 1–6:

Read the statement or passage and then choose the best answer to the question. Answer the question based on what is stated or implied in the statement or passage.

1. Wells provide water for drinking, bathing, and cleaning to many people across the world. When wells are being dug, there are several issues that must be taken into account to minimize the chance of potential problems down the road. First, it's important to be aware that groundwater levels differ, depending on the season. In general, groundwater levels will be higher during the winter. So if a well is being dug during the winter, it should be deep enough to remain functional during the summer, when water levels are lower. Well water that is used is replaced by melting snow and rain. If the well owners are using the water faster than it can be replaced, however, the water levels will be lowered. The only way to remedy this, aside from waiting for the groundwater to be replenished naturally, is to deepen the well.

From this passage, it can be concluded that

    A. It is better to have a well that is too deep than one that is too shallow.
    B. Most well owners will face significant water shortages every year.
    C. Most people who dig wells during the winter do not make them deep enough.
    D. Well water is safe to use for bathing and cleaning, but is not suitable for drinking.

2. Today's low-fat craze has led many people to assume that all fats are unhealthy, but this is simply not the case. Fat is an essential component of any healthy diet because it provides energy and helps the body process nutrients. While all fats should be consumed in moderation, there are good and bad fats. Good fats are what are known as unsaturated fats. They are found in olive oil, fatty fish like salmon, and nuts. Bad fats are saturated and trans fats. They are found in foods like butter, bacon, and ice cream. Consumption of foods that contain trans or saturated fats should be restricted or avoided altogether.

The main purpose of this passage is to

    A. Explain why fat is important for the body.
    B. Discuss some of the main sources of good fats.
    C. Talk about the different types of fats.
    D. Discuss examples of foods that should be avoided.

3. Satire is a genre that originated in the ancient world and is still popular today. Although satire is often humorous, its purposes and intentions go well beyond simply making people laugh. Satire is a way for the playwright, author, or television producer to criticize society, human nature, and individuals that he holds in contempt. Satire as we know it today developed in Ancient Greece and Rome. There were three main types. The first, Menippean satire, focused on criticizing aspects of human nature. This was done by introducing stereotypical, one-dimensional characters. Horatian satire can be viewed as gentle satire. It made fun of people and their habits but in a way that was not offensive. Juvenalian satire was written is such a way that the audience would experience feelings of disgust and aversion when they saw the characters and their actions. Some of the most popular satires today are fake news shows, like the *Daily Show* and the *Colbert Report*, and satirical comic strips like *Doonesbury*.

The main purpose of the passage is

- A. To discuss the history of satire.
- B. To present the major types of satire.
- C. To discuss modern examples of satire.
- D. To present the purposes of satire.

4. Many people believe that how we express our feelings is mainly determined by our upbringing and culture. Undoubtedly, this is true in some cases. In North America, for example, it is customary to shake hands when we meet somebody to express acceptance, whereas in other countries they may simply bow slightly to indicate this. Many feelings, however, are expressed in similar ways by people all over the world. These emotions include fear, anger, happiness, disgust, and sorrow. For example, if a person is experiencing fear, his or her eyes will widen and the pupils will dilate. This reaction is largely involuntary. The finding that people express many feelings in a similar manner, regardless of where they are from, indicates that facial expressions are influenced more by evolution than culture.

Based on the passage, it can be concluded that

- A. People often can't hide what they are feeling.
- B. People from other parts of the world express happiness differently.
- C. Fear is the only emotion that is felt by everybody in the world.
- D. Acceptance is a feeling invented by man.

5. Cities are typically warmer than the surrounding countryside, a phenomenon known as the heat island effect. There are numerous causes of this phenomenon, including emissions from cars and buildings. This creates a mini greenhouse effect. In rural areas, the standing water in marshes and ponds evaporates, which cools the air slightly. This does not occur to the same extent in the city. The tall buildings in the center of most cities block winds that would provide some relief from the excessive heat. Finally, the color and material of most roads and buildings absorbs rather than reflects heat. Although planting trees and using building materials that reflect heat may alleviate the problem somewhat, it will by no means eliminate it.

The main purpose of the passage is to

- A. Talk about how the problem of heat island can be solved.
- B. Argue that cities should make an effort to plant more trees.
- C. Present the major causes of the problem of heat island.
- D. Contrast the city environment to that of the countryside.

6. Marsupials resemble mammals in a number of ways. For one thing, they are warm-blooded creatures. They have hair, and the mothers feed their young by producing milk. However, one thing that separates marsupials from mammals is that their young are born when they are not yet fully developed. Most are born after only about four or five weeks. They finish their development in the pouch of their mother. Some of the more commonly known marsupials are koalas, kangaroos, and opossums. They are a diverse group, with many members having little in common besides their reproductive traits.

A major difference between marsupials and mammals is

    A.   Marsupials have hair, while mammals do not.
    B.   Mammals are a much more diverse group than marsupials.
    C.   Marsupials are born at an earlier stage of development.
    D.   Mammals feed their young by producing milk.

Questions 7–11 are based on the following passage:

Harriet Tubman was a runaway slave from Maryland who became known as the "Moses of her people." Over the course of 10 years, and at great personal risk, she led hundreds of slaves to freedom along the Underground Railroad, a secret network of safe houses where runaway slaves could stay on their journey north to freedom. She later became a leader in the abolitionist movement, and during the Civil War she was a spy for the federal forces in South Carolina as well as a nurse.

Harriet Tubman's name at birth was Araminta Ross. She was one of 11 children of Harriet and Benjamin Ross born into slavery in Dorchester County, Maryland. As a child, Ross was "hired out" by her master as a nursemaid for a small baby. Ross had to stay awake all night so that the baby wouldn't cry and wake the mother. If Ross fell asleep, the baby's mother whipped her. From a very young age, Ross was determined to gain her freedom.

As a slave, Araminta Ross was scarred for life when she refused to help in the punishment of another young slave. A young man had gone to the store without permission, and when he returned, the overseer wanted to whip him. He asked Ross to help but she refused. When the young man started to run away, the overseer picked up a heavy iron weight and threw it at him. He missed the young man and hit Ross instead. The weight nearly crushed her skull and left a deep scar. She was unconscious for days, and suffered from seizures for the rest of her life.

In 1844, Ross married a free black named John Tubman and took his last name. She also changed her first name, taking her mother's name, Harriet. In 1849, worried that she and the other slaves on the plantation were going to be sold, Tubman decided to run away. Her husband refused to go with her, so she set out with her two brothers, and followed the North Star in the sky to guide her north to freedom. Her brothers became frightened and turned back, but she continued on and reached Philadelphia. There she found work as a household servant and saved her money so she could return to help others escape.

7. This passage is mainly about

    A. slaves in the Civil War.

    B. how slaves escaped along the Underground Railroad.

    C. Harriet Tubman's role as an abolitionist leader.

    D. Harriet Tubman's life as a slave.

8. The author of the passage describes Harriet Tubman's life as a slave to show

    A. why she wanted to escape slavery.

    B. why she was a spy during the Civil War.

    C. why she suffered from seizures.

    D. how she loved babies.

9. Harriet Tubman's seizures were caused by

    A. a whipping.

    B. a severe head injury.

    C. loss of sleep.

    D. a birth defect.

10. How is this passage structured?

    A. cause and effect

    B. problem and solution

    C. chronological order

    D. compare and contrast

11. How did Araminta Ross come to be known as Harriet Tubman?

    A. She took her husband's last name and changed her first name to her mother's name.

    B. She was named after the plantation owner's wife.

    C. She changed her name because she was wanted as an Underground Railroad runner.

    D. She changed her name to remain anonymous as a Civil War spy.

Questions 12–16 are based on the following passage:

> There will come soft rains and the smell of the ground,
> And swallows circling with their shimmering sound;
>
> And frogs in the pools singing at night,
> And wild plum trees in tremulous white;
>
> Robins will wear their feathery fire
> Whistling their whims on a low fence-wire;
>
> And not one will know of the war, not one
> Will care at last when it is done.
>
> Not one would mind, neither bird nor tree
> If mankind perished utterly;
>
> And Spring herself, when she woke at dawn,
> Would scarcely know that we were gone.

12. How many stanzas does this poem have?

    A. 2
    B. 4
    C. 6
    D. 10

13. Which line uses personification?

    A. Line 2
    B. Line 4
    C. Line 7
    D. Line 11

14. The "we" used in line 12 refers to

    A. all of mankind.
    B. the victors of the war.
    C. Americans.
    D. the poet and the reader.

15. This poem is an example of a(n)

    A. sonnet.
    B. rhymed verse.
    C. free verse.
    D. lyric.

16. Which of these statements offers the best summary of the poem?

    A. Nature does not care about the affairs of mankind.
    B. It is the government's responsibility to fight a war.
    C. War has a devastating impact on nature.
    D. Wars should not be fought in the spring.

Questions 17–20 refer to the following passage:

Grapes are one of the oldest cultivated fruits. Hieroglyphics show that Egyptians were involved in grape and wine production. Also, the early Romans were known to have developed many grape varieties.

Grapes have been grown in California for more than 200 years. The tradition of viticulture (growing grapes) began in 1769 when Spanish friars established missions throughout California.

In California, the boom in grapes planted for eating arose in the early 1800s. William Wolfskill, founder of California's citrus industry, planted the first table grape vineyard in 1839 near Los Angeles.

By the 1850s, the United States had officially acquired California from Mexico and 80,000 gold prospectors had moved to the region, a few of them realizing that there was money in grapes as well as in gold.

Today, California wine, table grapes and raisins are all important agricultural commodities, with approximately 700,000 acres planted in vineyards.

About 85% of California's table grape production is in the southern San Joaquin Valley region with the Coachella Valley region accounting for most of the remaining production.

17. This passage is mainly about

    A. how Egyptians grew wine grapes.
    B. how to make raisins from grapes.
    C. William Wolfskill's life as a farmer.
    D. the history of growing grapes in California.

18. The best title for this passage is

    A. Early Wine Production.
    B. California Table Grapes.
    C. Viticulture in California.
    D. The California Missions.

19. Most of California's table grapes are grown in

    A. the San Joaquin Valley region.
    B. the Coachella Valley region.
    C. Los Angeles.
    D. the California missions.

20. William Wolfskill is credited with

    A. deciphering hieroglyphics about grape and wine production.
    B. helping the United States acquire California.
    C. planting the first table grape vineyard in California.
    D. farming 700,000 acres of vineyards.

Questions 21–24 pertain to the following passage:

How are Hypotheses Confirmed?

Most scientists agree that while the scientific method is an invaluable methodological tool, it is not a perfect method for arriving at objectively true universals. For example, a scientist may be interested in demonstrating that all members of a given category *x* are also members of a given category *y*. However, a hypothesis of the form "all *x* are also *y*" cannot be proven true by observing instances of x and demonstrating that they are also y. Even if one were able to observe all instances of *x* in the universe and demonstrate that each one was also *y*, this still falls short of proving the hypothesis *all x are y*, because it is still possible that at some point in the past, there existed an *x* that was not *y*, or that at some point in the future, there will exist an *x* that is not *y*.

Leaving that issue aside, though, consider the impact on the hypothesis of two separate pieces of data: 1) an *x* that is *y*; 2) an *x* that is not *y*. The first is just one of many pieces of data that must be assembled in order to give weight to the hypothesis. The second is a single piece of data that independently invalidates the hypothesis. The problem, though, is not with the evidence or with reality, but with the way we have chosen to approach the issue.

As an alternative to this true/false paradigm, we can instead choose to form our hypotheses in such a way that we are not seeking to make universal claims of fact but instead are seeking to make probabilistic claims of likelihood. Consider the difference between "all *x* are also *y*" and "a given *x* is also *y*." The answer to the first must be universally *yes* or universally *no*. The answer to the second is a percentage based on probability. Before going further, we will assign example parameters to the terms *x* and *y*. Consider instead the two hypotheses: 1) all monkeys have hair; 2) a given monkey will have hair. With our first hypothesis, as we have already seen, we would have to investigate every monkey in existence in our attempt to prove the hypothesis. A single instance of a hairless monkey would invalidate the hypothesis. With the second hypothesis, however, we can investigate a representative sample of monkeys and make an estimate of the probability of hair within the population (all monkeys) based on the results. This approach does two things for us. First, it allows us to make a prediction about any given monkey without checking the entire population. Second, it allows us to keep making this prediction even if a hairless monkey is found, because we are only stating the likelihood of a monkey having hair, rather than making a universal claim.

The fact that a hairless monkey could one day be discovered does not invalidate Hypothesis 2 as it would Hypothesis 1. Rather, it is expected that there may be rare "disconfirming" occurrences since the hypothesis is only stated as a likelihood rather than a certainty. Because of the impossibility of stating with certainty that a certain event has never happened, does not currently exist, and never will exist, scientific hypotheses are frequently confirmed as probabilities rather than universal truths.

21. What is the main idea of the third paragraph?

A. One hairy monkey proves the hypothesis "All monkeys are hairy."
B. The same piece of evidence can both confirm and disconfirm a hypothesis.
C. Rather than making a universal claim, a hypothesis can be stated as probability.
D. The scientific method is not a failsafe method for arriving at objective truth.

22. The closest synonym for the word "disconfirming" in the fourth paragraph would be:

A. proving
B. dissipating
C. distilling
D. disproving

23. Which of the following is true of hypotheses of the form "All x are also y"?

A. Something that is neither x nor y disproves the hypothesis.
B. Something that is both x and y disproves the hypothesis.
C. Something that is x but not y disproves the hypothesis.
D. Something that is y but not x disproves the hypothesis.

24. Using the same reasoning as that in the passage, which of the following hypotheses can be confirmed as probabilities?

    I. All automobiles have four wheels.
    II. A specific automobile has four wheels.
    III. No automobiles have four wheels.

A. I only
B. II only
C. Both I and II
D. I, II, and III

Writing

Alberto wrote this essay about a memorable teacher. He would like you to read his paper and look for corrections and improvements he should make. When you finish reading, answer questions 1–10.

(1) I had the same teacher for both third and 4th grades, which were difficult years for me. (2) My teacher and I did not get along, and I don't think she liked me. (3) Every day, I thought she was treating me unfairly and being mean. (4) Because I felt that way, I think I acted out and stopped doing my work. (5) In the middle of fourth grade, my family moved to a new town, and I had Mr. Shanbourne as my new teacher.

(6) From the very first day in Mr. Shanbourne's class, I was on guard. (7) I was expecting to hate my teacher and for him to hate me back when I started his class. (8) Mr. Shanbourne took me by surprise right away when he asked me if I wanted to stand up and introduce myself. (9) I said no, probably in a surly voice, and he just nodded and began teaching the first lesson of the day.

(10) I wasn't sure how to take this. (11) My old teacher forced me to do things and gave me detention if I didn't. (12) She loved detention and gave it to me for anything I did—talking back, working too loudly, forgetting an assignment. (13) Mr. Shanbourne obviously didn't believe in detention, and I tried him! (14) During my first two weeks at my new school I did my best to get in trouble. (15) I zoned out in class, turned work in late, talked out in class, and handed in assignments after the due date. (16) Mr. Shanbourne just nodded.

(17) Mr. Shanbourne asked me to stay in during recess. (18) *This is it*, I thought. I was going to get in trouble, get the detention my ten-year-old self had practically been begging for. (19) After all of the other kids ran outside, I walked up to Mr. Shanbourne's desk.

(20) "How are you doing, Alberto," he said.

(21) I mumbled something.

(22) He told me he was disappointed in my behavior over the last two weeks. (23) I had expected this and just took it. (24) The detention was coming any second. (25) Than Mr. Shanbourne took me by surprise. (26) He told me that even though he didn't know me very well, he believed I could be a hard worker and that I could be successful in his class. (27) He asked me how he could help me listen better and turn my work in on time.

(28) I told him I had to think about it and rushed out to recess. (29) Even though my answer seemed rude, I was stunned. (30) I hadn't had a teacher in years who seemed to care about me, and said he believed in my abilities.

(31) To be honest, my behavior did not improve right away and I still turned in many of my assignments late. (32) But over the last few months of fourth grade, things changed. (33) Mr. Shanbourne continued to believe in me, encourage me, and help me, and I responded by doing my best. (34) I had a different teacher for fifth grade, but whenever I was struggling I walked down to Mr. Shanbourne's classroom to get his advice. (35) I'll never forget how Mr. Shanbourne helped me, and I hope he'll never forget me either.

1. What change should be made to sentence 1?

   A. Change *teacher* to *teachers*
   B. Change *4ᵗʰ* to *fourth*
   C. Delete the comma after *grades*
   D. Change *years* to *year's*

2. What is the most effective way to revise sentence 7?

   A. I started his class expecting my teacher to hate me back and for me to hate him.
   B. Expecting to hate my teacher, I started his class expecting him to hate me back.
   C. Starting his class expecting to hate my teacher, I also expected to hate him back.
   D. I started his class expecting to hate my teacher and for him to hate me back.

3. What is the most effective way to combine sentences 10 and 11?

   A. I wasn't sure how to take this, and my old teacher forced me to do things and gave me detention if I didn't.
   B. I wasn't sure how to take this, although my old teacher forced me to do things and gave me detention if I didn't.
   C. I wasn't sure how to take this because my old teacher forced me to do things and gave me detention if I didn't.
   D. I wasn't sure how to take this as a result of my old teacher forced me to do things and gave me detention if I didn't.

4. Which phrase, if any, can be deleted from sentence 15 without changing the meaning of the sentence?

   A. zoned out in class
   B. turned work in late
   C. talked out in class
   D. No change

5. What transition should be added to the beginning of sentence 16?

   A. Surprisingly
   B. Actually
   C. Furthermore
   D. Instead

6. Which version of sentence 20 is correctly punctuated?

   A. "How are you doing, Alberto?" he said.
   B. "How are you doing, Alberto? he said."
   C. "How are you doing, Alberto." he said.
   D. No change.

7. What change should be made to sentence 25?
  A. Change *Than* to *Then*.
  B. Change *Shanbourne* to *Shanbourne's*.
  C. Add a comma after *Shanbourne*.
  D. Change *by* to *bye*.

8. What change should be made to sentence 30?
  A. Change *hadn't* to *haven't*.
  B. Change *who* to *whom*.
  C. Delete the comma after *me*.
  D. Change *believed* to *beleived*.

9. What change should be made to sentence 31?
  A. Delete the comma after *honest*.
  B. Change *did* to *does*.
  C. Add a comma after *away*.
  D. Change *many* to *much*.

10. What change should be made to sentence 33?
  A. Change *continued* to *continues*.
  B. Delete the comma after *in me*.
  C. Change *encuorage* to *encourage*.
  D. Delete the comma after *help me*.

For questions 11–15, select the best option for replacing the underlined portion of the sentence. The first option listed is always the same as the current version of the sentence.

11. Several theories <u>about what caused dinosaurs to have extinction exist</u>, but scientists are still unable to reach a concrete conclusion.
  A. about what caused dinosaurs to have extinction exist
  B. about what caused dinosaurs to become extinct exist
  C. about the causes of the dinosaur extinction exists
  D. in regards to the extinction cause of dinosaurs exist

12. <u>Although most persons</u> prefer traditional pets like cats and dogs, others gravitate towards exotic animals like snakes and lizards.
  A. Although most persons
  B. Because most people
  C. While most people
  D. Maybe some persons

13. It is important that software companies offer tech support <u>to customers who are encountering problems</u>.
  A. to customers who are encountering problems
  B. because not all customers encounter problems
  C. with customers who encounter problems
  D. to customer who is encountering difficulties

14. The fact <u>that children eat high fat diets and watch excessive amount of television are a cause of concern</u> for many parents.

    A. that children eat high fat diets and watch excessive amount of television are a cause of concern

    B. the children eat high fat diets and watches excessive amount of television are a cause of concern

    C. is children eat high fat diets and watch excessive amount of television is a cause for concern

    D. that children eat high fat diets and watch excessive amounts of television is a cause for concern

15. <u>Contrarily to popular beliefs</u>, bats do not actually entangle themselves in the hair of humans on purpose.

    A. Contrarily to popular beliefs

    B. Contrary to popular belief

    C. Contrary to popularity belief

    D. Contrary to popular believing

16. Mitosis is the process of cell division, and if there are errors during this process, it can result in serious complications.

Rewrite, beginning with

<u>Serious complications can result</u> ...

The next words will be

    A. during the process of cell division

    B. if there are errors during the process

    C. in the process of mitosis

    D. when this process leads to errors

17. It was a very tough decision, but Sharon finally decided after much consideration to study biology at Yale University.

Rewrite, beginning with

<u>After much consideration</u> ...

The next words will be

    A. Sharon finally decided to study

    B. it was a very tough decision

    C. Sharon studied biology at Yale University

    D. a very tough study was decided.

18. Small business owners must compete with larger stores by providing excellent service, because department store prices are simply too low for owners of small businesses to match them.

Rewrite, beginning with

<u>Prices in department stores are simply too low for owners of small businesses to match them, ...</u>

The next words will be

    A. so small business owners must
    B. while small business owners must
    C. when small business owners must
    D. because small business owners must

19. Ants are fascinating creatures, and some of their unique characteristics are their strength, organizational skills, and construction talents.

Rewrite, beginning with

<u>Strength, organizational skills, and construction talents</u> ...

The next words will be

    A. are some of the unique characteristics
    B. are possessed by fascinating creatures
    C. of ants are fascinating characteristics
    D. are unique characteristics of their

20. Many people do not regularly wear their seatbelts, even though law enforcement professionals warn motorists about the dangers of not doing so.

Rewrite, beginning with

<u>Despite warnings by law enforcement professionals</u> ...

The next words will be

    A. motorists ignore the dangers of not doing so
    B. many people do not regularly wear their seatbelts
    C. about the people who don't wear seatbelts
    D. even though motorists do not wear seatbelts

Essay

In the United States, elections are decided by majority vote, with the candidate who receives over 50% of the vote winning the entire seat. However, in many other countries, the election system is proportional, with parties receiving a particular number of seats based on the percentage of the vote they receive. Please write a multiple-paragraph persuasive essay (approximately 350–500 words) discussing which system you believe to be better and why.

Answers and Explanations for Test #5

Math

1. A: When graphing an inequality, a solid circle at an endpoint means that the number at that endpoint is included in the range, while a hollow circle means it is not. Since the inequality says that x is strictly greater than 2, the circle at 2 should be hollow; since the inequality says that x is less than *or equal to* 4, the circle at 4 should be solid. $2 < x \leq 4$ indicates that x is between 2 and 4, so the area between the circles should be shaded; the two end rays in choice D would instead represent the pair of inequalities "$x < 2$ or $x \geq 4$".

2. D: To simplify the inequality $3 - 2x < 5$, we can first subtract 3 from both sides: $3 - 2x - 3 < 5 - 3 \Rightarrow -2x < 2$. Now, we can divide both sides of the inequality by -2. When an inequality is multiplied or divided by a negative number, its direction changes ($<$ becomes $>$, $\leq$ becomes $\geq$, and vice versa). So $-2x < 2$ becomes $\frac{-2x}{-2} > \frac{2}{-2}$, or $x > -1$.

3. C: If the exam has 30 questions, and the student answered C questions correctly and left B questions blank, then the number of questions the student answered incorrectly must be $30 - B - C$. He gets one point for each correct question, or $1 \cdot C = C$ points, and loses $\frac{1}{2}$ point for each incorrect question, or $\frac{1}{2}(30 - B - C)$ points. Since the blank questions do not affect his score, one way to express his total score is $C - \frac{1}{2}(30 - B - C)$.

4. B: Call the number of people present at the meeting x. If each person hands out a card to every *other* person (that is, every person besides himself), then each person hands out $x - 1$ cards. The total number of cards handed out is therefore $(x - 1)$. Since we are told there are a total of 30 cards handed out, we have the equation $x(x - 1) = 30$, which we can rewrite as the quadratic equation $x^2 - x - 30 = 0$. We can solve this equation by factoring the quadratic expression. One way to do this is to find two numbers that add to the coefficient of x (in this case -1) and that multiply to the constant term (in this case -30). Those two numbers are 5 and -6. Our factored equation is therefore $(x + 5)(x - 6) = 0$. To make the equation true, one or both of the factors must be zero: either $x + 5 = 0$, in which case $x = -5$, or $x - 6 = 0$, in which case $x = 6$. Obviously, the number of people at the meeting cannot be negative, so the second solution, $x = 6$, must be correct.

5. B: First, let's distribute the x and y that are outside the parentheses and then combine like terms: $x(y - 2) + y(3 - x) = (xy - 2x) + (3y - xy) = -2x + 3y + xy - xy = -2x + 3y$.

6. B: The average is the total amount spent divided by the number of students. The first three students spend an average of $10, so the total amount they spend is $3 \cdot \$10 = \$30$. The other six students spend an average of $4, so the total amount they spend is $6 \cdot \$4 = \$24$. The total amount spent by all nine students is $\$30 + \$24 = \$54$, and the average amount they spend is $\$54 \div 9 = \$6$.

7. B: Dividing both sides of the equation by $\frac{1}{3}\pi h$ gives $r^2 = \frac{V}{\frac{1}{3}\pi h}$. Solving for r gives $r = \sqrt{\frac{V}{\frac{1}{3}\pi h}}$ or $r = \sqrt{\frac{3V}{\pi h}}$.

8. C: We can cross-multiply to obtain: $2x = 3(x + 4)$ or $2x = 3x + 12$. Solving for x gives $x = -12$.

256

9. D: The radical equation may be solved by first subtracting 8 from both sides of the equation. Doing so gives $4\sqrt{x} = 16$. Dividing both sides of the equation by 4 gives $\sqrt{x} = 4$. Squaring both sides gives $x = 16$.

10. C: Using the method of elimination to solve the system of linear equations, each term in the top equation may be multiplied by −2, while each term in the bottom equation may be multiplied by 5. Doing so produces two new equations with x-terms that will add to 0. The sum of $-10x - 18y = 14$ and $10x - 20y = 100$ may be written as $-38y = 114$, so $y = -3$. Substituting the y-value of −3 into the top, original equation gives $5x + 9(-3) = -7$. Solving for x gives $x = 4$. Thus, the solution is $x = 4$, $y = -3$.

11. B: Use the Pythagorean Theorem to solve this problem: $a^2 + b^2 = c^2$ where c is the hypotenuse while a and b are the legs of the triangle.

$$5^2 + 12^2 = c^2$$

$$25 + 144 = c^2 = 169$$

$$c = \sqrt{169} = 13$$

12. B: Angles that form a straight line add up to 180 degrees. Such angles are sometimes referred to as being "supplementary."

$$60 + 2x = 180$$

$$2x = 120$$

$$x = 60$$

13. C: The formula for circumference (C) is $C = \pi \cdot diameter$. The diameter is 12.2 and π is approximately 3.14, so 12 and 3 are reasonable approximations for this problem:

$$3 \cdot 12 = 36$$

14. D: As rectangle $ABCD$ is moved from Quadrant I into Quadrant II, it is rotated in a counterclockwise manner. Therefore, rectangle $ABCD$ can be carried onto its image $A'B'C'D'$ by a 90° counterclockwise rotation about the origin.

15. A: If two triangles are similar, then all pairs of corresponding sides are proportional. For ΔRST to be similar to ΔXYZ, we need $\frac{RS}{XY} = \frac{RT}{XZ} = \frac{ST}{YZ}$. Substituting in for those values becomes $\frac{24}{8} = \frac{12}{4} = \frac{30}{YZ}$. Simplifying the fractions results in $\frac{3}{1} = \frac{3}{1} = \frac{30}{YZ}$. Therefore, in order for the triangles to be similar, we need $\frac{3}{1} = \frac{30}{YZ}$. After cross-multiplying the terms, it becomes $3(YZ) = 30(1)$, so $3(YZ) = 30$. Divide both sides by 3 to get $YZ = 10$. Answer B is obtained by noting that 30 is 6 more than 24 and then incorrectly adding 6 to 8 to get 14. Answer C incorrectly sets up the scale factor as $\frac{24}{8} = \frac{2}{1}$ and sets $\frac{2}{1} = \frac{30}{YZ}$ to get $YZ = 15$. Answer D notes that 30 is 18 more than 12 and then incorrectly adds 18 to 4 to get 22.

16. C: Hiking due west at 3 miles/hour, the first hiker will have gone 6 miles after 2 hours. Hiking due north at 4 miles/hour, the second hiker will have gone 8 miles after 2 hours. Since one hiker headed west and the other headed north, their distance from each other can be drawn as:

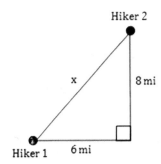

Since the distance between the two hikers is the hypotenuse of a right triangle and we know the lengths of the two legs of the right triangle, the Pythagorean Theorem ($a^2 + b^2 = c^2$) is used to find the value of x. Therefore, $6^2 + 8^2 = x^2 \Rightarrow 36 + 64 = x^2 \Rightarrow 100 = x^2 \Rightarrow 10 = x$. Answer A is the distance between the hikers after only 1 hour of hiking. Answer B incorrectly adds the distances hiked after 1 hour. Answer D incorrectly adds the distances hiked after 2 hours.

17. A: The frequency table for Choice A correctly shows the frequencies represented by the histogram. The frequencies of values falling between 1 and 10 is 3, between 11 and 20 is 9, between 21 and 30 is 8, between 31 and 40 is 6, and between 41 and 50 is 4.

18. A: The probability of non-mutually exclusive events, A or B, occurring may be written as $P(A \text{ or } B) = P(A) + P(B) - P(A \text{ and } B)$. There are 3 even numbers on the die so the probability of rolling an even number is $\frac{3}{6}$. There are 2 numbers greater than 4 so this probability is $\frac{2}{6}$. There is 1 number, 6, that is both even and greater than 4, so this probability is $\frac{1}{6}$. Thus, $P(A \text{ or } B) = \frac{3}{6} + \frac{2}{6} - \frac{1}{6} = \frac{2}{3}$.

19. C: The expected value is equal to the sum of the products of the probability of rolling each number and the number's value. Thus, the expected value is $\left(1 \cdot \frac{1}{10}\right) + \left(2 \cdot \frac{1}{10}\right) + \left(3 \cdot \frac{1}{10}\right) + \left(4 \cdot \frac{1}{10}\right) + \left(5 \cdot \frac{1}{10}\right) + \left(6 \cdot \frac{1}{10}\right) + \left(7 \cdot \frac{1}{10}\right) + \left(8 \cdot \frac{1}{10}\right) + \left(9 \cdot \frac{1}{10}\right) + \left(10 \cdot \frac{1}{10}\right)$. The expected value is 5.5.

20. B: The expected value is equal to the sum of the products of the probabilities and the amount she will lose or win. Each probability is equal to $\frac{2}{6}$. Thus, the expected value may be written as $\left(-6 \cdot \frac{2}{6}\right) + \left(3 \cdot \frac{2}{6}\right) + \left(-9 \cdot \frac{2}{6}\right)$. Thus, the expected value is –$4.

Reading

1. A: The passage discusses two problems that can occur with wells. Both of the problems mentioned are associated with wells that are too shallow; there is no mention of problems associated with wells that are too deep. Therefore, it seems safe to conclude that a deeper well would be more desirable than a shallow one. The passage does not indicate that most well owners have water shortages every year (choice B), but rather discusses how to deal with a shortage. Nor does it imply that most wells dug during the winter are not deep enough (choice C), though it advises to plan ahead for summer. Choice D is contradicted in the first sentence.

2. C: Choice A is mentioned only briefly in the passage. Choices B and D are mentioned, but this information does not fit into the overall purpose of the passage, which is to discuss the different types of fats, both good and bad.

3. B: Choices C and D are mentioned only briefly. Although the history of satire is discussed (choice A), most of the passage focuses on discussing the three major forms of satire that originated in Ancient Greece and Rome, making B the best choice.

4. A: Answer choice B is incorrect because the passage states that happiness is expressed similarly by people all over the world. Choice C is incorrect because the passage states that there are many emotions felt and expressed by people all over the world. Choice D is incorrect because, although people may express acceptance differently, that is not sufficient to conclude it is not a natural emotion. Choice A is correct. We can conclude that people can't always hide what they are feeling because of the statement in the passage that the facial expressions associated with emotions like fear are largely involuntary.

5. C: C is the correct answer because the passage mainly focuses on discussing the causes of heat islands. Choices A, B, and D are touched upon only in passing.

6. C: Answer choices A and D are incorrect because the passage states that these are characteristics that marsupials and mammals share. Choice B can be eliminated, because it is not mentioned in the passage. C is the correct choice, as the passage states that "one thing that separates marsupials from mammals is that their young are born when they are not yet fully developed."

7. D: Answer choice D best summarizes the main topic discussed here. While choice C is a fact given about Tubman in the passage, it is not the main focus. Choices A and B are not discussed in the passage.

8. A: The author uses phrases like Tubman "was determined to gain her freedom" and "worried that she and the other slaves on the plantation were going to be sold" as he or she describes Tubman's life as a slave. The reader can deduce that the author included these descriptions to illustrate why Harriet Tubman wanted to escape slavery, choice A. Choices B and D are not discussed in the passage. Choice C is a supporting detail, not the main point.

9. B: Paragraph 3 describes why Harriet Tubman suffered from seizures. An overseer threw a heavy weight and hit her in the head. The weight nearly crushed her skull. She suffered from seizures for the rest of her life. While whippings (choice A) and sleep loss (choice C) are mentioned, they are not the direct cause of the seizures. Birth defects (choice D) are not discussed.

10. C: Clue words and phrases such as *as a child* and *later*, as well as the use of dates, indicates that this passage is arranged in chronological order.

11. A: Paragraph 4 explains how Araminta Ross became known as Harriet Tubman. She married John Tubman and took his last name. She also changed her first name to her mother's name.

12. C: A stanza consists of a grouping of lines, set off by a space, that usually has a set pattern of meter and rhyme. This poem has six stanzas.

13. D: Personification is a metaphor in which a thing or abstraction is represented as a person. Personification is used throughout this poem. However, of the answer choices given, line 11 is the best choice. The author personifies spring as a female.

14. A: The fifth stanza gives clues to whom *we* refers with the word *mankind*. The war (choice B) is mentioned but is not in reference to *we*. Americans (choice C) are not mentioned, and the scope of the poem is broad, not merely speaking to the reader (choice D).

15. B: This is an example of a rhymed verse poem. The last word of each line rhymes with the last word of the other line in every stanza. A sonnet (choice A) is a poem of fourteen lines following a set rhyme scheme and logical structure. Often, poets use iambic pentameter when writing sonnets. A free verse poem (choice C) is written without using strict meter or rhyme. A lyric poem (choice D) is a short poem that expresses personal feelings, which may or may not be set to music.

16. A: Answer choice A gives the best summary of the poem, demonstrated by the phrases about things in nature not caring about war or the extinction of humanity. There is no discussion of government (choice B). While war is mentioned, there is no discussion of its effect on nature (choice C); rather, the poem focuses on the peaceful beauty of nature despite man's effects. The mention of spring has nothing to do with war (choice D).

17. D: Answer choice (D) best summarizes what this passage is mainly about. Egypt (choice A), raisins (choice B), and William Wolfskill (choice C) are briefly mentioned, but are not the main subject.

18. C: Answer choice (C) is the best title for the passage because it best summarizes all the topics covered in the passage. The other answer choices are details mentioned in the passage, but are not the main focus of the passage.

19. A: The last paragraph of the passage answers this detail question. The Coachella Valley Region (choice B) is where most of the other grapes are grown. Los Angeles (choice C) is the approximate site of the first table grape vineyard. The California missions (choice D) are not specifically associate with table grapes in the passage.

20. C: The third paragraph of the passage answers this detail question. Wolfskill is not associated with the details in any of the other answer choices.

21. C: The main idea is often found in the opening sentence of a paragraph. This sentence states that hypotheses can be formed not as universal claims but as probabilities. The rest of the paragraph explains this statement. Answer choice C best captures this thought. Choices A and B give statements that contradict the passage. Choice D refers to a statement from the first paragraph.

22. D: To answer this question, it is helpful to break the word apart. From the passage, it is clear that *confirming* is synonymous with *proving*. The prefix *dis* means *not*. So we can infer that *disconfirming* refers to *disproving*. Choice A is inappropriate because it is an antonym. Choice B is inappropriate because *dissipating* means *breaking or spreading apart*. Choice C is inappropriate because *distilling* means *purifying or breaking down*.

23. C: Choice C is a good choice because, using the monkey example, a monkey (x) that has no hair (y) disproves the hypothesis "all monkeys are hairy." Choice A is inappropriate because something that is neither x nor y is irrelevant to the passage. Choice B is inappropriate because something that is both x and y helps to confirm the hypothesis. Choice D is inappropriate because items that are y (hairy) but not x (monkeys) are irrelevant to the passage.

24. B: Statement I makes a universal claim. As the passage states, it is impossible to confirm a hypothesis that makes a universal claim because that involves testing all past, present, and future occurrences. Statement III also makes a universal claim, though it is a negative claim. Only

Statement II correctly states a hypothesis that can be confirmed as a probability, as demonstrated in the third paragraph of the passage.

Writing

1. B: The word *fourth* should be written out to match the form of *third*. While the word *teacher* could become plural, choice A is incorrect because the second sentence of the passage shows that Alberto is talking about a single teacher. Choice C is incorrect because the comma correctly separates two independent clauses. Choice D is incorrect because Alberto is talking about several years rather than the possessive of one year. Therefore, the form of *years* should be plural rather than possessive.

2. D: Answer choice D uses proper word order to get the point across. This sentence begins with a subject and verb and follows the verb by two objects. Choice A is incorrect because the phrases *my teacher to hate me back* and *for me to hate him* are written in reverse order. It is more logical for *for me to hate him* to be written first. Choice B is incorrect because the subject and verb separate Alberto's two emotions (*expecting to hate my teacher* and *expecting him to hate me back*). This separation makes the sentence more difficult to read and understand. Choice C is incorrect because Alberto states twice that he expected to hate Mr. Shanbourne.

3. C: The word *because* combines the sentence by showing that the second clause is an explanation for the first clause. Choice A is incorrect because the conjunction *and* doesn't show how the two clauses are connected. Choice B is incorrect because the word *although* implies contrast rather than explanation. Although *as a result of* has a similar meaning to *because* and could be used to effectively combine the sentences, choice D is incorrect because the verbs *forced* and *gave* should be changed to *forcing* and *giving* in order for *as a result of* to be used correctly.

4. B: The phrase *turned in work late* is redundant with the phrase *handed in assignments after the due date*; only one of those phrases needs to be in the sentence. Choices A and C are incorrect because both phrases add unique information to the sentence. Choice D is incorrect because the sentence has two redundant phrases, and one of them should be deleted.

5. A: The transition "surprisingly" indicates that the reaction was unexpected, or even contradictory to the circumstance of the speaker not turning his work in on time and talking out in class. The other answer choices do not make as much sense to coordinate these two sentences.

6. A: This answer correctly punctuates the dialogue with a question mark and with the quotation marks in the correct spot. Choice B is incorrect because the end quotes should be after *Alberto* rather than after *said*. Choices C and D are incorrect because the clause *How are you doing, Alberto* is a question and should be punctuated with a question mark rather than a period or comma.

7. A: *Than* is a comparative word and *then* is a word that shows a sequence of events. Since the sentence shows the next step in a sequence of events, *then* is the correct word to use. Choice B is incorrect because *Shanbourne* is not possessive in this context. Choice C is incorrect because a comma should not separate a subject and verb. Choice D is incorrect because *bye* is the spelling used to say good-bye and *by* is the spelling used for prepositions.

8. C: A comma should only be used before a conjunction (the word *and* in sentence 29) if the clause following the conjunction is an independent clause, which means it can be written as a complete sentence. Since *said he believed in my abilities* does not have a subject, it is not an independent clause. Choice A is incorrect because this essay is written in the past tense, so *hadn't* is a more consistent verb choice. Choice B is incorrect because the word *who* should be used when it refers to a subject. Since one could write a sentence such as "The teacher seemed to care about me"—which replaces *who* with a noun to create a subject—*who* is correct. *Whom* would be correct if the word referred to the object of the sentence. Choice D is incorrect because the correct spelling of *believed* has an *i* before an *e*.

9. C: A comma should be added before a conjunction (*and*) that precedes an independent clause. Choice A is incorrect because the comma after *honest* correctly separates a nonessential phrase from the rest of the sentence. Choice B is incorrect because the passage is written in past tense rather than present. Choice D is incorrect because *many* refers to a number of items (such as a number of homework assignments) while *much* refers to an abstract amount.

10. C: *Encourage* is the correct spelling (the *o* should come before the *u*). Choice A is incorrect because the word *responded*, used later in the sentence, shows that Alberto is still writing in the past tense. Choice B is incorrect because the comma is needed to separate items in the series. Choice D is incorrect because the comma is needed before *and* because *and* is a conjunction that precedes an independent clause.

11. B: The phrase *to have extinction* in choice A is grammatically incorrect. In choice C, *causes* is plural, and so the word should be *exist* rather than *exists*. D is not the best choice because it is somewhat awkward. B sounds the best and is also grammatically correct.

12. C: C is the best answer because it indicates a contrast and is grammatically correct.

13. A: A is the best answer because it denotes the party to whom companies are offering tech support and because the verb *are* agrees with the noun *customers*. Choice B does not make sense. Choice C is incorrect because it uses *with* instead of *to*. Choice D is missing the article *a* before *customer*.

14. D: D is the best choice. The phrases *high-fat diets* and *excessive amounts of television* agree with each other because they are both plural. The word *is* refers to *the fact that*, so these also agree with each other.

15. B: This is a well-known phrase meaning *despite what most people believe*. The word *contrarily* in choice A makes it incorrect. *Popularity* in choice C is incorrect, and *believing* in choice D is incorrect.

16. B: The original sentence states that serious complications can result if there are errors during the process of cell division. Choices A and C refer to the process of cell division only, and not the errors that must be made for complications to occur. Choice D indicates that the process leads to errors, rather than that the errors occur during the process.

17. A: The original sentence states that after much consideration a decision was made, which is why A is the best choice. The decision wasn't still difficult after much consideration, as choice B indicates, and she didn't immediately attend university, as is indicated by choice C. Choice D simply doesn't make sense in the context of the statement.

18. A: A is the best choice because it is the only one that indicates a cause/effect relationship. Small business owners must do something *because* prices in department stores are too low for small business owners to match them.

19. A: The rewritten sentence begins with examples of some of the unique characteristics of ants. Choice B does not indicate that they are unique characteristics. Choice C describes them as

262

fascinating rather than unique. Choice D does not make sense in the context of the sentence because of the phrase *of their* that follows *are unique characteristics*.

20. B: The word *despite* indicates that something is done in spite of warnings by law enforcement professionals, which eliminates choices C and D. Choice A does not indicate precisely what motorists are failing to do, which eliminates that choice. Choice B is the correct answer.

How to Overcome Test Anxiety

Just the thought of taking a test is enough to make most people a little nervous. A test is an important event that can have a long-term impact on your future, so it's important to take it seriously and it's natural to feel anxious about performing well. But just because anxiety is normal, that doesn't mean that it's helpful in test taking, or that you should simply accept it as part of your life. Anxiety can have a variety of effects. These effects can be mild, like making you feel slightly nervous, or severe, like blocking your ability to focus or remember even a simple detail.

If you experience test anxiety—whether severe or mild—it's important to know how to beat it. To discover this, first you need to understand what causes test anxiety.

Causes of Test Anxiety

While we often think of anxiety as an uncontrollable emotional state, it can actually be caused by simple, practical things. One of the most common causes of test anxiety is that a person does not feel adequately prepared for their test. This feeling can be the result of many different issues such as poor study habits or lack of organization, but the most common culprit is time management. Starting to study too late, failing to organize your study time to cover all of the material, or being distracted while you study will mean that you're not well prepared for the test. This may lead to cramming the night before, which will cause you to be physically and mentally exhausted for the test. Poor time management also contributes to feelings of stress, fear, and hopelessness as you realize you are not well prepared but don't know what to do about it.

Other times, test anxiety is not related to your preparation for the test but comes from unresolved fear. This may be a past failure on a test, or poor performance on tests in general. It may come from comparing yourself to others who seem to be performing better or from the stress of living up to expectations. Anxiety may be driven by fears of the future—how failure on this test would affect your educational and career goals. These fears are often completely irrational, but they can still negatively impact your test performance.

Review Video: 3 Reasons You Have Test Anxiety
Visit mometrix.com/academy and enter code: 428468

264

Elements of Test Anxiety

As mentioned earlier, test anxiety is considered to be an emotional state, but it has physical and mental components as well. Sometimes you may not even realize that you are suffering from test anxiety until you notice the physical symptoms. These can include trembling hands, rapid heartbeat, sweating, nausea, and tense muscles. Extreme anxiety may lead to fainting or vomiting. Obviously, any of these symptoms can have a negative impact on testing. It is important to recognize them as soon as they begin to occur so that you can address the problem before it damages your performance.

> **Review Video: 3 Ways to Tell You Have Test Anxiety**
> Visit mometrix.com/academy and enter code: 927847

The mental components of test anxiety include trouble focusing and inability to remember learned information. During a test, your mind is on high alert, which can help you recall information and stay focused for an extended period of time. However, anxiety interferes with your mind's natural processes, causing you to blank out, even on the questions you know well. The strain of testing during anxiety makes it difficult to stay focused, especially on a test that may take several hours. Extreme anxiety can take a huge mental toll, making it difficult not only to recall test information but even to understand the test questions or pull your thoughts together.

> **Review Video: How Test Anxiety Affects Memory**
> Visit mometrix.com/academy and enter code: 609003

Effects of Test Anxiety

Test anxiety is like a disease—if left untreated, it will get progressively worse. Anxiety leads to poor performance, and this reinforces the feelings of fear and failure, which in turn lead to poor performances on subsequent tests. It can grow from a mild nervousness to a crippling condition. If allowed to progress, test anxiety can have a big impact on your schooling, and consequently on your future.

Test anxiety can spread to other parts of your life. Anxiety on tests can become anxiety in any stressful situation, and blanking on a test can turn into panicking in a job situation. But fortunately, you don't have to let anxiety rule your testing and determine your grades. There are a number of relatively simple steps you can take to move past anxiety and function normally on a test and in the rest of life.

> **Review Video: How Test Anxiety Impacts Your Grades**
> Visit mometrix.com/academy and enter code: 939819

Physical Steps for Beating Test Anxiety

While test anxiety is a serious problem, the good news is that it can be overcome. It doesn't have to control your ability to think and remember information. While it may take time, you can begin taking steps today to beat anxiety.

Just as your first hint that you may be struggling with anxiety comes from the physical symptoms, the first step to treating it is also physical. Rest is crucial for having a clear, strong mind. If you are tired, it is much easier to give in to anxiety. But if you establish good sleep habits, your body and mind will be ready to perform optimally, without the strain of exhaustion. Additionally, sleeping well helps you to retain information better, so you're more likely to recall the answers when you see the test questions.

Getting good sleep means more than going to bed on time. It's important to allow your brain time to relax. Take study breaks from time to time so it doesn't get overworked, and don't study right before bed. Take time to rest your mind before trying to rest your body, or you may find it difficult to fall asleep.

Review Video: The Importance of Sleep for Your Brain
Visit mometrix.com/academy and enter code: 319338

Along with sleep, other aspects of physical health are important in preparing for a test. Good nutrition is vital for good brain function. Sugary foods and drinks may give a burst of energy but this burst is followed by a crash, both physically and emotionally. Instead, fuel your body with protein and vitamin-rich foods.

Also, drink plenty of water. Dehydration can lead to headaches and exhaustion, especially if your brain is already under stress from the rigors of the test. Particularly if your test is a long one, drink water during the breaks. And if possible, take an energy-boosting snack to eat between sections.

Review Video: How Diet Can Affect your Mood
Visit mometrix.com/academy and enter code: 624317

Along with sleep and diet, a third important part of physical health is exercise. Maintaining a steady workout schedule is helpful, but even taking 5-minute study breaks to walk can help get your blood pumping faster and clear your head. Exercise also releases endorphins, which contribute to a positive feeling and can help combat test anxiety.

When you nurture your physical health, you are also contributing to your mental health. If your body is healthy, your mind is much more likely to be healthy as well. So take time to rest, nourish your body with healthy food and water, and get moving as much as possible. Taking these physical steps will make you stronger and more able to take the mental steps necessary to overcome test anxiety.

Review Video: How to Stay Healthy and Prevent Test Anxiety
Visit mometrix.com/academy and enter code: 877894

Mental Steps for Beating Test Anxiety

Working on the mental side of test anxiety can be more challenging, but as with the physical side, there are clear steps you can take to overcome it. As mentioned earlier, test anxiety often stems from lack of preparation, so the obvious solution is to prepare for the test. Effective studying may be the most important weapon you have for beating test anxiety, but you can and should employ several other mental tools to combat fear.

First, boost your confidence by reminding yourself of past success—tests or projects that you aced. If you're putting as much effort into preparing for this test as you did for those, there's no reason you should expect to fail here. Work hard to prepare; then trust your preparation.

Second, surround yourself with encouraging people. It can be helpful to find a study group, but be sure that the people you're around will encourage a positive attitude. If you spend time with others who are anxious or cynical, this will only contribute to your own anxiety. Look for others who are motivated to study hard from a desire to succeed, not from a fear of failure.

Third, reward yourself. A test is physically and mentally tiring, even without anxiety, and it can be helpful to have something to look forward to. Plan an activity following the test, regardless of the outcome, such as going to a movie or getting ice cream.

When you are taking the test, if you find yourself beginning to feel anxious, remind yourself that you know the material. Visualize successfully completing the test. Then take a few deep, relaxing breaths and return to it. Work through the questions carefully but with confidence, knowing that you are capable of succeeding.

Developing a healthy mental approach to test taking will also aid in other areas of life. Test anxiety affects more than just the actual test—it can be damaging to your mental health and even contribute to depression. It's important to beat test anxiety before it becomes a problem for more than testing.

Review Video: <u>Test Anxiety and Depression</u>
Visit mometrix.com/academy and enter code: 904704

Study Strategy

Being prepared for the test is necessary to combat anxiety, but what does being prepared look like? You may study for hours on end and still not feel prepared. What you need is a strategy for test prep. The next few pages outline our recommended steps to help you plan out and conquer the challenge of preparation.

STEP 1: SCOPE OUT THE TEST

Learn everything you can about the format (multiple choice, essay, etc.) and what will be on the test. Gather any study materials, course outlines, or sample exams that may be available. Not only will this help you to prepare, but knowing what to expect can help to alleviate test anxiety.

STEP 2: MAP OUT THE MATERIAL

Look through the textbook or study guide and make note of how many chapters or sections it has. Then divide these over the time you have. For example, if a book has 15 chapters and you have five days to study, you need to cover three chapters each day. Even better, if you have the time, leave an extra day at the end for overall review after you have gone through the material in depth.

If time is limited, you may need to prioritize the material. Look through it and make note of which sections you think you already have a good grasp on, and which need review. While you are studying, skim quickly through the familiar sections and take more time on the challenging parts. Write out your plan so you don't get lost as you go. Having a written plan also helps you feel more in control of the study, so anxiety is less likely to arise from feeling overwhelmed at the amount to cover.

STEP 3: GATHER YOUR TOOLS

Decide what study method works best for you. Do you prefer to highlight in the book as you study and then go back over the highlighted portions? Or do you type out notes of the important information? Or is it helpful to make flashcards that you can carry with you? Assemble the pens, index cards, highlighters, post-it notes, and any other materials you may need so you won't be distracted by getting up to find things while you study.

If you're having a hard time retaining the information or organizing your notes, experiment with different methods. For example, try color-coding by subject with colored pens, highlighters, or post-it notes. If you learn better by hearing, try recording yourself reading your notes so you can listen while in the car, working out, or simply sitting at your desk. Ask a friend to quiz you from your flashcards, or try teaching someone the material to solidify it in your mind.

STEP 4: CREATE YOUR ENVIRONMENT

It's important to avoid distractions while you study. This includes both the obvious distractions like visitors and the subtle distractions like an uncomfortable chair (or a too-comfortable couch that makes you want to fall asleep). Set up the best study environment possible: good lighting and a comfortable work area. If background music helps you focus, you may want to turn it on, but otherwise keep the room quiet. If you are using a computer to take notes, be sure you don't have any other windows open, especially applications like social media, games, or anything else that could distract you. Silence your phone and turn off notifications. Be sure to keep water close by so you stay hydrated while you study (but avoid unhealthy drinks and snacks).

Also, take into account the best time of day to study. Are you freshest first thing in the morning? Try to set aside some time then to work through the material. Is your mind clearer in the afternoon or evening? Schedule your study session then. Another method is to study at the same time of day that you will take the test, so that your brain gets used to working on the material at that time and will be ready to focus at test time.

STEP 5: STUDY!

Once you have done all the study preparation, it's time to settle into the actual studying. Sit down, take a few moments to settle your mind so you can focus, and begin to follow your study plan. Don't give in to distractions or let yourself procrastinate. This is your time to prepare so you'll be ready to fearlessly approach the test. Make the most of the time and stay focused.

Of course, you don't want to burn out. If you study too long you may find that you're not retaining the information very well. Take regular study breaks. For example, taking five minutes out of every hour to walk briskly, breathing deeply and swinging your arms, can help your mind stay fresh.

As you get to the end of each chapter or section, it's a good idea to do a quick review. Remind yourself of what you learned and work on any difficult parts. When you feel that you've mastered the material, move on to the next part. At the end of your study session, briefly skim through your notes again.

But while review is helpful, cramming last minute is NOT. If at all possible, work ahead so that you won't need to fit all your study into the last day. Cramming overloads your brain with more information than it can process and retain, and your tired mind may struggle to recall even previously learned information when it is overwhelmed with last-minute study. Also, the urgent nature of cramming and the stress placed on your brain contribute to anxiety. You'll be more likely to go to the test feeling unprepared and having trouble thinking clearly.

So don't cram, and don't stay up late before the test, even just to review your notes at a leisurely pace. Your brain needs rest more than it needs to go over the information again. In fact, plan to finish your studies by noon or early afternoon the day before the test. Give your brain the rest of the day to relax or focus on other things, and get a good night's sleep. Then you will be fresh for the test and better able to recall what you've studied.

STEP 6: TAKE A PRACTICE TEST

Many courses offer sample tests, either online or in the study materials. This is an excellent resource to check whether you have mastered the material, as well as to prepare for the test format and environment.

Check the test format ahead of time: the number of questions, the type (multiple choice, free response, etc.), and the time limit. Then create a plan for working through them. For example, if you have 30 minutes to take a 60-question test, your limit is 30 seconds per question. Spend less time on the questions you know well so that you can take more time on the difficult ones.

If you have time to take several practice tests, take the first one open book, with no time limit. Work through the questions at your own pace and make sure you fully understand them. Gradually work up to taking a test under test conditions: sit at a desk with all study materials put away and set a timer. Pace yourself to make sure you finish the test with time to spare and go back to check your answers if you have time.

After each test, check your answers. On the questions you missed, be sure you understand why you missed them. Did you misread the question (tests can use tricky wording)? Did you forget the information? Or was it something you hadn't learned? Go back and study any shaky areas that the practice tests reveal.

Taking these tests not only helps with your grade, but also aids in combating test anxiety. If you're already used to the test conditions, you're less likely to worry about it, and working through tests until you're scoring well gives you a confidence boost. Go through the practice tests until you feel comfortable, and then you can go into the test knowing that you're ready for it.

Test Tips

On test day, you should be confident, knowing that you've prepared well and are ready to answer the questions. But aside from preparation, there are several test day strategies you can employ to maximize your performance.

First, as stated before, get a good night's sleep the night before the test (and for several nights before that, if possible). Go into the test with a fresh, alert mind rather than staying up late to study.

Try not to change too much about your normal routine on the day of the test. It's important to eat a nutritious breakfast, but if you normally don't eat breakfast at all, consider eating just a protein bar. If you're a coffee drinker, go ahead and have your normal coffee. Just make sure you time it so that the caffeine doesn't wear off right in the middle of your test. Avoid sugary beverages, and drink enough water to stay hydrated but not so much that you need a restroom break 10 minutes into the test. If your test isn't first thing in the morning, consider going for a walk or doing a light workout before the test to get your blood flowing.

Allow yourself enough time to get ready, and leave for the test with plenty of time to spare so you won't have the anxiety of scrambling to arrive in time. Another reason to be early is to select a good seat. It's helpful to sit away from doors and windows, which can be distracting. Find a good seat, get out your supplies, and settle your mind before the test begins.

When the test begins, start by going over the instructions carefully, even if you already know what to expect. Make sure you avoid any careless mistakes by following the directions.

Then begin working through the questions, pacing yourself as you've practiced. If you're not sure on an answer, don't spend too much time on it, and don't let it shake your confidence. Either skip it and come back later, or eliminate as many wrong answers as possible and guess among the remaining ones. Don't dwell on these questions as you continue—put them out of your mind and focus on what lies ahead.

Be sure to read all of the answer choices, even if you're sure the first one is the right answer. Sometimes you'll find a better one if you keep reading. But don't second-guess yourself if you do immediately know the answer. Your gut instinct is usually right. Don't let test anxiety rob you of the information you know.

If you have time at the end of the test (and if the test format allows), go back and review your answers. Be cautious about changing any, since your first instinct tends to be correct, but make sure you didn't misread any of the questions or accidentally mark the wrong answer choice. Look over any you skipped and make an educated guess.

At the end, leave the test feeling confident. You've done your best, so don't waste time worrying about your performance or wishing you could change anything. Instead, celebrate the successful

completion of this test. And finally, use this test to learn how to deal with anxiety even better next time.

> **Review Video: 5 Tips to Beat Test Anxiety**
> Visit mometrix.com/academy and enter code: 570656

Important Qualification

Not all anxiety is created equal. If your test anxiety is causing major issues in your life beyond the classroom or testing center, or if you are experiencing troubling physical symptoms related to your anxiety, it may be a sign of a serious physiological or psychological condition. If this sounds like your situation, we strongly encourage you to seek professional help.

How to Overcome Your Fear of Math

The word *math* is enough to strike fear into most hearts. How many of us have memories of sitting through confusing lectures, wrestling over mind-numbing homework, or taking tests that still seem incomprehensible even after hours of study? Years after graduation, many still shudder at these memories.

The fact is, math is not just a classroom subject. It has real-world implications that you face every day, whether you realize it or not. This may be balancing your monthly budget, deciding how many supplies to buy for a project, or simply splitting a meal check with friends. The idea of daily confrontations with math can be so paralyzing that some develop a condition known as *math anxiety*.

But you do NOT need to be paralyzed by this anxiety! In fact, while you may have thought all your life that you're not good at math, or that your brain isn't wired to understand it, the truth is that you may have been conditioned to think this way. From your earliest school days, the way you were taught affected the way you viewed different subjects. And the way math has been taught has changed.

Several decades ago, there was a shift in American math classrooms. The focus changed from traditional problem-solving to a conceptual view of topics, de-emphasizing the importance of learning the basics and building on them. The solid foundation necessary for math progression and confidence was undermined. Math became more of a vague concept than a concrete idea. Today, it is common to think of math, not as a straightforward system, but as a mysterious, complicated method that can't be fully understood unless you're a genius.

This is why you may still have nightmares about being called on to answer a difficult problem in front of the class. Math anxiety is a very real, though unnecessary, fear.

Math anxiety may begin with a single class period. Let's say you missed a day in 6th grade math and never quite understood the concept that was taught while you were gone. Since math is cumulative, with each new concept building on past ones, this could very well affect the rest of your math career. Without that one day's knowledge, it will be difficult to understand any other concepts that link to it. Rather than realizing that you're just missing one key piece, you may begin to believe that you're simply not capable of understanding math.

This belief can change the way you approach other classes, career options, and everyday life experiences, if you become anxious at the thought that math might be required. A student who loves science may choose a different path of study upon realizing that multiple math classes will be required for a degree. An aspiring medical student may hesitate at the thought of going through the necessary math classes. For some this anxiety escalates into a more extreme state known as *math phobia*.

Math anxiety is challenging to address because it is rooted deeply and may come from a variety of causes: an embarrassing moment in class, a teacher who did not explain concepts well and contributed to a shaky foundation, or a failed test that contributed to the belief of math failure.

These causes add up over time, encouraged by society's popular view that math is hard and unpleasant. Eventually a person comes to firmly believe that he or she is simply bad at math. This belief makes it difficult to grasp new concepts or even remember old ones. Homework and test grades begin to slip, which only confirms the belief. The poor performance is not due to lack of ability but is caused by math anxiety.

Math anxiety is an emotional issue, not a lack of intelligence. But when it becomes deeply rooted, it can become more than just an emotional problem. Physical symptoms appear. Blood pressure may rise and heartbeat may quicken at the sight of a math problem – or even the thought of math! This fear leads to a mental block. When someone with math anxiety is asked to perform a calculation, even a basic problem can seem overwhelming and impossible. The emotional and physical response to the thought of math prevents the brain from working through it logically.

The more this happens, the more a person's confidence drops, and the more math anxiety is generated. This vicious cycle must be broken!

The first step in breaking the cycle is to go back to very beginning and make sure you really understand the basics of how math works and why it works. It is not enough to memorize rules for multiplication and division. If you don't know WHY these rules work, your foundation will be shaky and you will be at risk of developing a phobia. Understanding mathematical concepts not only promotes confidence and security, but allows you to build on this understanding for new concepts. Additionally, you can solve unfamiliar problems using familiar concepts and processes.

Why is it that students in other countries regularly outperform American students in math? The answer likely boils down to a couple of things: the foundation of mathematical conceptual understanding and societal perception. While students in the US are not expected to *like* or *get* math, in many other nations, students are expected not only to understand math but also to excel at it.

Changing the American view of math that leads to math anxiety is a monumental task. It requires changing the training of teachers nationwide, from kindergarten through high school, so that they learn to teach the *why* behind math and to combat the wrong math views that students may develop. It also involves changing the stigma associated with math, so that it is no longer viewed as unpleasant and incomprehensible. While these are necessary changes, they are challenging and will take time. But in the meantime, math anxiety is not irreversible—it can be faced and defeated, one person at a time.

False Beliefs

One reason math anxiety has taken such hold is that several false beliefs have been created and shared until they became widely accepted. Some of these unhelpful beliefs include the following:

There is only one way to solve a math problem. In the same way that you can choose from different driving routes and still arrive at the same house, you can solve a math problem using different methods and still find the correct answer. A person who understands the reasoning behind math calculations may be able to look at an unfamiliar concept and find the right answer, just by applying logic to the knowledge they already have. This approach may be different than what is taught in the classroom, but it is still valid. Unfortunately, even many teachers view math as a subject where the best course of action is to memorize the rule or process for each problem rather than as a place for students to exercise logic and creativity in finding a solution.

Many people don't have a mind for math. A person who has struggled due to poor teaching or math anxiety may falsely believe that he or she doesn't have the mental capacity to grasp mathematical concepts. Most of the time, this is false. Many people find that when they are relieved of their math anxiety, they have more than enough brainpower to understand math.

Men are naturally better at math than women. Even though research has shown this to be false, many young women still avoid math careers and classes because of their belief that their math abilities are inferior. Many girls have come to believe that math is a male skill and have given up trying to understand or enjoy it.

Counting aids are bad. Something like counting on your fingers or drawing out a problem to visualize it may be frowned on as childish or a crutch, but these devices can help you get a tangible understanding of a problem or a concept.

Sadly, many students buy into these ideologies at an early age. A young girl who enjoys math class may be conditioned to think that she doesn't actually have the brain for it because math is for boys, and may turn her energies to other pursuits, permanently closing the door on a wide range of opportunities. A child who finds the right answer but doesn't follow the teacher's method may believe that he is doing it wrong and isn't good at math. A student who never had a problem with math before may have a poor teacher and become confused, yet believe that the problem is because she doesn't have a mathematical mind.

Students who have bought into these erroneous beliefs quickly begin to add their own anxieties, adapting them to their own personal situations:

I'll never use this in real life. A huge number of people wrongly believe that math is irrelevant outside the classroom. By adopting this mindset, they are handicapping themselves for a life in a mathematical world, as well as limiting their career choices. When they are inevitably faced with real-world math, they are conditioning themselves to respond with anxiety.

I'm not quick enough. While timed tests and quizzes, or even simply comparing yourself with other students in the class, can lead to this belief, speed is not an indicator of skill level. A person can work very slowly yet understand at a deep level.

If I can understand it, it's too easy. People with a low view of their own abilities tend to think that if they are able to grasp a concept, it must be simple. They cannot accept the idea that they are capable of understanding math. This belief will make it harder to learn, no matter how intelligent they are.

I just can't learn this. An overwhelming number of people think this, from young children to adults, and much of the time it is simply not true. But this mindset can turn into a self-fulfilling prophecy that keeps you from exercising and growing your math ability.

The good news is, each of these myths can be debunked. For most people, they are based on emotion and psychology, NOT on actual ability! It will take time, effort, and the desire to change, but change is possible. Even if you have spent years thinking that you don't have the capability to understand math, it is not too late to uncover your true ability and find relief from the anxiety that surrounds math.

Math Strategies

It is important to have a plan of attack to combat math anxiety. There are many useful strategies for pinpointing the fears or myths and eradicating them:

Go back to the basics. For most people, math anxiety stems from a poor foundation. You may think that you have a complete understanding of addition and subtraction, or even decimals and percentages, but make absolutely sure. Learning math is different from learning other subjects. For example, when you learn history, you study various time periods and places and events. It may be important to memorize dates or find out about the lives of famous people. When you move from US history to world history, there will be some overlap, but a large amount of the information will be new. Mathematical concepts, on the other hand, are very closely linked and highly dependent on each other. It's like climbing a ladder – if a rung is missing from your understanding, it may be difficult or impossible for you to climb any higher, no matter how hard you try. So go back and make sure your math foundation is strong. This may mean taking a remedial math course, going to a tutor to work through the shaky concepts, or just going through your old homework to make sure you really understand it.

Speak the language. Math has a large vocabulary of terms and phrases unique to working problems. Sometimes these are completely new terms, and sometimes they are common words, but are used differently in a math setting. If you can't speak the language, it will be very difficult to get a thorough understanding of the concepts. It's common for students to think that they don't understand math when they simply don't understand the vocabulary. The good news is that this is fairly easy to fix. Brushing up on any terms you aren't quite sure of can help bring the rest of the concepts into focus.

Check your anxiety level. When you think about math, do you feel nervous or uncomfortable? Do you struggle with feelings of inadequacy, even on concepts that you know you've already learned? It's important to understand your specific math anxieties, and what triggers them. When you catch yourself falling back on a false belief, mentally replace it with the truth. Don't let yourself believe that you can't learn, or that struggling with a concept means you'll never understand it. Instead, remind yourself of how much you've already learned and dwell on that past success. Visualize grasping the new concept, linking it to your old knowledge, and moving on to the next challenge. Also, learn how to manage anxiety when it arises. There are many techniques for coping with the irrational fears that rise to the surface when you enter the math classroom. This may include controlled breathing, replacing negative thoughts with positive ones, or visualizing success. Anxiety interferes with your ability to concentrate and absorb information, which in turn contributes to greater anxiety. If you can learn how to regain control of your thinking, you will be better able to pay attention, make progress, and succeed!

Don't go it alone. Like any deeply ingrained belief, math anxiety is not easy to eradicate. And there is no need for you to wrestle through it on your own. It will take time, and many people find that speaking with a counselor or psychiatrist helps. They can help you develop strategies for responding to anxiety and overcoming old ideas. Additionally, it can be very helpful to take a short course or seek out a math tutor to help you find and fix the missing rungs on your ladder and make sure that you're ready to progress to the next level. You can also find a number of math aids online: courses that will teach you mental devices for figuring out problems, how to get the most out of your math classes, etc.

Check your math attitude. No matter how much you want to learn and overcome your anxiety, you'll have trouble if you still have a negative attitude toward math. If you think it's too hard, or just have general feelings of dread about math, it will be hard to learn and to break through the anxiety. Work on cultivating a positive math attitude. Remind yourself that math is not just a hurdle to be cleared, but a valuable asset. When you view math with a positive attitude, you'll be much more likely to understand and even enjoy it. This is something you must do for yourself. You may find it helpful to visit with a counselor. Your tutor, friends, and family may cheer you on in your endeavors. But your greatest asset is yourself. You are inside your own mind – tell yourself what you need to hear. Relive past victories. Remind yourself that you are capable of understanding math. Root out any false beliefs that linger and replace them with positive truths. Even if it doesn't feel true at first, it will begin to affect your thinking and pave the way for a positive, anxiety-free mindset.

Aside from these general strategies, there are a number of specific practical things you can do to begin your journey toward overcoming math anxiety. Something as simple as learning a new note-taking strategy can change the way you approach math and give you more confidence and understanding. New study techniques can also make a huge difference.

Math anxiety leads to bad habits. If it causes you to be afraid of answering a question in class, you may gravitate toward the back row. You may be embarrassed to ask for help. And you may procrastinate on assignments, which leads to rushing through them at the last moment when it's too late to get a better understanding. It's important to identify your negative behaviors and replace them with positive ones:

Prepare ahead of time. Read the lesson before you go to class. Being exposed to the topics that will be covered in class ahead of time, even if you don't understand them perfectly, is extremely helpful in increasing what you retain from the lecture. Do your homework and, if you're still shaky, go over some extra problems. The key to a solid understanding of math is practice.

Sit front and center. When you can easily see and hear, you'll understand more, and you'll avoid the distractions of other students if no one is in front of you. Plus, you're more likely to be sitting with students who are positive and engaged, rather than others with math anxiety. Let their positive math attitude rub off on you.

Ask questions in class and out. If you don't understand something, just ask. If you need a more in-depth explanation, the teacher may need to work with you outside of class, but often it's a simple concept you don't quite understand, and a single question may clear it up. If you wait, you may not be able to follow the rest of the day's lesson. For extra help, most professors have office hours outside of class when you can go over concepts one-on-one to clear up any uncertainties. Additionally, there may be a *math lab* or study session you can attend for homework help. Take advantage of this.

Review. Even if you feel that you've fully mastered a concept, review it periodically to reinforce it. Going over an old lesson has several benefits: solidifying your understanding, giving you a confidence boost, and even giving some new insights into material that you're currently learning! Don't let yourself get rusty. That can lead to problems with learning later concepts.

Teaching Tips

While the math student's mindset is the most crucial to overcoming math anxiety, it is also important for others to adjust their math attitudes. Teachers and parents have an enormous influence on how students relate to math. They can either contribute to math confidence or math anxiety.

As a parent or teacher, it is very important to convey a positive math attitude. Retelling horror stories of your own bad experience with math will contribute to a new generation of math anxiety. Even if you don't share your experiences, others will be able to sense your fears and may begin to believe them.

Even a careless comment can have a big impact, so watch for phrases like *He's not good at math* or *I never liked math*. You are a crucial role model, and your children or students will unconsciously adopt your mindset. Give them a positive example to follow. Rather than teaching them to fear the math world before they even know it, teach them about all its potential and excitement.

Work to present math as an integral, beautiful, and understandable part of life. Encourage creativity in solving problems. Watch for false beliefs and dispel them. Cross the lines between subjects: integrate history, English, and music with math. Show students how math is used every day, and how the entire world is based on mathematical principles, from the pull of gravity to the shape of seashells. Instead of letting students see math as a necessary evil, direct them to view it as an imaginative, beautiful art form – an art form that they are capable of mastering and using.

Don't give too narrow a view of math. It is more than just numbers. Yes, working problems and learning formulas is a large part of classroom math. But don't let the teaching stop there. Teach students about the everyday implications of math. Show them how nature works according to the laws of mathematics, and take them outside to make discoveries of their own. Expose them to math-related careers by inviting visiting speakers, asking students to do research and presentations, and learning students' interests and aptitudes on a personal level.

Demonstrate the importance of math. Many people see math as nothing more than a required stepping stone to their degree, a nuisance with no real usefulness. Teach students that algebra is used every day in managing their bank accounts, in following recipes, and in scheduling the day's events. Show them how learning to do geometric proofs helps them to develop logical thinking, an invaluable life skill. Let them see that math surrounds them and is integrally linked to their daily lives: that weather predictions are based on math, that math was used to design cars and other machines, etc. Most of all, give them the tools to use math to enrich their lives.

Make math as tangible as possible. Use visual aids and objects that can be touched. It is much easier to grasp a concept when you can hold it in your hands and manipulate it, rather than just listening to the lecture. Encourage math outside of the classroom. The real world is full of measuring, counting, and calculating, so let students participate in this. Keep your eyes open for numbers and patterns to discuss. Talk about how scores are calculated in sports games and how far apart plants are placed in a garden row for maximum growth. Build the mindset that math is a normal and interesting part of daily life.

Finally, find math resources that help to build a positive math attitude. There are a number of books that show math as fascinating and exciting while teaching important concepts, for example: *The Math Curse; A Wrinkle in Time; The Phantom Tollbooth;* and *Fractals, Googols and Other Mathematical Tales*. You can also find a number of online resources: math puzzles and games, videos that show math in nature, and communities of math enthusiasts. On a local level, students can compete in a variety of math competitions with other schools or join a math club.

The student who experiences math as exciting and interesting is unlikely to suffer from math anxiety. Going through life without this handicap is an immense advantage and opens many doors that others have closed through their fear.

Self-Check

Whether you suffer from math anxiety or not, chances are that you have been exposed to some of the false beliefs mentioned above. Now is the time to check yourself for any errors you may have accepted. Do you think you're not wired for math? Or that you don't need to understand it since you're not planning on a math career? Do you think math is just too difficult for the average person?

Find the errors you've taken to heart and replace them with positive thinking. Are you capable of learning math? Yes! Can you control your anxiety? Yes! These errors will resurface from time to time, so be watchful. Don't let others with math anxiety influence you or sway your confidence. If you're having trouble with a concept, find help. Don't let it discourage you!

Create a plan of attack for defeating math anxiety and sharpening your skills. Do some research and decide if it would help you to take a class, get a tutor, or find some online resources to fine-tune your knowledge. Make the effort to get good nutrition, hydration, and sleep so that you are operating at full capacity. Remind yourself daily that you are skilled and that anxiety does not control you. Your mind is capable of so much more than you know. Give it the tools it needs to grow and thrive.

Thank You

We at Mometrix would like to extend our heartfelt thanks to you, our friend and patron, for allowing us to play a part in your journey. It is a privilege to serve people from all walks of life who are unified in their commitment to building the best future they can for themselves.

The preparation you devote to these important testing milestones may be the most valuable educational opportunity you have for making a real difference in your life. We encourage you to put your heart into it—that feeling of succeeding, overcoming, and yes, conquering will be well worth the hours you've invested.

We want to hear your story, your struggles and your successes, and if you see any opportunities for us to improve our materials so we can help others even more effectively in the future, please share that with us as well. **The team at Mometrix would be absolutely thrilled to hear from you!** So please, send us an email (support@mometrix.com) and let's stay in touch.

> If you'd like some additional help, check out these other resources we offer for your exam:
> http://MometrixFlashcards.com/TSI

Additional Bonus Material

Due to our efforts to try to keep this book to a manageable length, we've created a link that will give you access to all of your additional bonus material.

Please visit http://www.mometrix.com/bonus948/tsi to access the information.